PIANO • VOCAL • GUITAR

2 C.C. Rider
8 Burning Love
11 Something
14 You Gave Me a Mountain
18 Steamroller Blues
21 My Way
26 Love Me
28 It's Over
33 Blue Suede Shoes
36 I'm So Lonesome I Could Cry
38 I Can't Stop Loving You
41 Hound Dog
44 What Now My Love
49 Fever
52 Welcome to My World
55 Suspicious Minds
61 I'll Remember You
66 Long Tall Sally
64 Whole Lotta Shakin' Goin' On
69 An American Trilogy
73 A Big Hunk O' Love
77 Can't Help Falling in Love
81 Blue Hawaii
88 Ku-U-I-Po
85 No More
90 The Hawaiian Wedding Song
93 Early Mornin' Rain

ISBN 978-1-4950-0252-6

7777 W. Bluemound Rd. P.O. Box 13819 Milwaukee, WI 53213

Visit Hal Leonard Online at
www.halleonard.com

www.elvis.com

C.C. RIDER

Arranged by
ELVIS PRESLEY

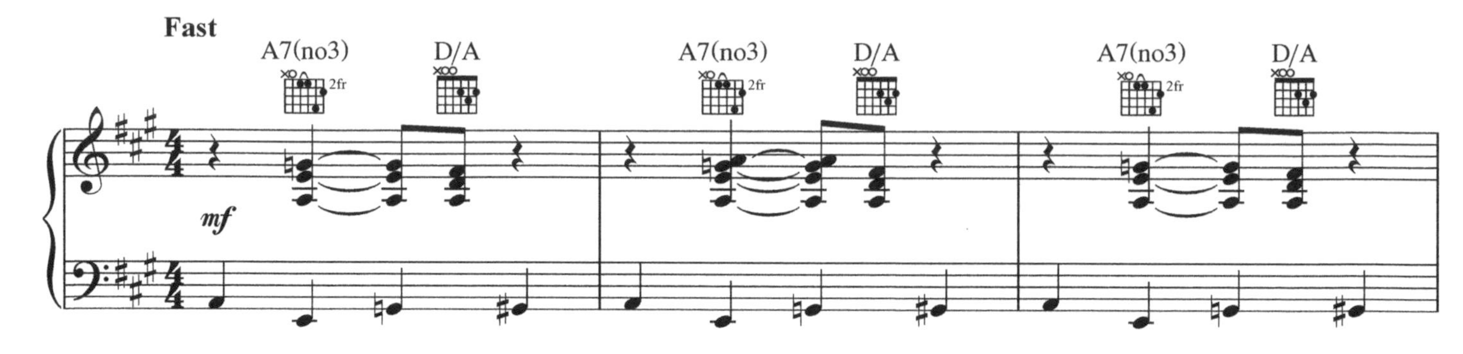

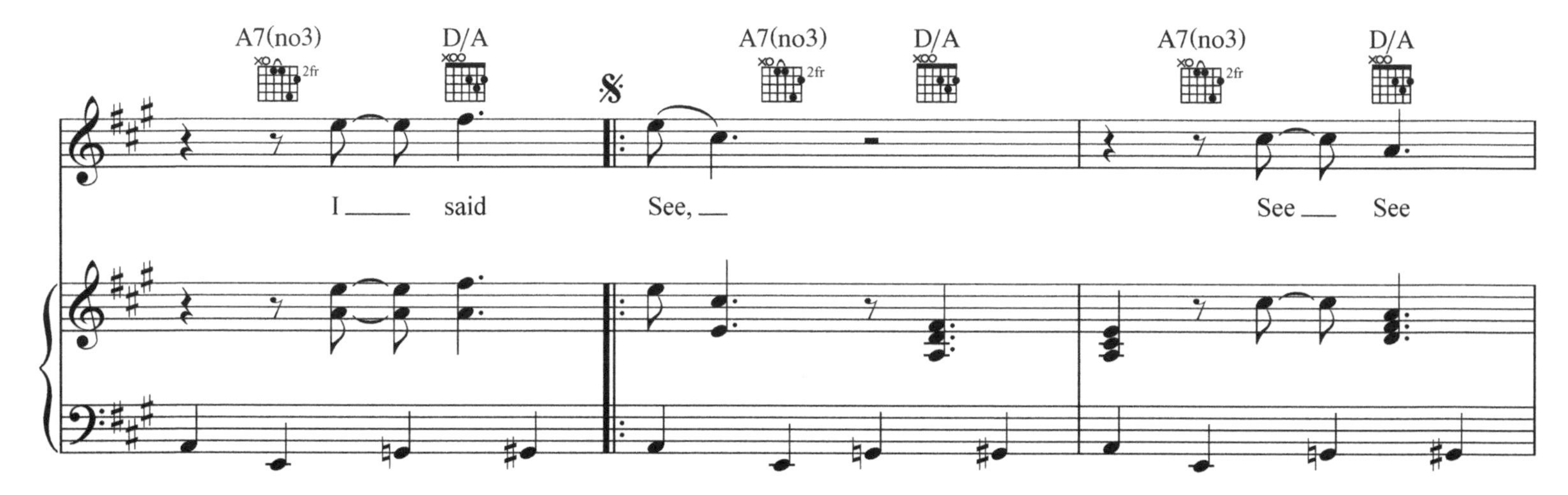

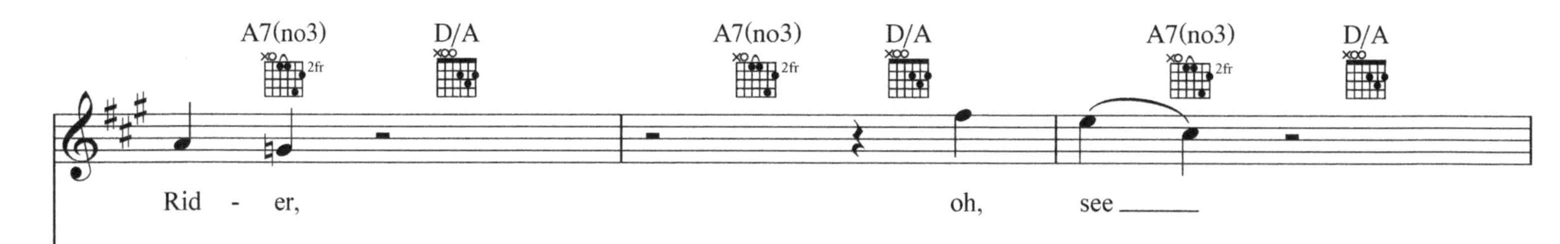

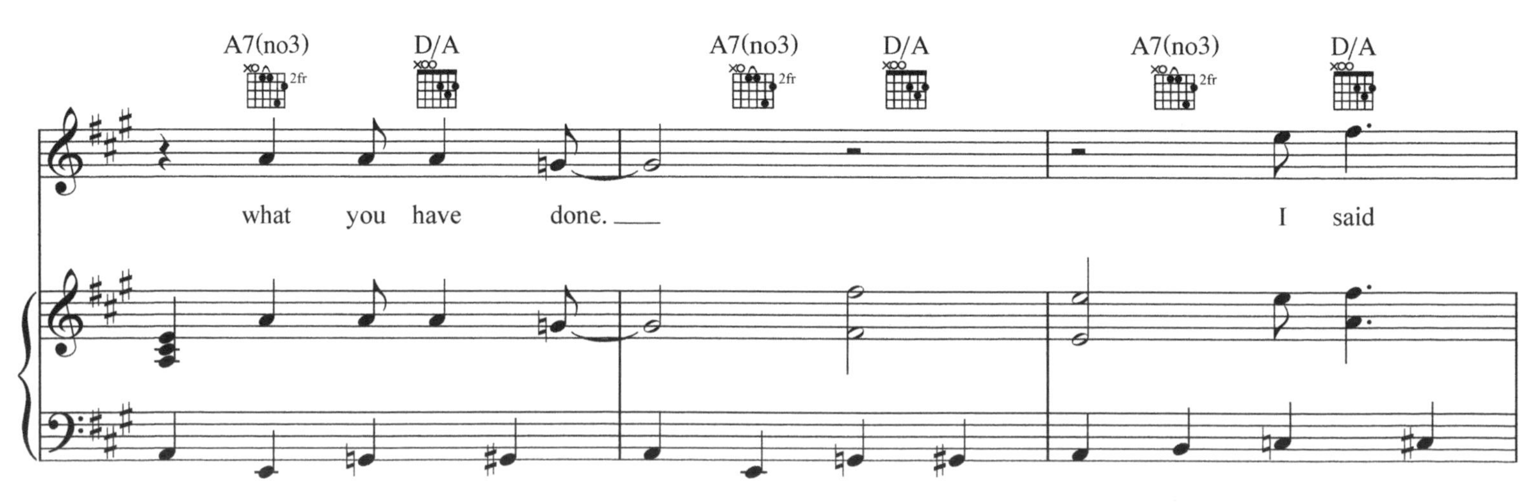

D7
See, See See Rid - er, oh,

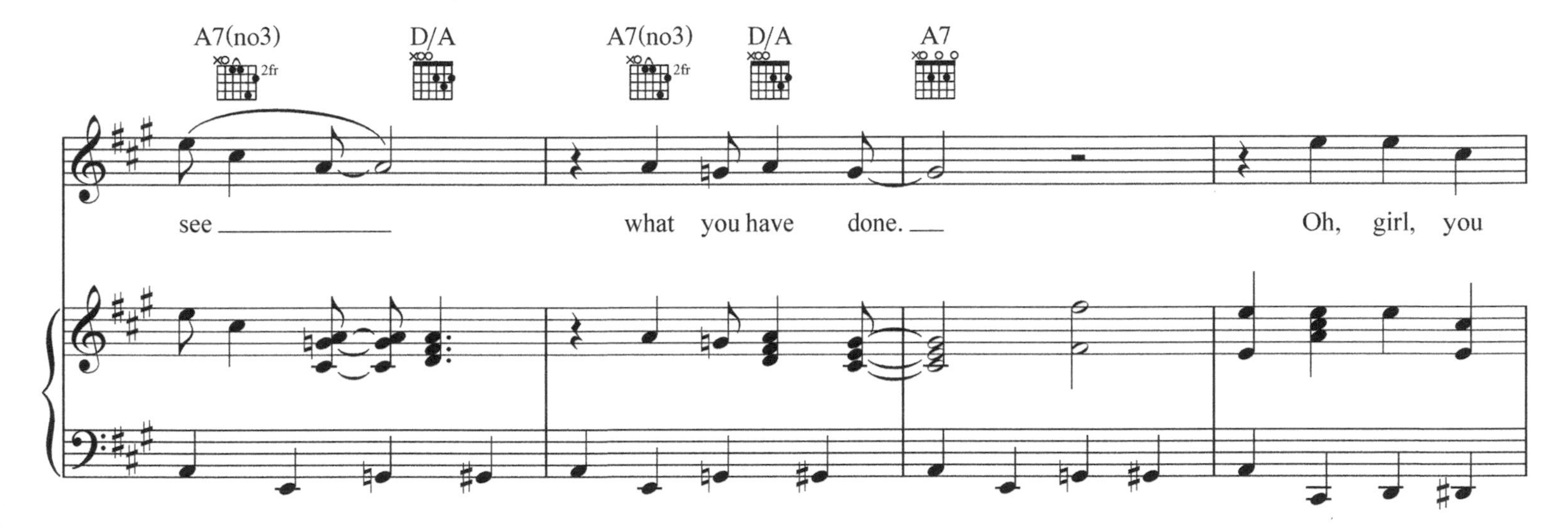
A7(no3)
D/A
A7(no3)
D/A
A7
2fr
see what you have done. Oh, girl, you

E7
D7/E
3fr
D7
made me love you. Now, now, now your lov - in' man has gone.

To Coda
A7(no3)
D/A
2fr
Well, what I say.
Well, I'm
Instrumental solo

A7
go - in'
a - way,
ba - by,

and I won't
be back till fall.

D7
And I'm go - in'

a - way,
ba - by,
and I won't

A7
be back till fall.
Well, if I find

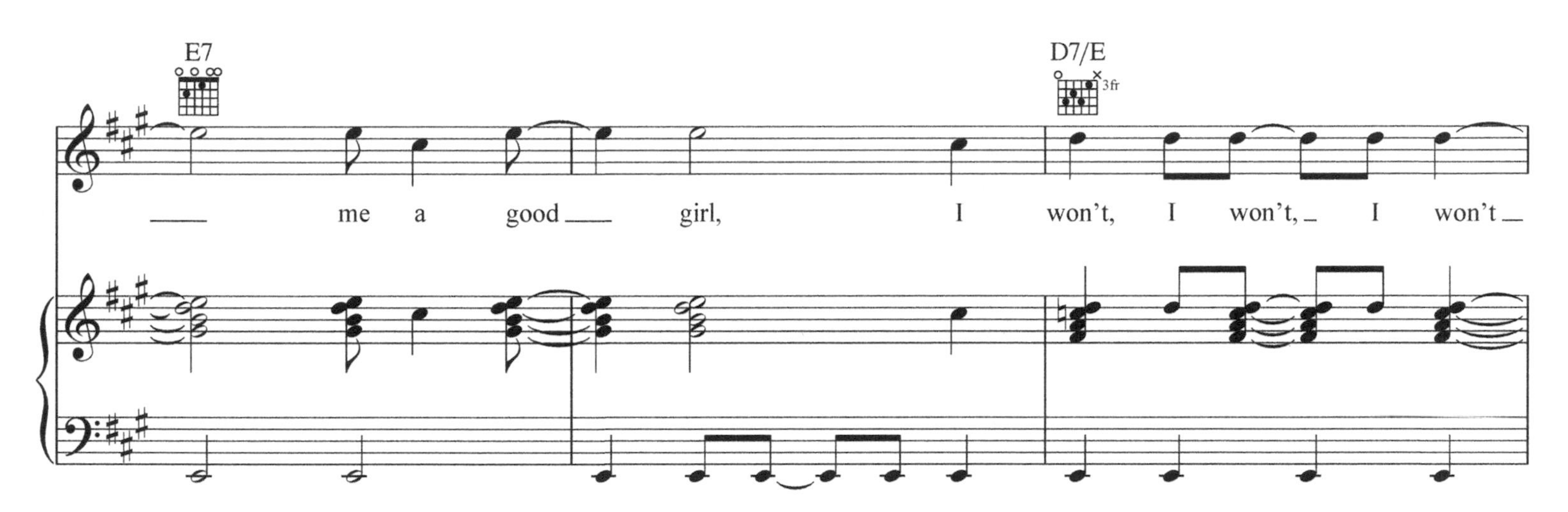
E7
D7/E
3fr
me a good girl,
I won't, I won't, I won't

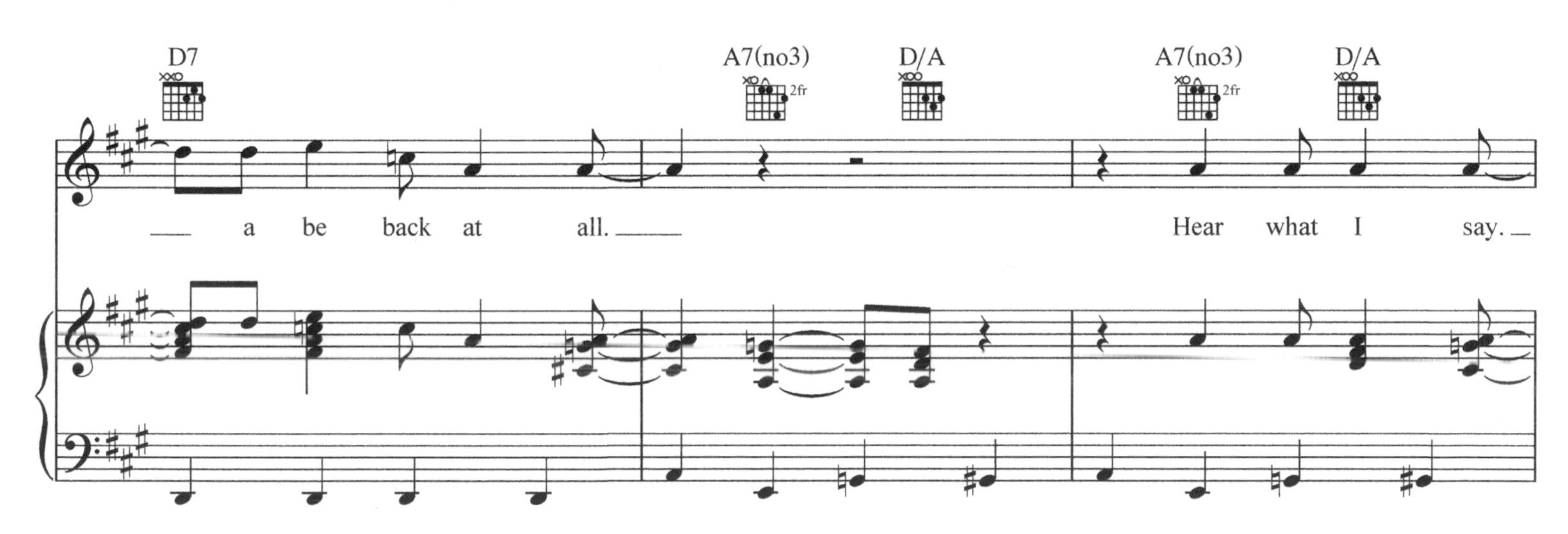
D7
A7(no3)
2fr
D/A
A7(no3)
2fr
D/A
a be back at all.
Hear what I say.

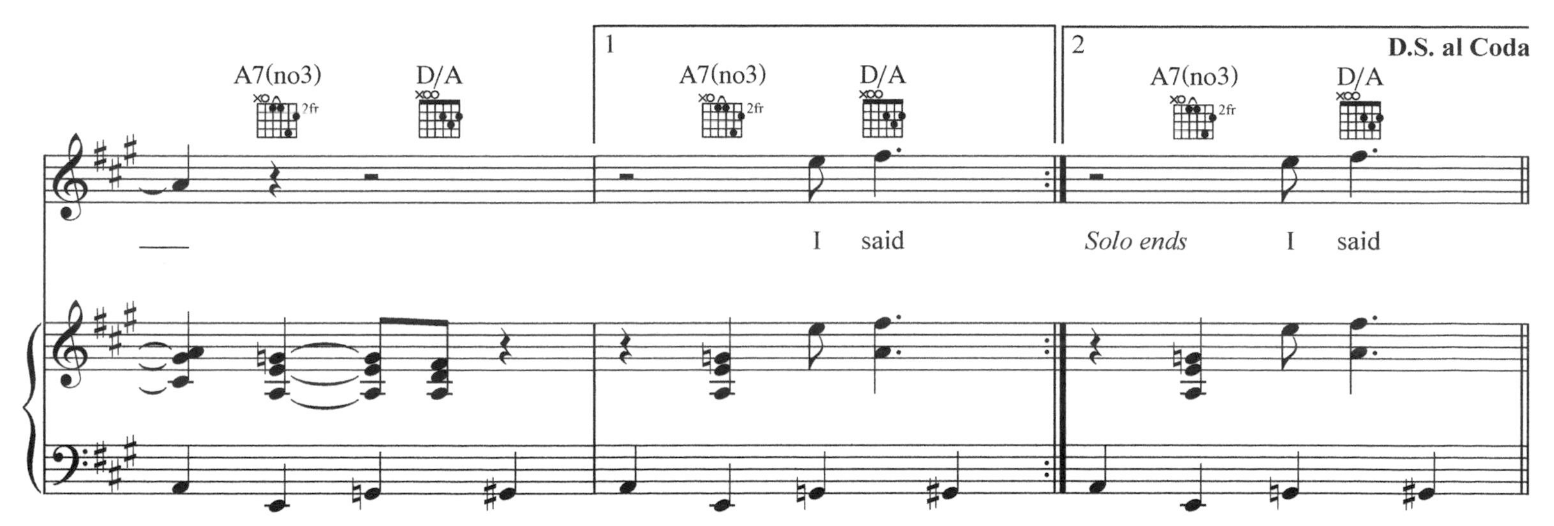
A7(no3)
2fr
D/A
1
A7(no3)
2fr
D/A
2
A7(no3)
2fr
D/A
D.S. al Coda
I said
Solo ends
I said

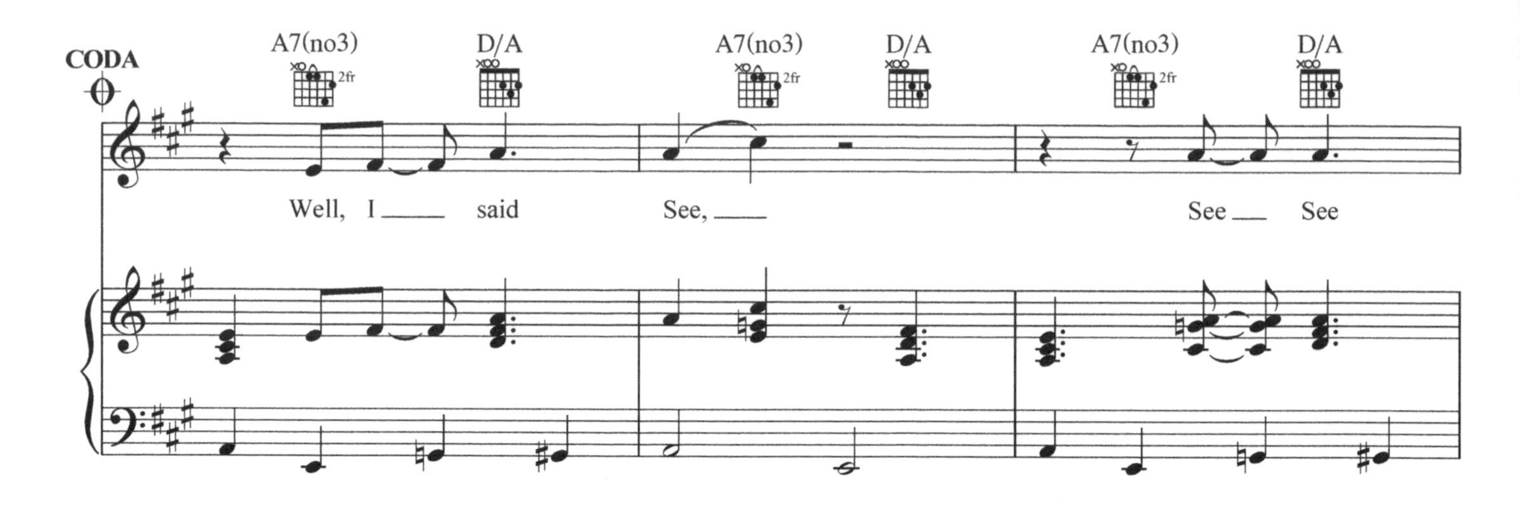
CODA
A7(no3)
D/A
2fr
Well, I said See, See See

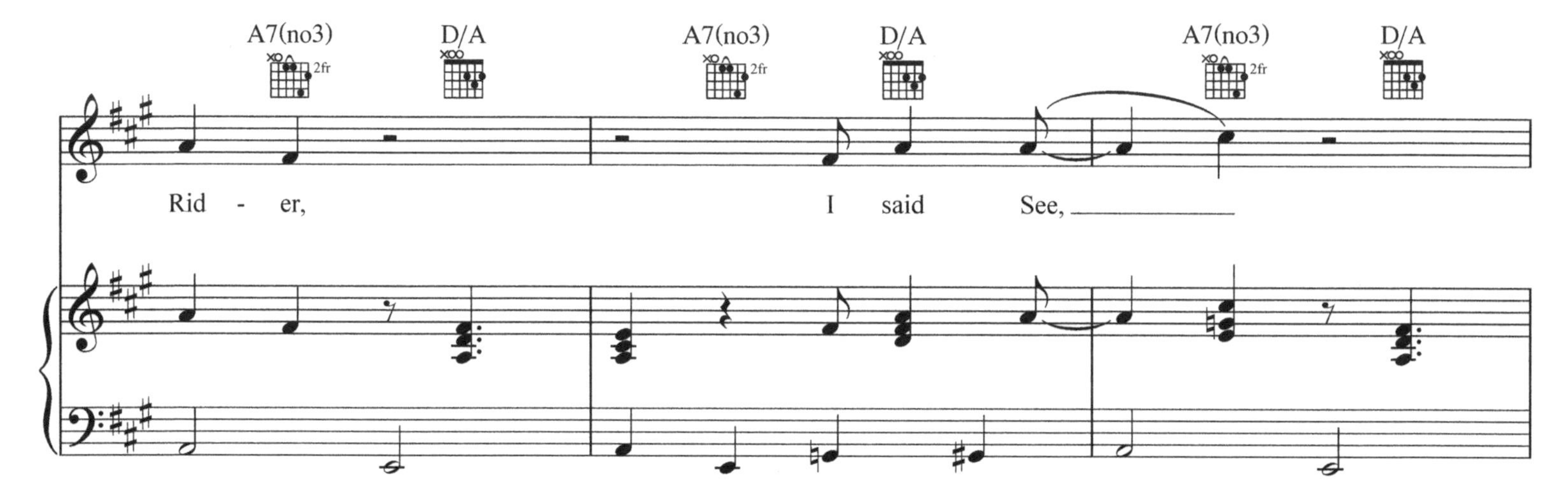
A7(no3)
D/A
2fr
Rid - er, I said See,

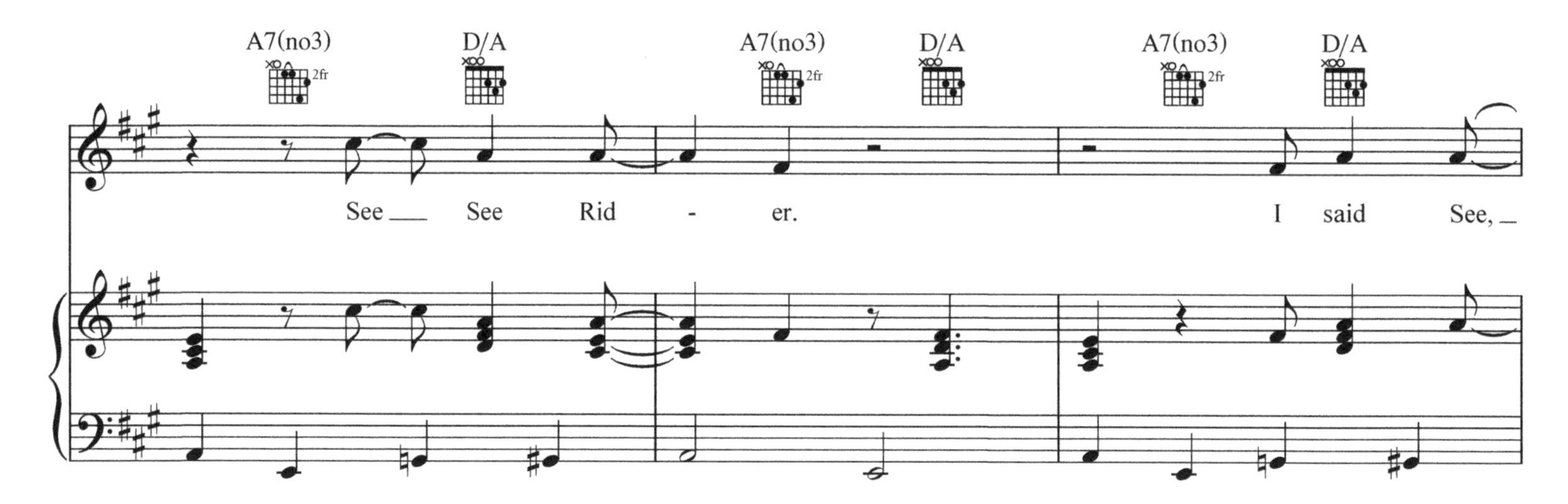
A7(no3)
D/A
2fr
See See Rid - er. I said See,

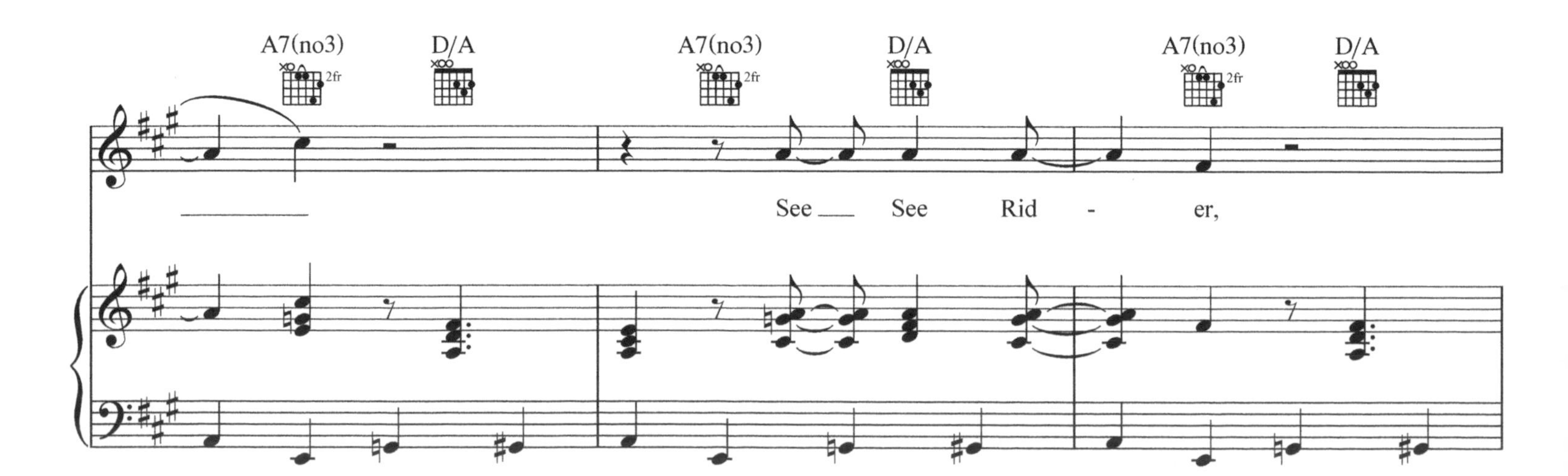
A7(no3)
D/A
2fr
See See Rid - er,

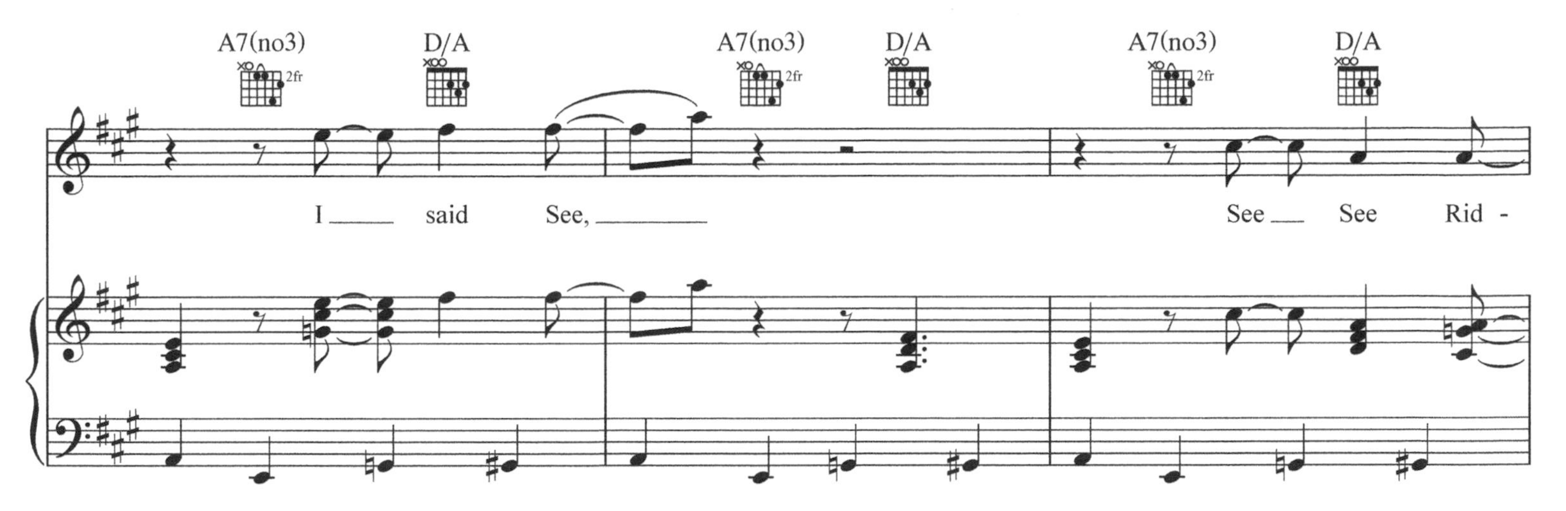
A7(no3)
D/A
A7(no3)
D/A
A7(no3)
D/A
2fr
I said See,
See See Rid -

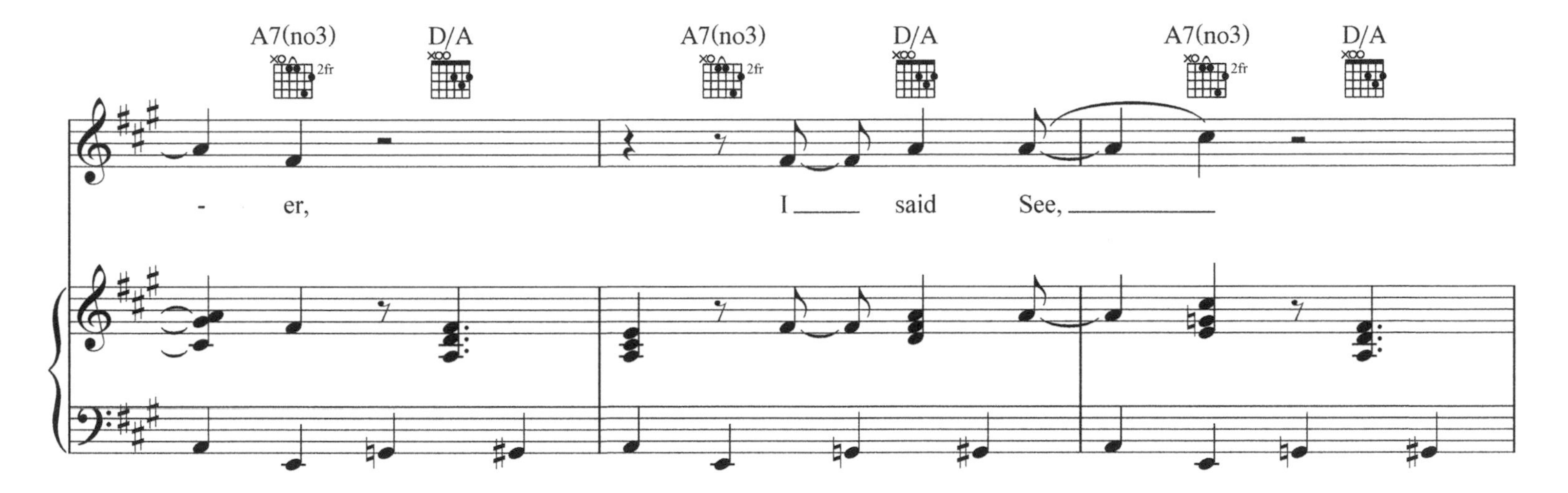
A7(no3)
D/A
A7(no3)
D/A
A7(no3)
D/A
2fr
- er,
I said See,

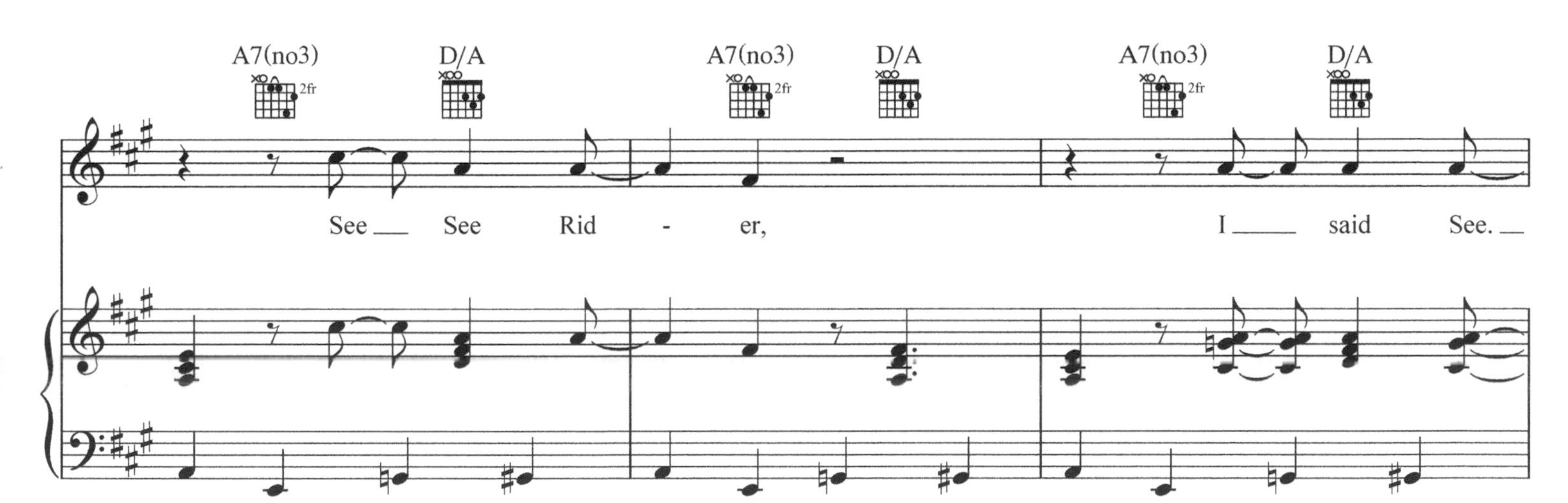
A7(no3)
D/A
A7(no3)
D/A
A7(no3)
D/A
2fr
See See Rid - er,
I said See.

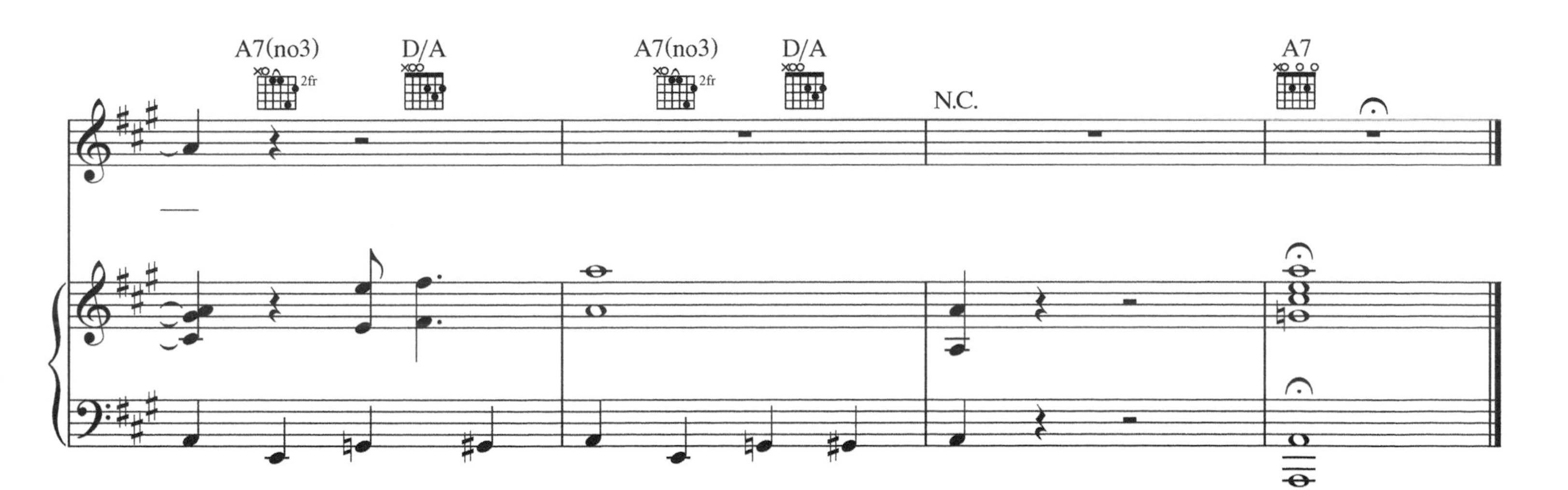
A7(no3)
D/A
A7(no3)
D/A
N.C.
A7
2fr

BURNING LOVE

Words and Music by
DENNIS LINDE

G
A
D
you've gone and set me on fire.
My
burn - in' and noth - in' can cool me.
I
and my chest is a heav - in'.
G
A
D
brain is flam - in', I don't know which way to go.
just might turn to smoke but I feel fine.
Lord, have mer - cy, I'm burn - in' a hole where I lay.
Bm
A
G
Your
'Cause your
Your
kiss - es lift me high - er, like the

Bm
A
G
Bm
A
sweet song of a choir, and you light my morn - in' sky

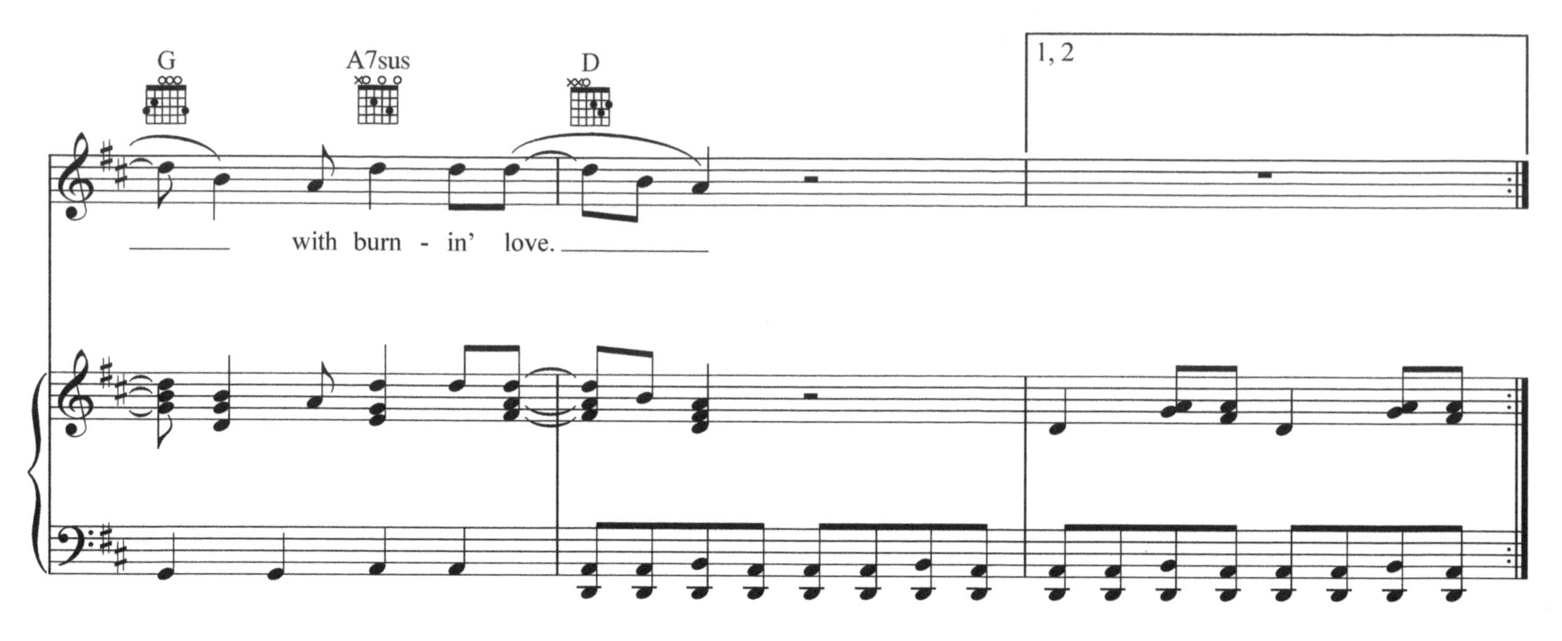
G
A7sus
D
1, 2
with burn - in' love.

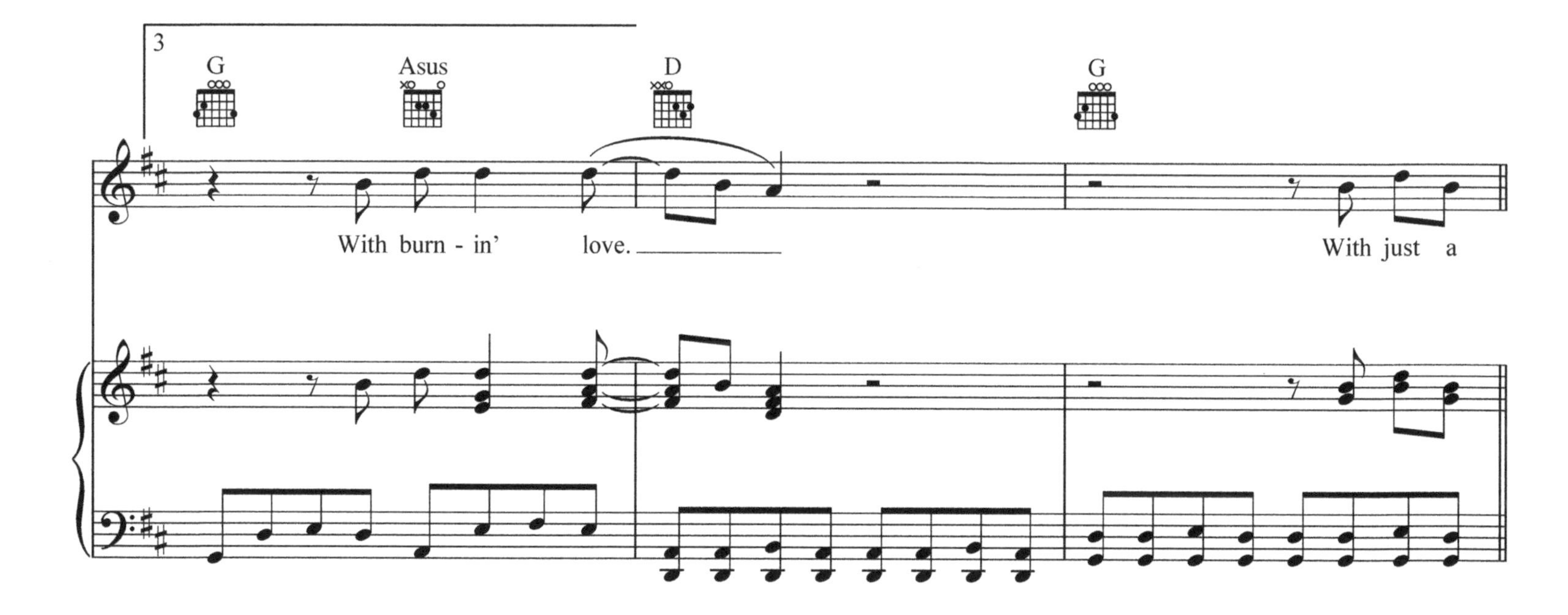
3
G
Asus
D
G
With burn - in' love.
With just a

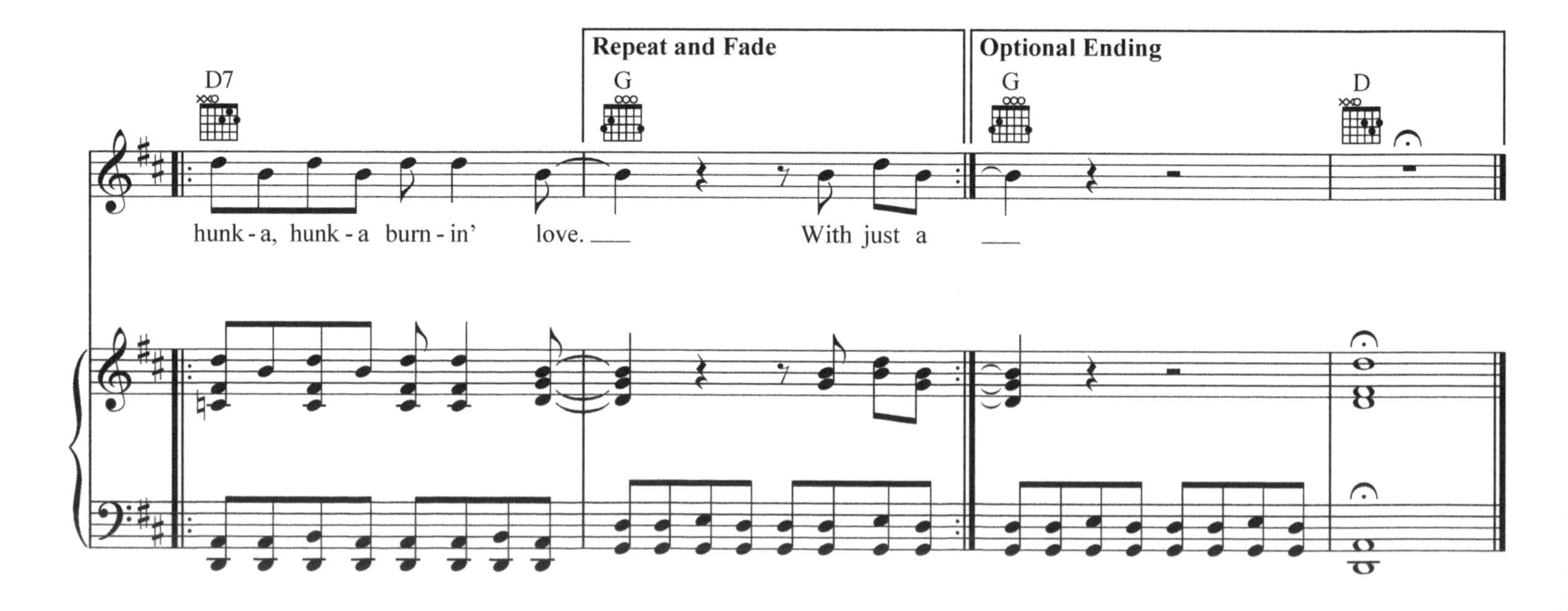
D7
Repeat and Fade
G
Optional Ending
G
D
hunk - a, hunk - a burn - in' love.
With just a

SOMETHING

Words and Music by
GEORGE HARRISON

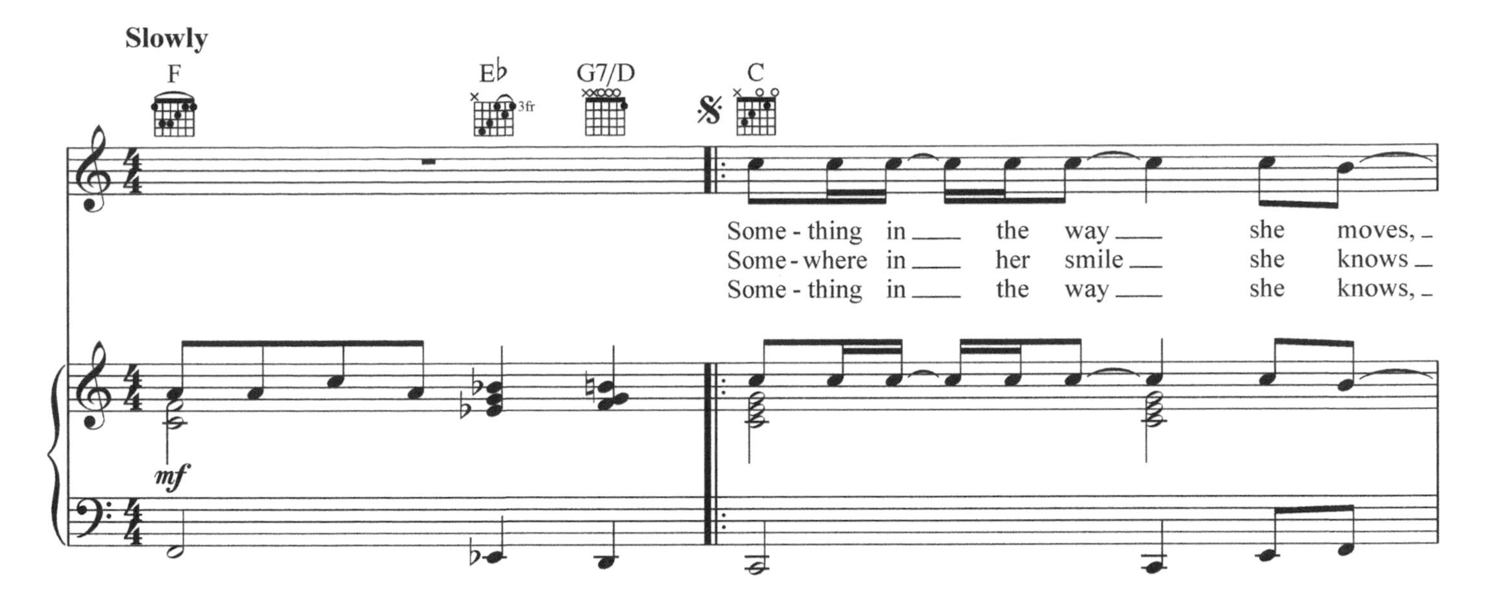

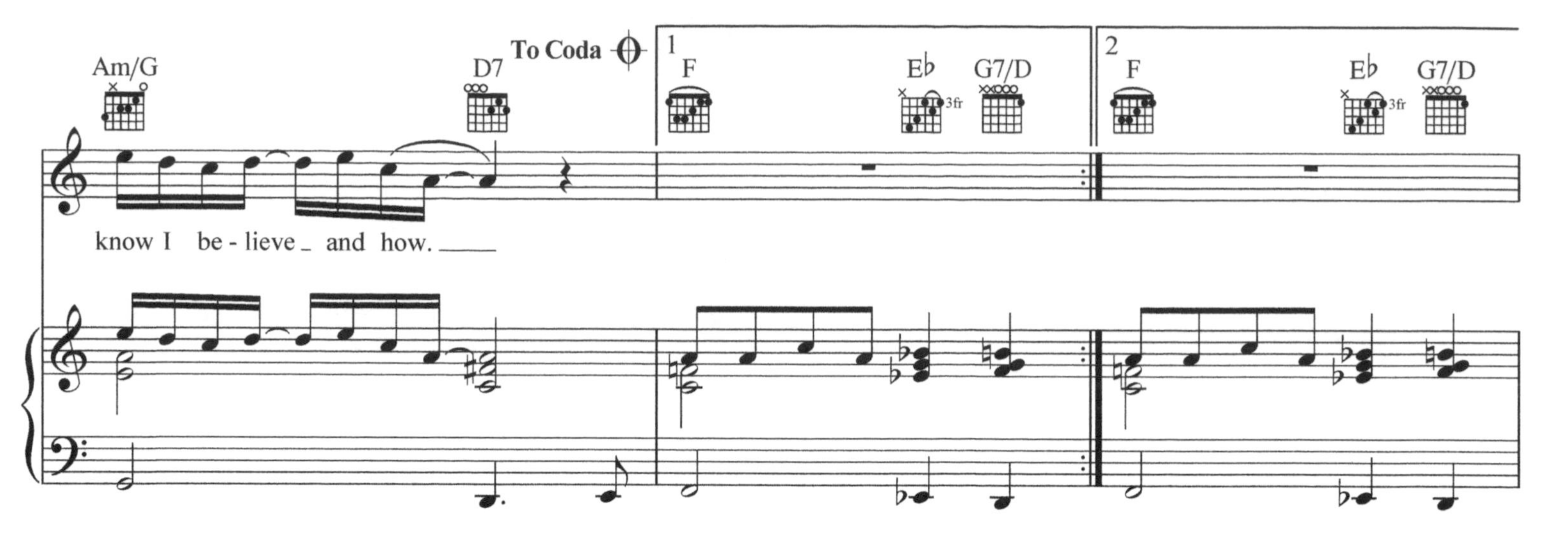
Am/G
D7
To Coda
F
E♭
G7/D
F
E♭
G7/D
know I be - lieve _ and how. ___

A
C♯m/G♯
F♯m
F♯m/E
You're ask-ing me _ will my _ love grow, I don't know, _

D
G
A
C♯m/G♯
_____ I ___ don't know. You stick a - round _ now, it may

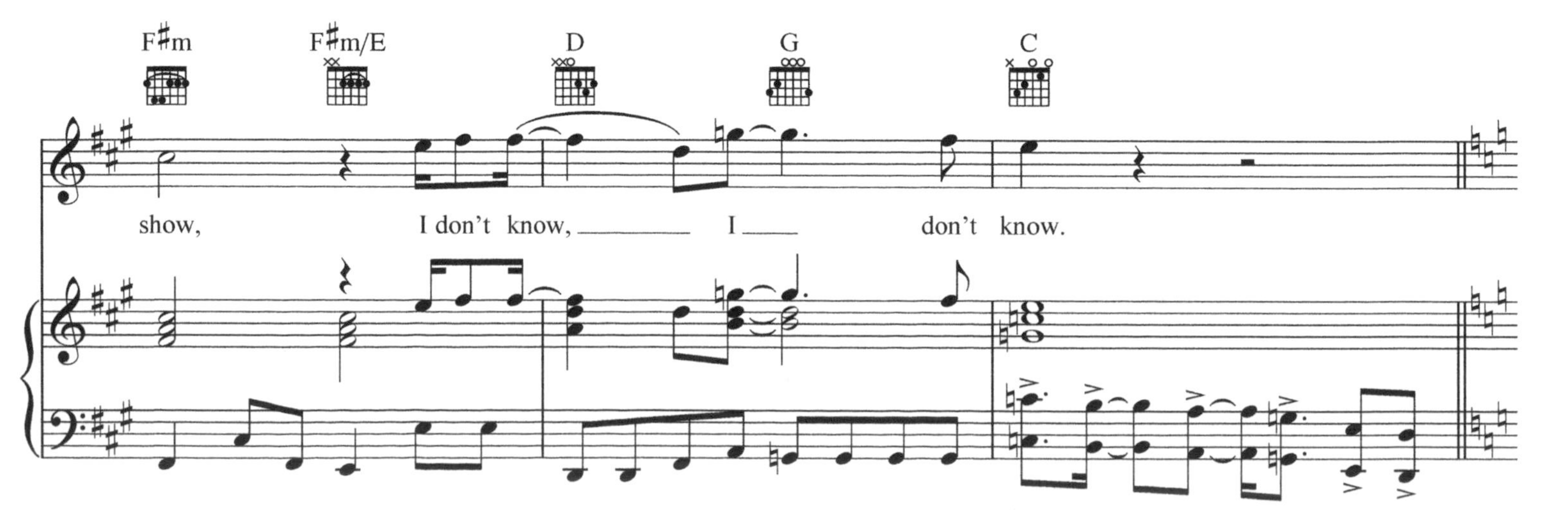
F♯m
F♯m/E
D
G
C
show, I don't know, ______ I ___ don't know.

Cmaj7
C7

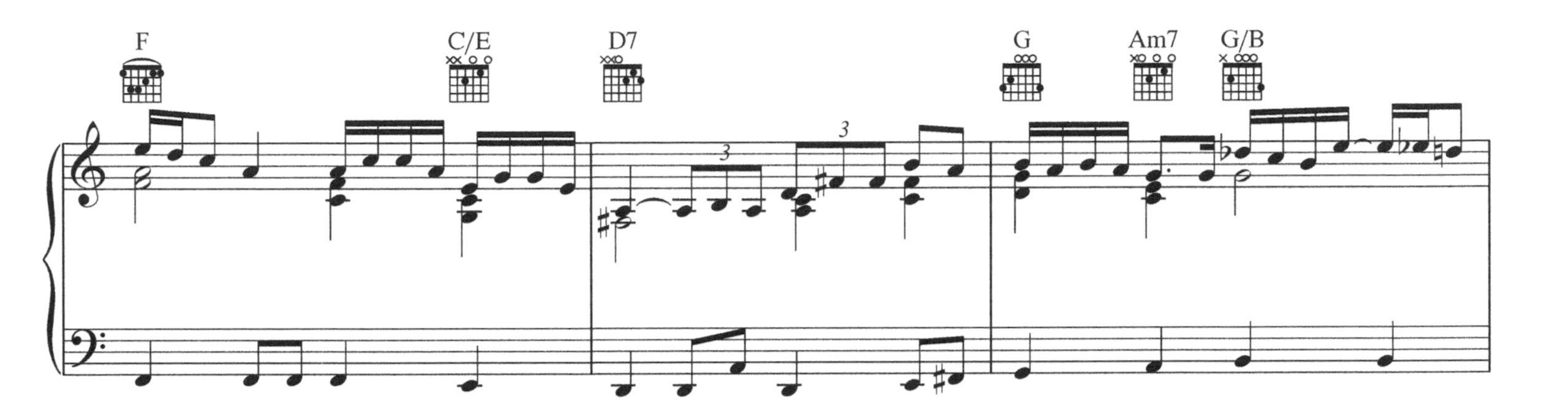
F
C/E
D7
G
Am7
G/B

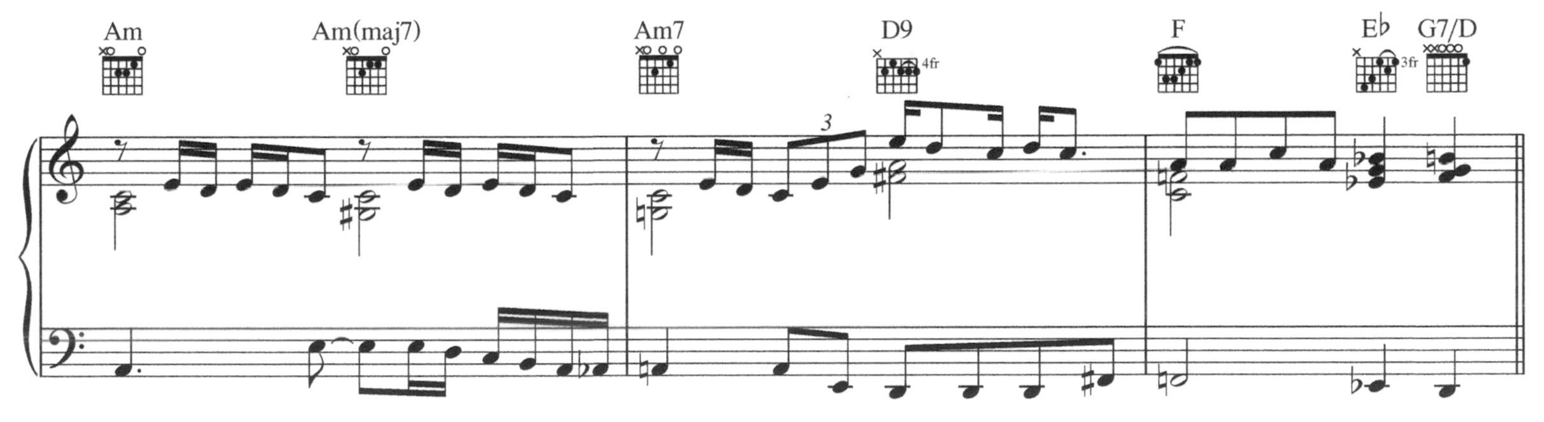
D.S. al Coda
Am
Am(maj7)
Am7
D9
F
E♭
G7/D

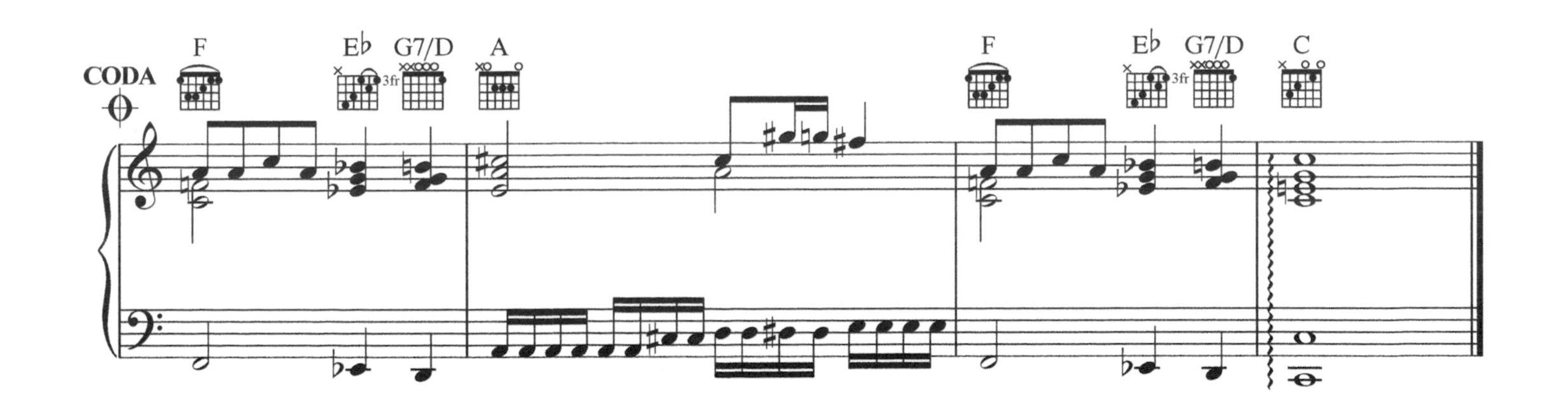
CODA
F
E♭
G7/D
A
F
E♭
G7/D
C

YOU GAVE ME A MOUNTAIN

Words and Music by
MARTY ROBBINS

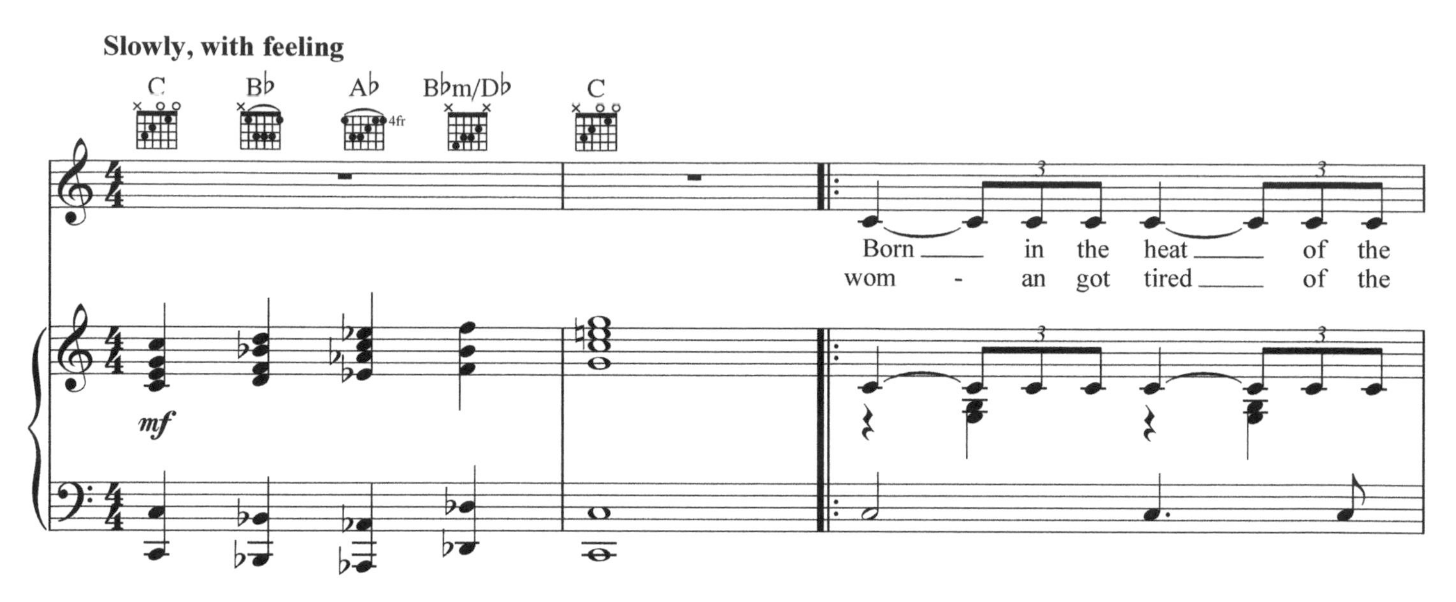

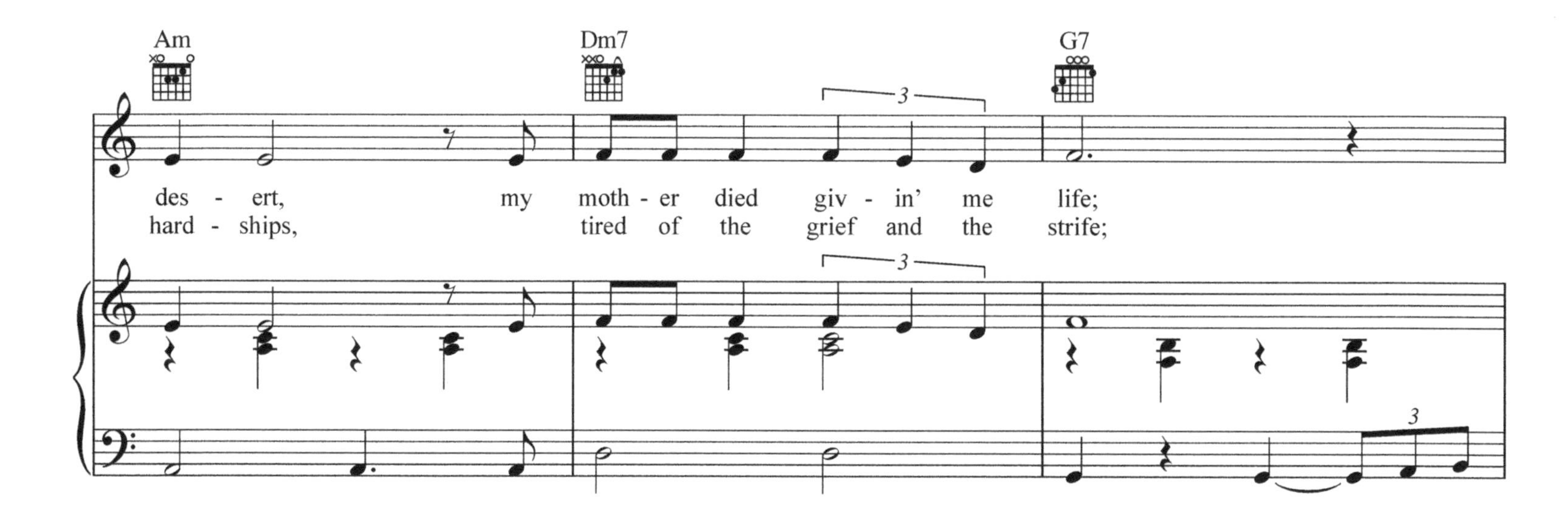

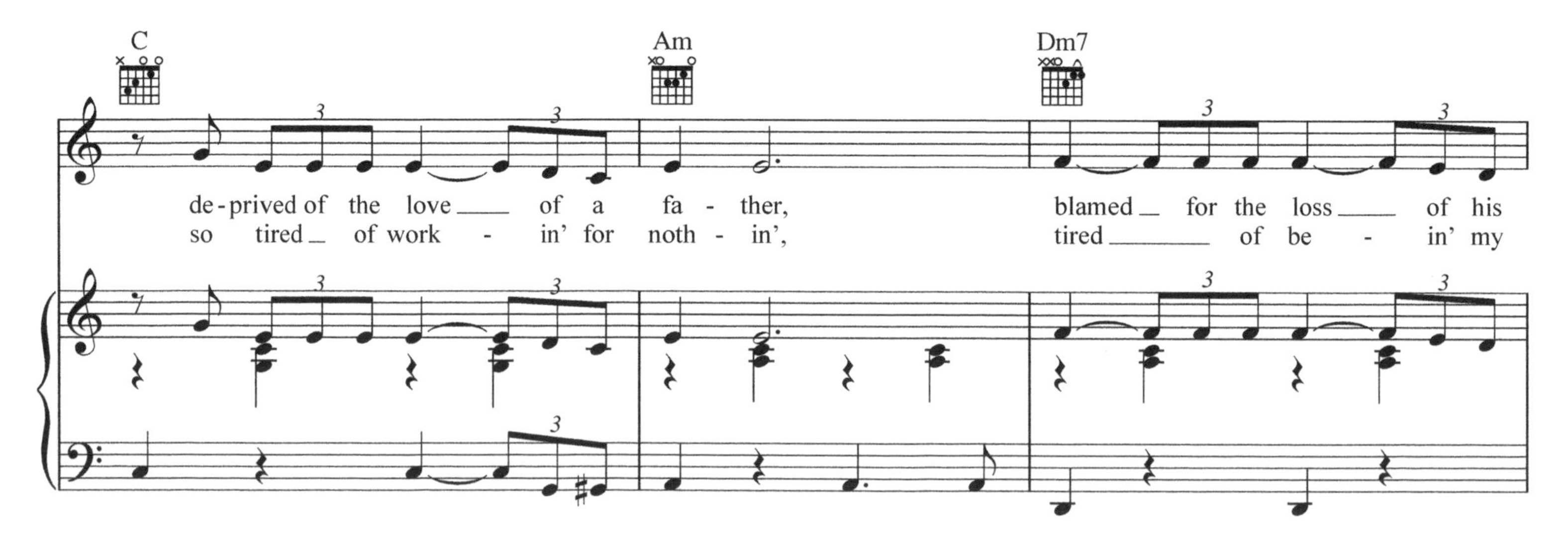

G7
C
Am7
wife. You know, Lord, I've been in a pris - on for
wife. She took my one ray of sun - shine. She

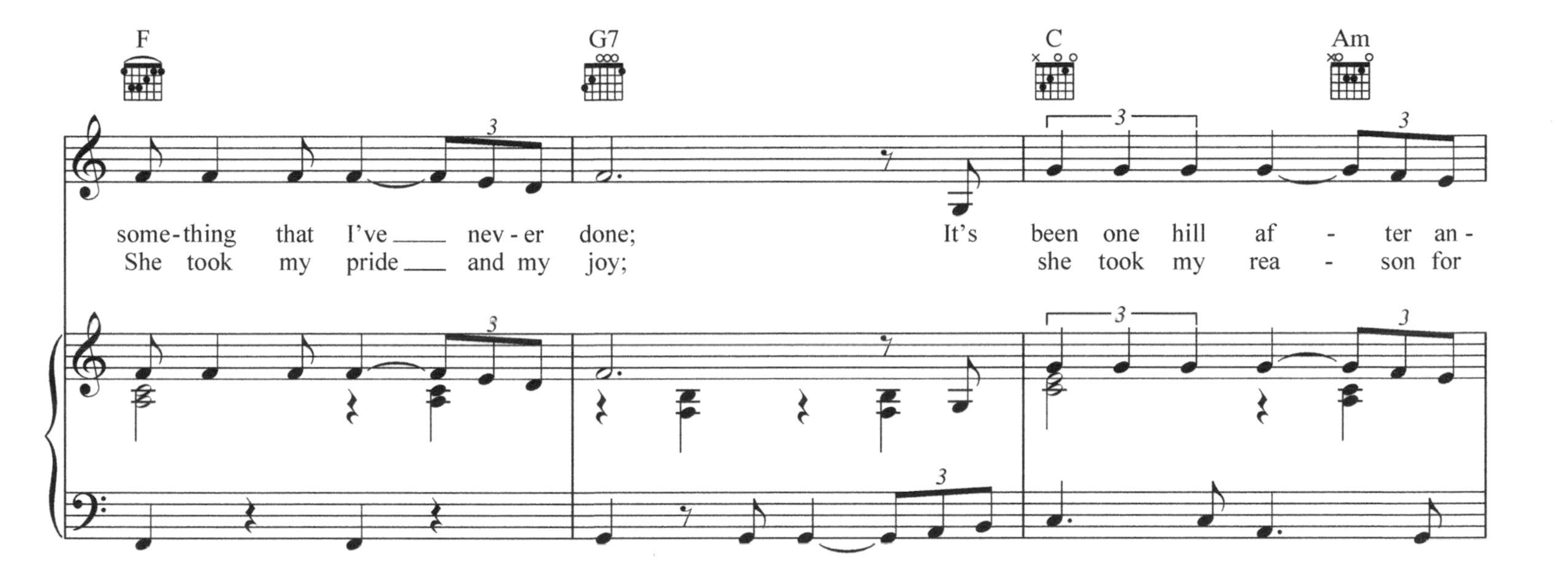
F
G7
C
Am
some - thing that I've nev - er done; It's been one hill af - ter an -
She took my pride and my joy; she took my rea - son for

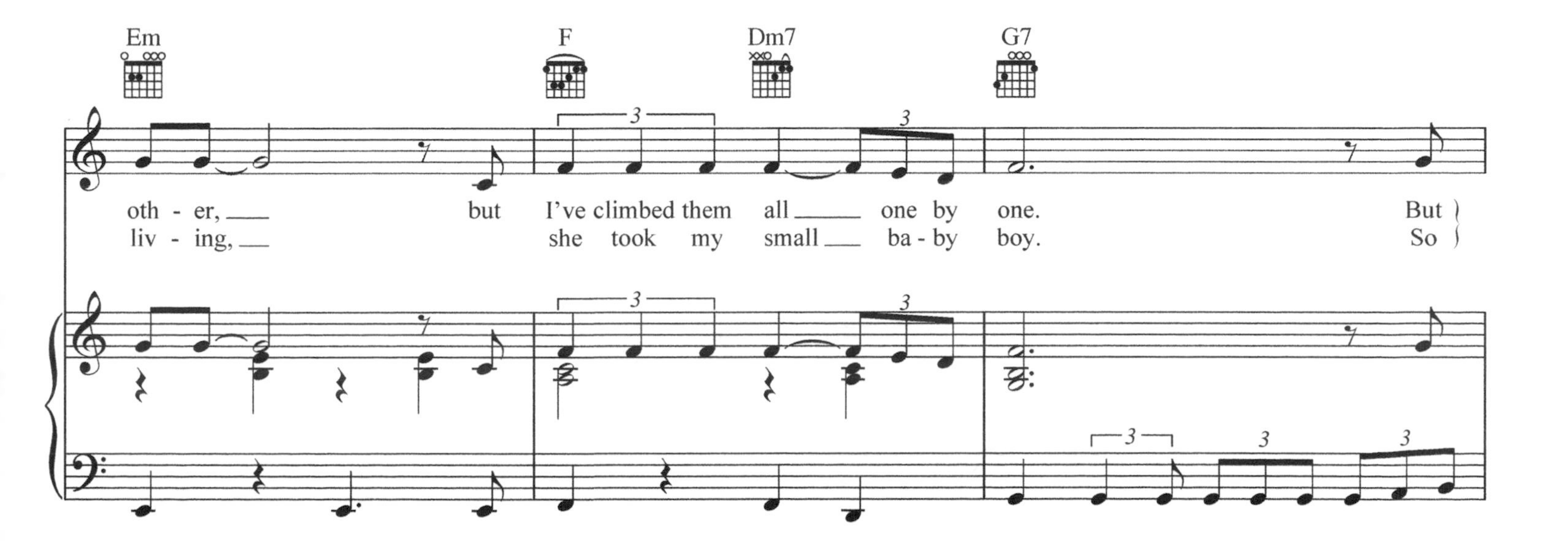
Em
F
Dm7
G7
oth - er, but I've climbed them all one by one. But
liv - ing, she took my small ba - by boy. So

C
F
this time, Lord, you gave me a

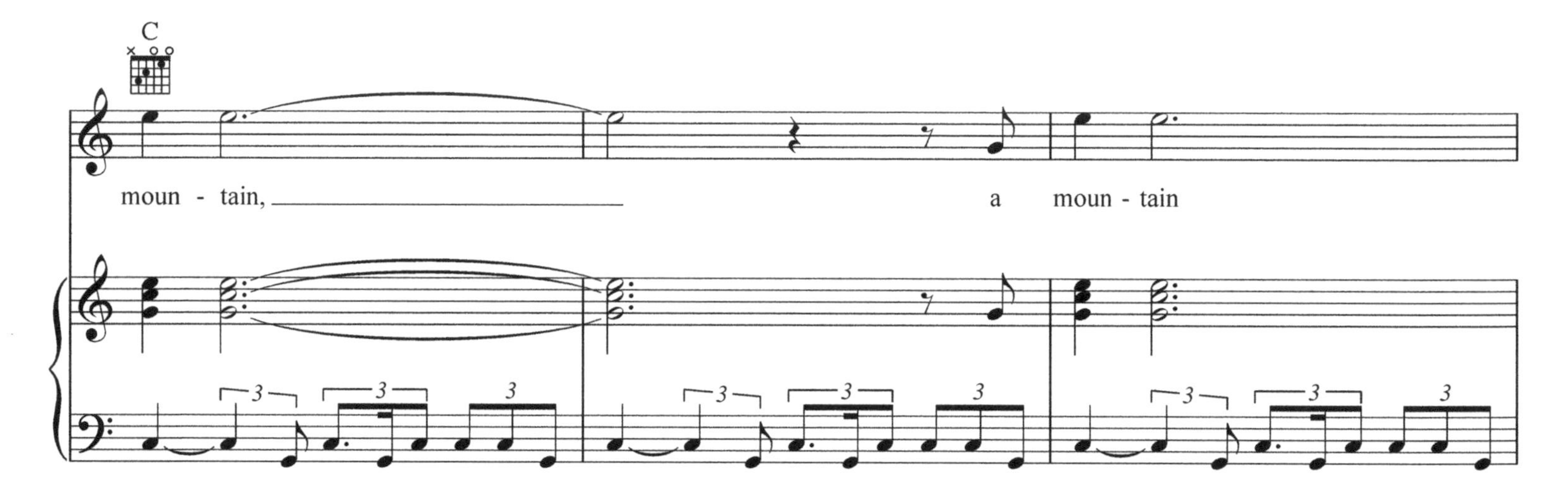
C
moun - tain, a moun - tain

F
C
I may nev - er climb.

And it is - n't a

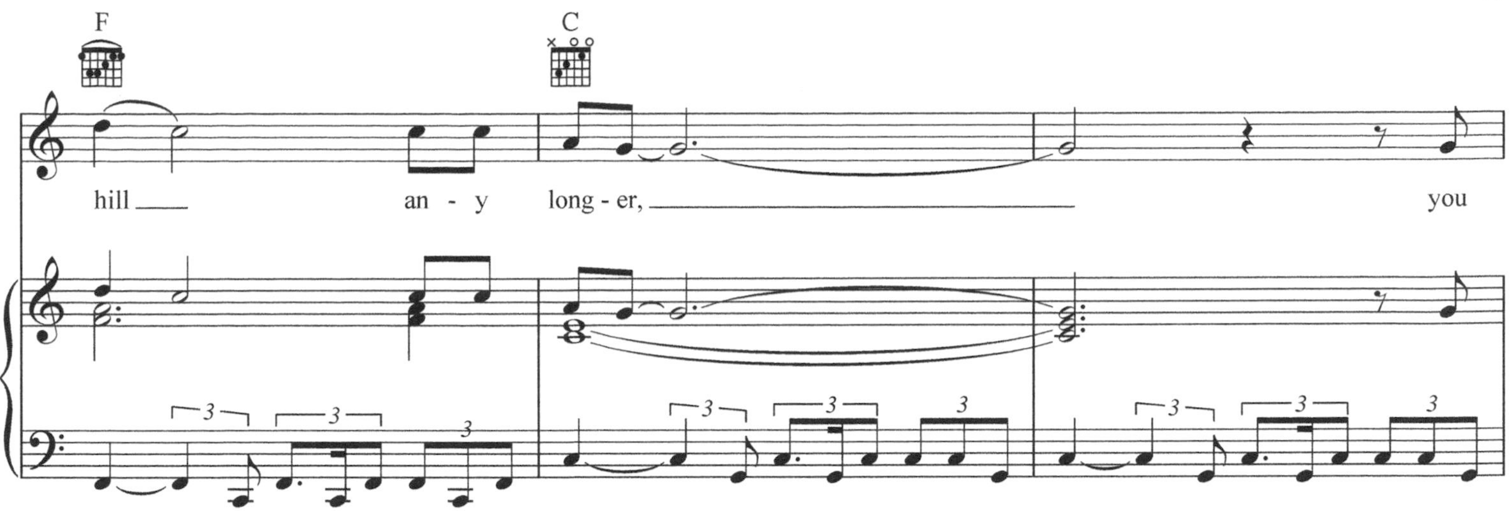
F
C
hill any - y long - er, you

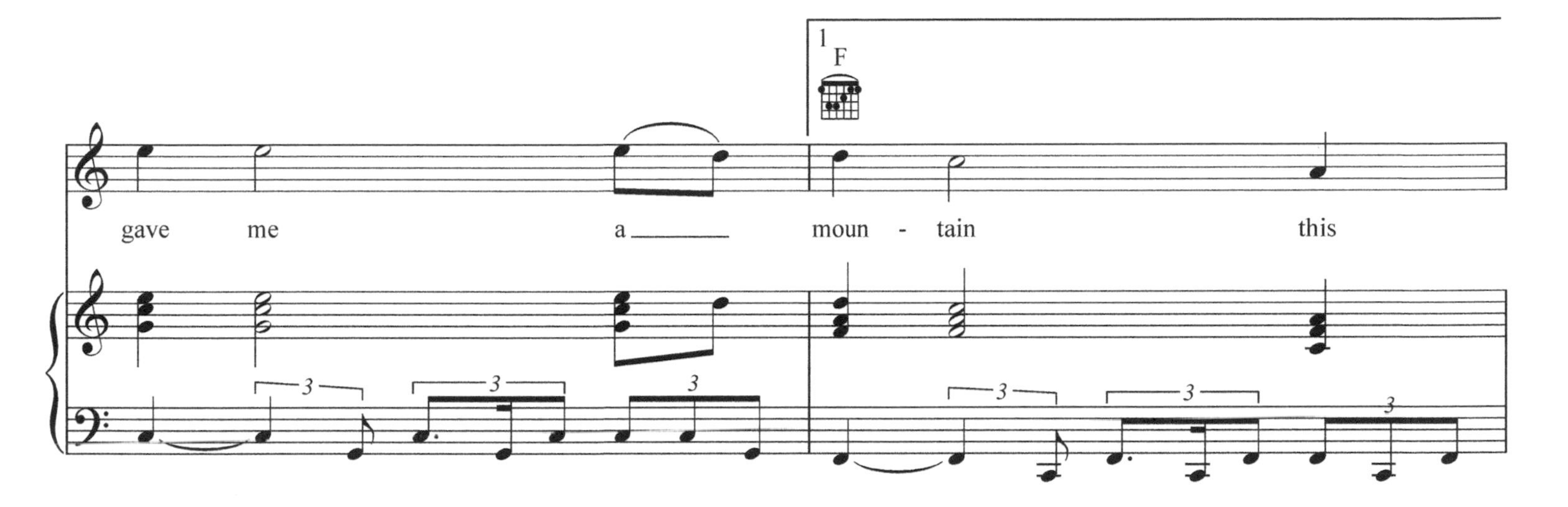
1
F
gave me a moun - tain this

C
time. My

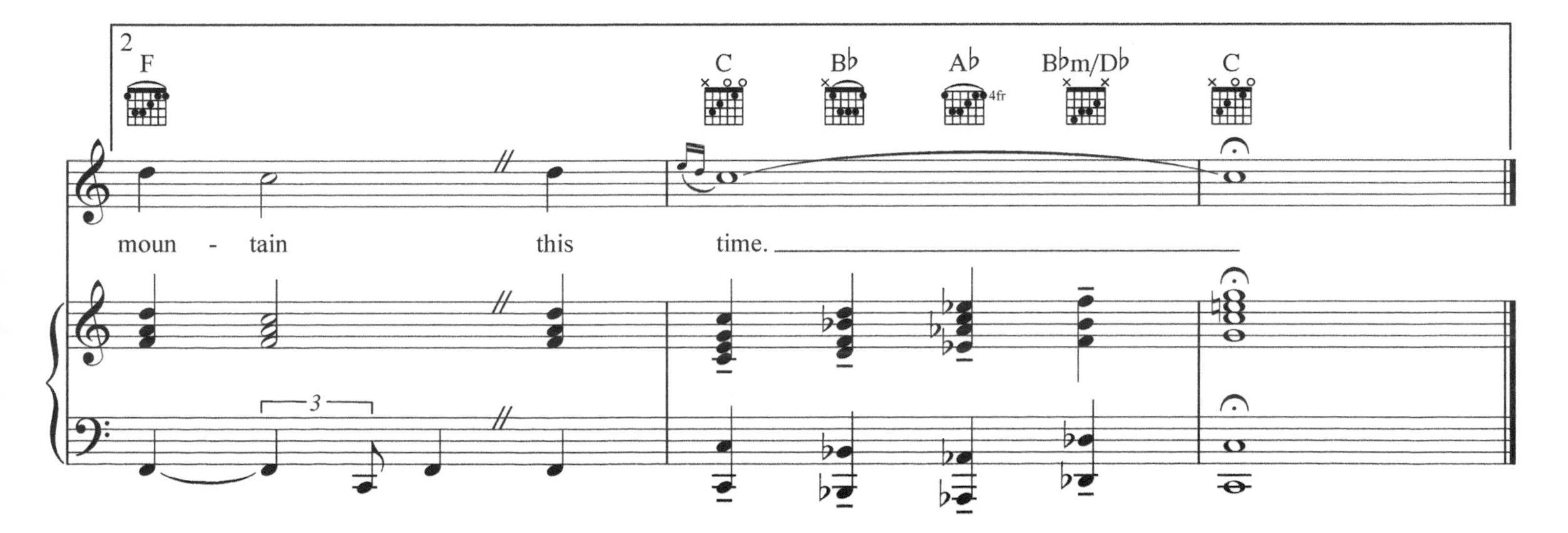
2
F
C
B♭
A♭
B♭m/D♭
C
4fr
moun - tain this time.

STEAMROLLER
(Steamroller Blues)

Words and Music by
JAMES TAYLOR

Moderate Blues

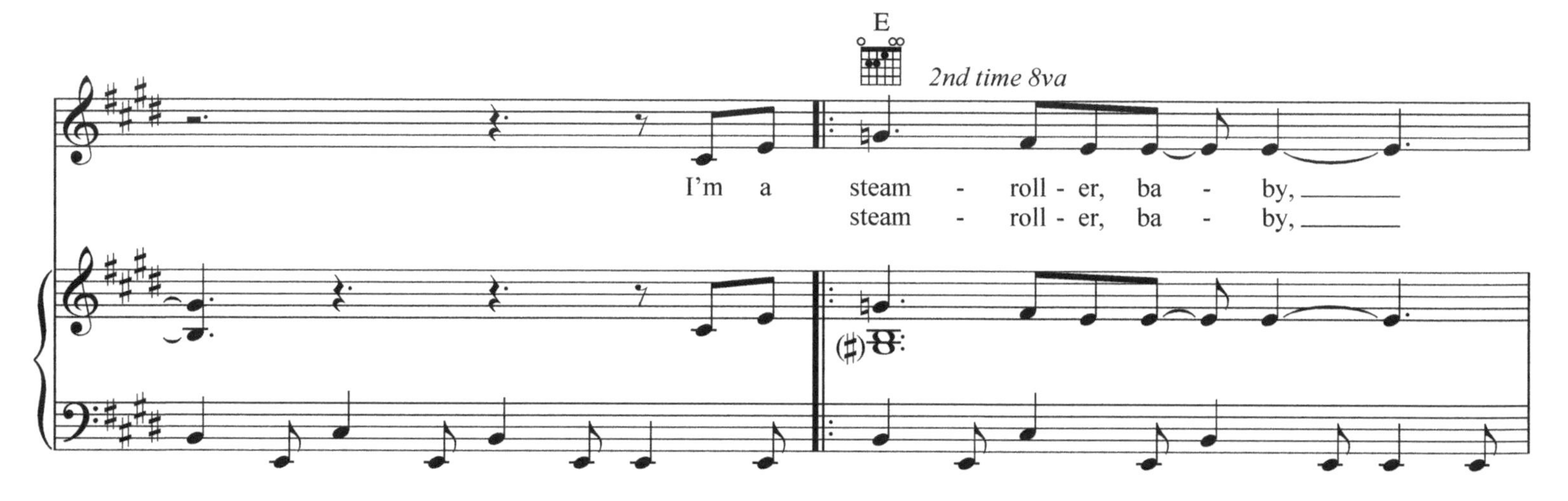

E
you.
you.
I'm gon - na in -
I'm gon - na in -

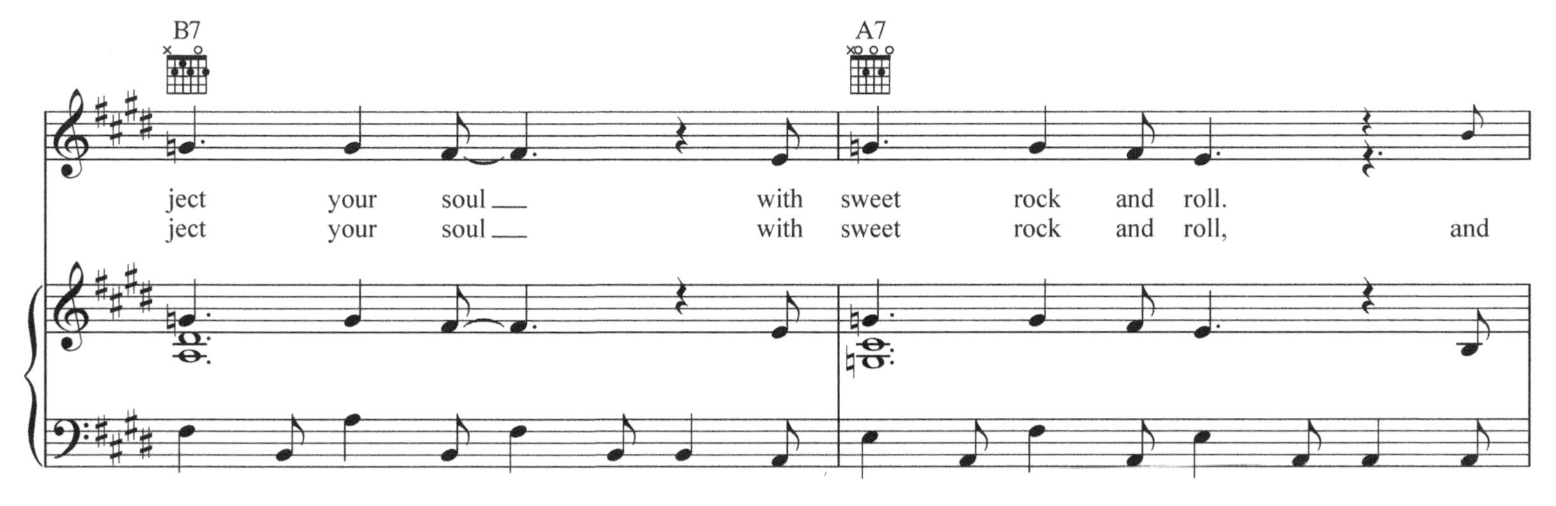
B7
A7
ject your soul with sweet rock and roll.
ject your soul with sweet rock and roll, and

E
B7
Hum.
shoot you full of rhy - thm and blues.
I'm a
I'm a

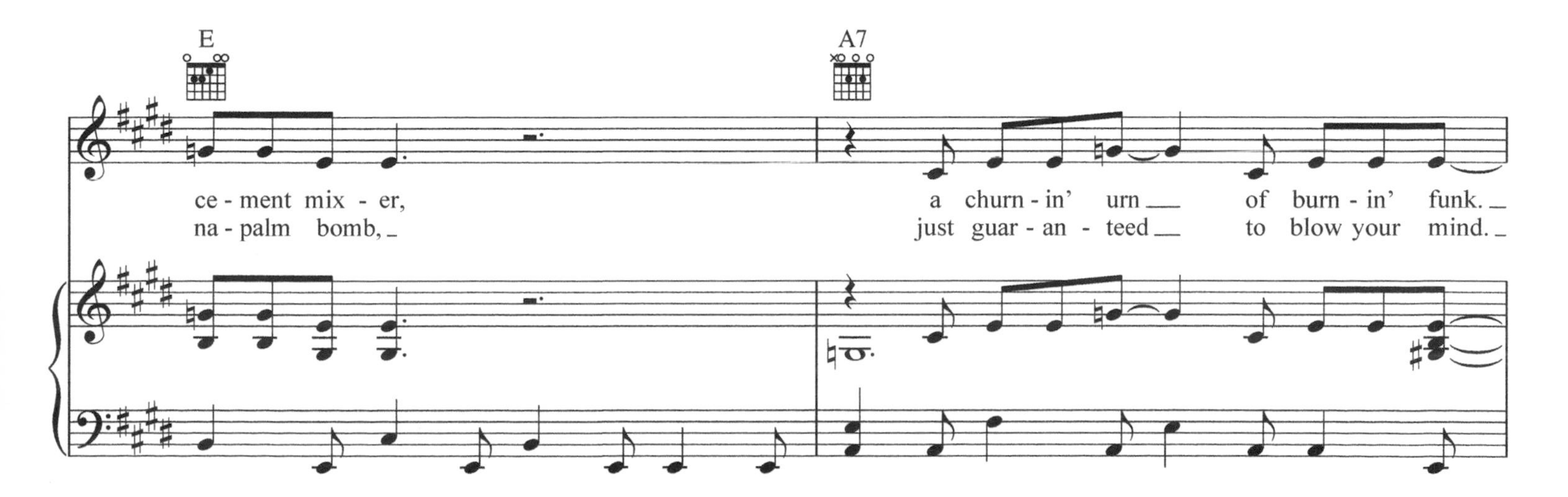
E
A7
ce - ment mix - er,
na - palm bomb,
a churn - in' urn of burn - in' funk.
just guar - an - teed to blow your mind.

E
A7
I'm a ce - ment mix - er,
I'm a na - palm bomb, __
E
a churn - in' urn __ of burn - in' funk. __
just guar - an - teed __ to blow your mind. __
I'm a
If I can't
B7
A7
1
E
4
dem - o - li - tion der - by, __
a heft - y hunk __ of steam - in' junk.
have your love now, ba - by, __
there won't be noth - ing left be -
B7
2
E
D9
E♭9
E9
4fr
I'm a
hind. __

MY WAY

English Words by PAUL ANKA
Original French Words by GILLES THIBAULT
Music by JACQUES REVAUX and CLAUDE FRANÇOIS

C
C7
cer - tain. I've lived a life that's full, I trav - eled
emp - tion. I planned each chart - ed course, each care - ful
F
Fm/B♭
C
each and ev - 'ry high - way, and more, much more than
step a - long the by - way, and more, much more than
G7
1
F6
C
2
F6
this, I did it my way. Re -
this, I did it my
3
C
C7
way. Yes, there were times, I'm sure you knew, when I bit

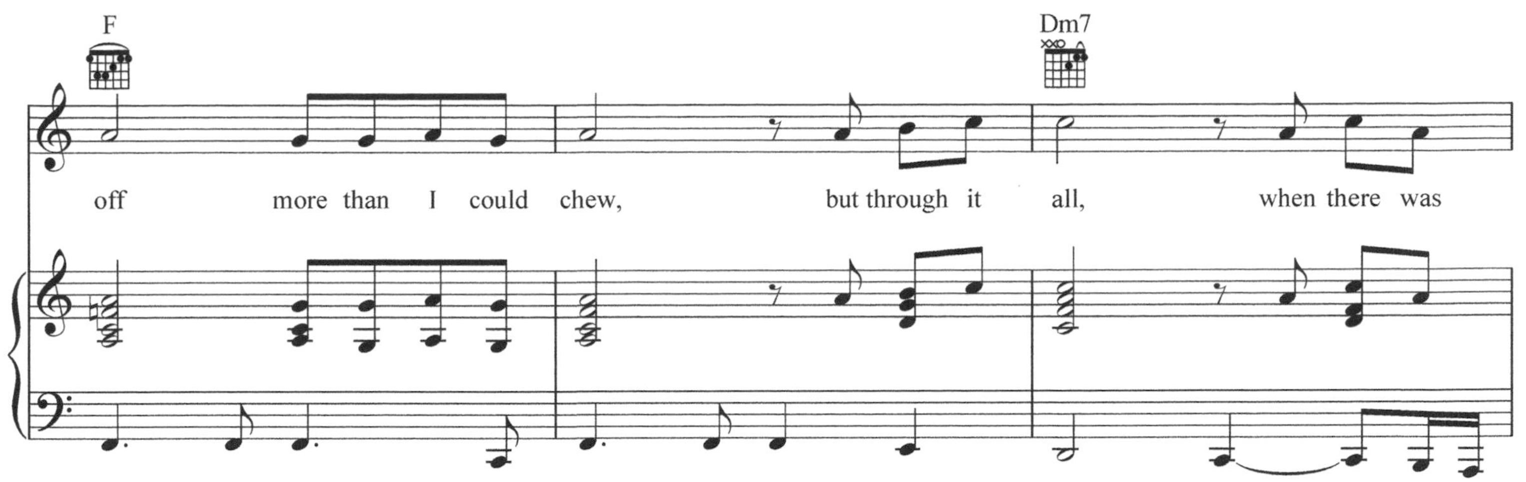
F
Dm7
off more than I could chew, but through it all, when there was

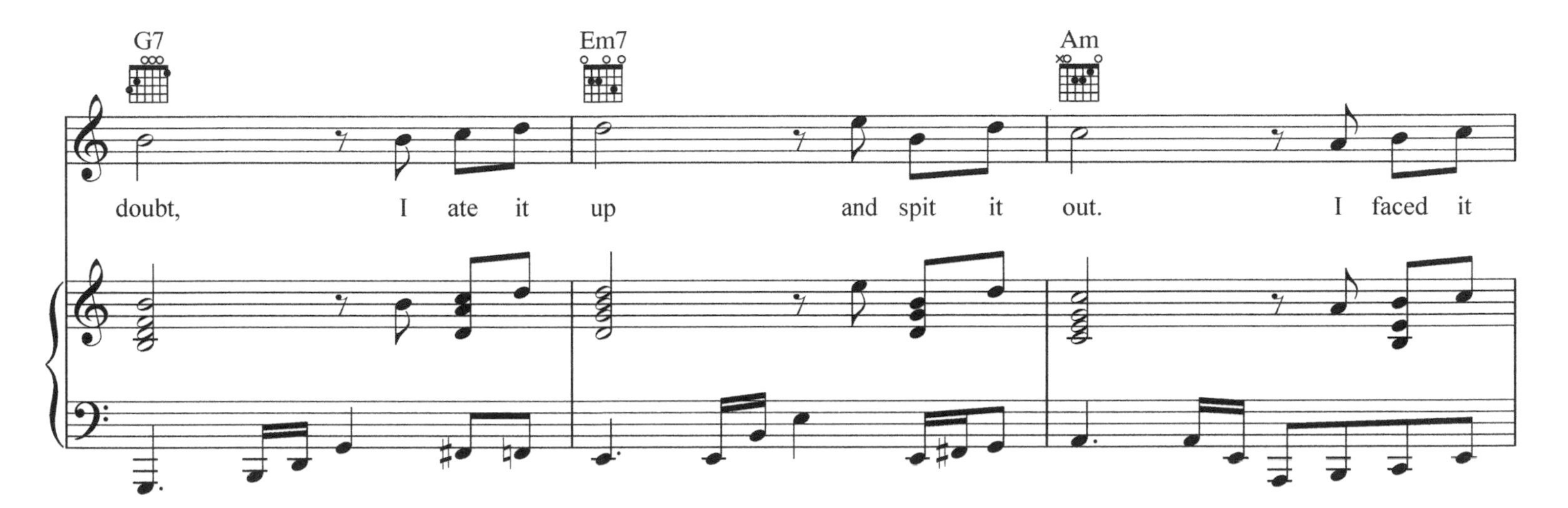
G7
Em7
Am
doubt, I ate it up and spit it out. I faced it

Dm7
G7
F6
C
all and I stood tall, and did it my way. I've

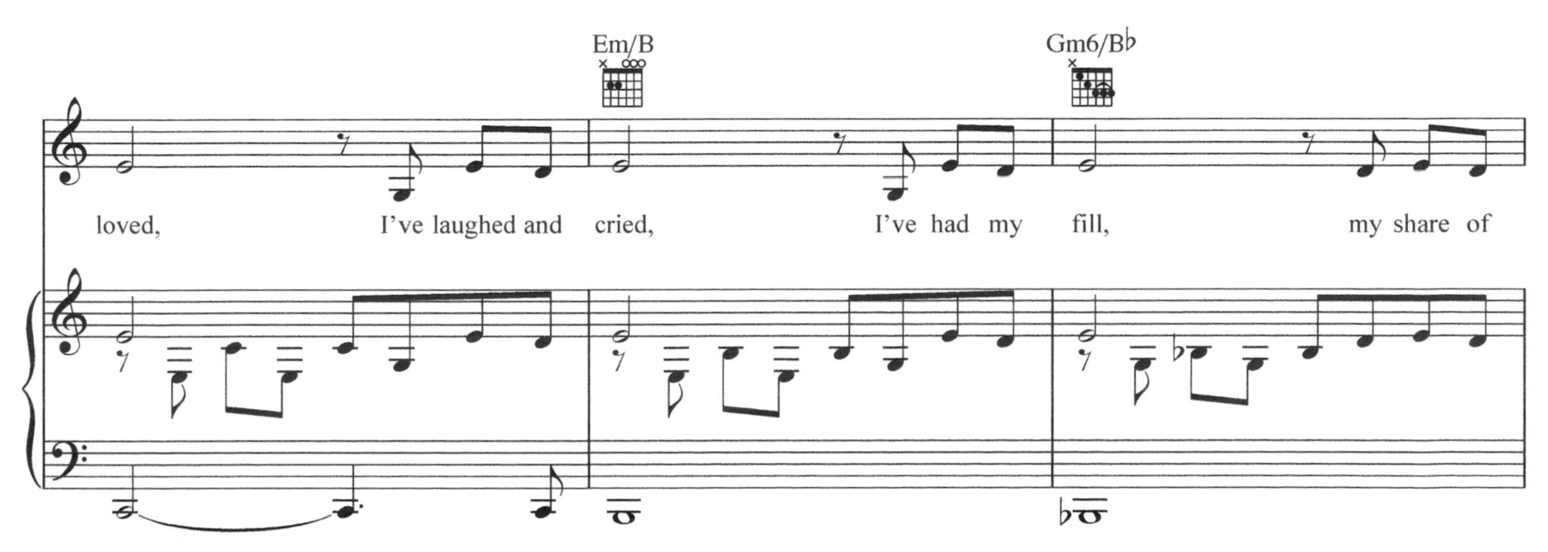
Em/B
Gm6/B♭
loved, I've laughed and cried, I've had my fill, my share of

A7
Dm
Dm(maj7)/C♯
los - ing. And now, as tears sub - side, I find it
Dm7/C
G7
C
all so a - mus - ing. To think I did all
C7
F
Fm/B♭
that, and may I say, not in a shy way, "Oh

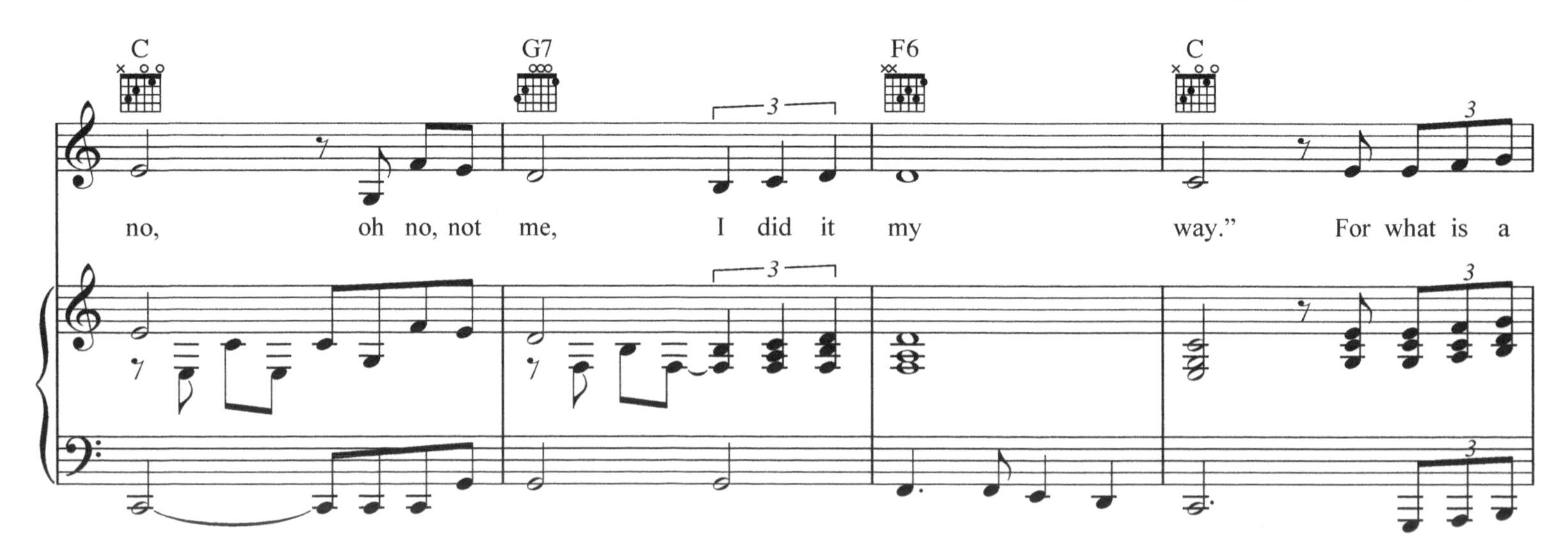
C
G7
F6
C
no, oh no, not me, I did it my way." For what is a

C7
F
man, what has he got? If not him - self, then he has

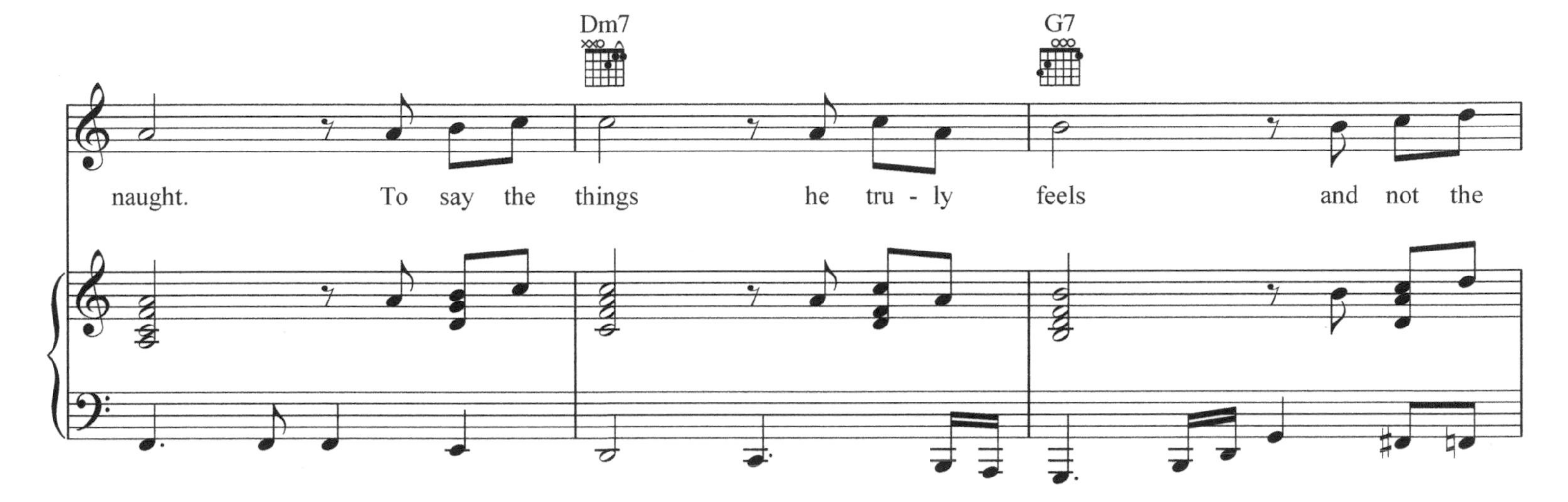
Dm7
G7
naught. To say the things he tru - ly feels and not the

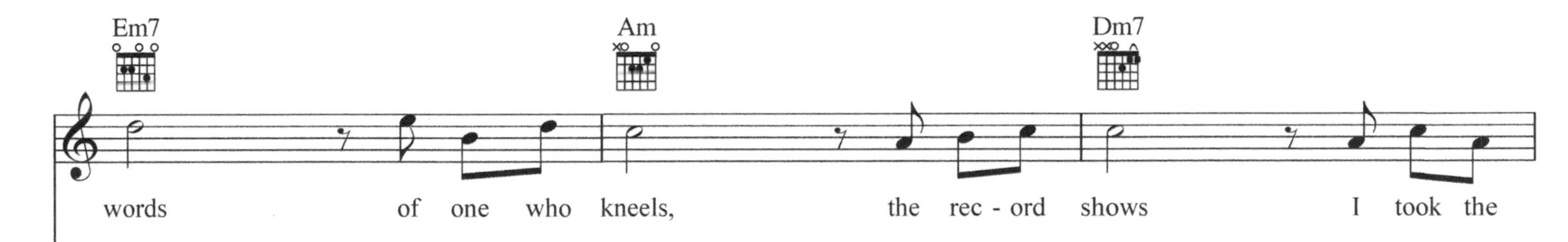
Em7
Am
Dm7
words of one who kneels, the rec - ord shows I took the

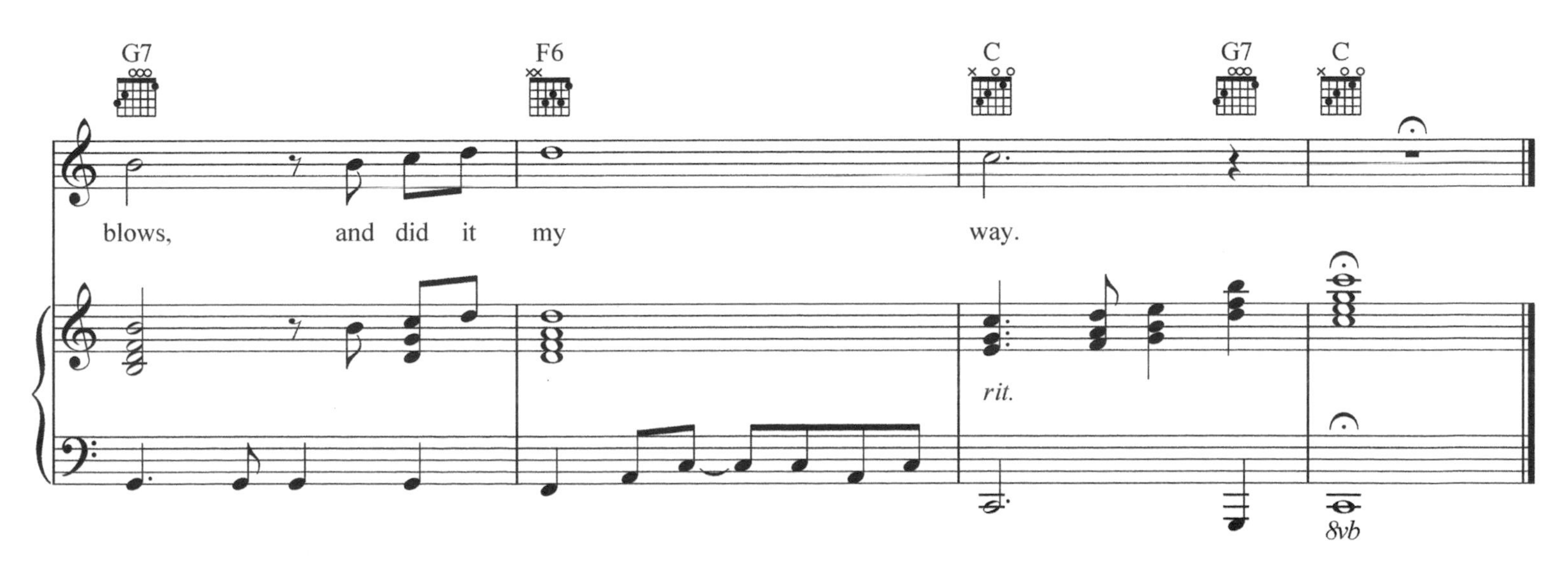
G7
F6
C
G7
C
blows, and did it my way.
rit.
8vb

LOVE ME

Words and Music by JERRY LEIBER
and MIKE STOLLER

2, 3
To Coda
F
B♭
F/A
Gm7
F
you, dear, on - ly. I would beg and
please, please love me.

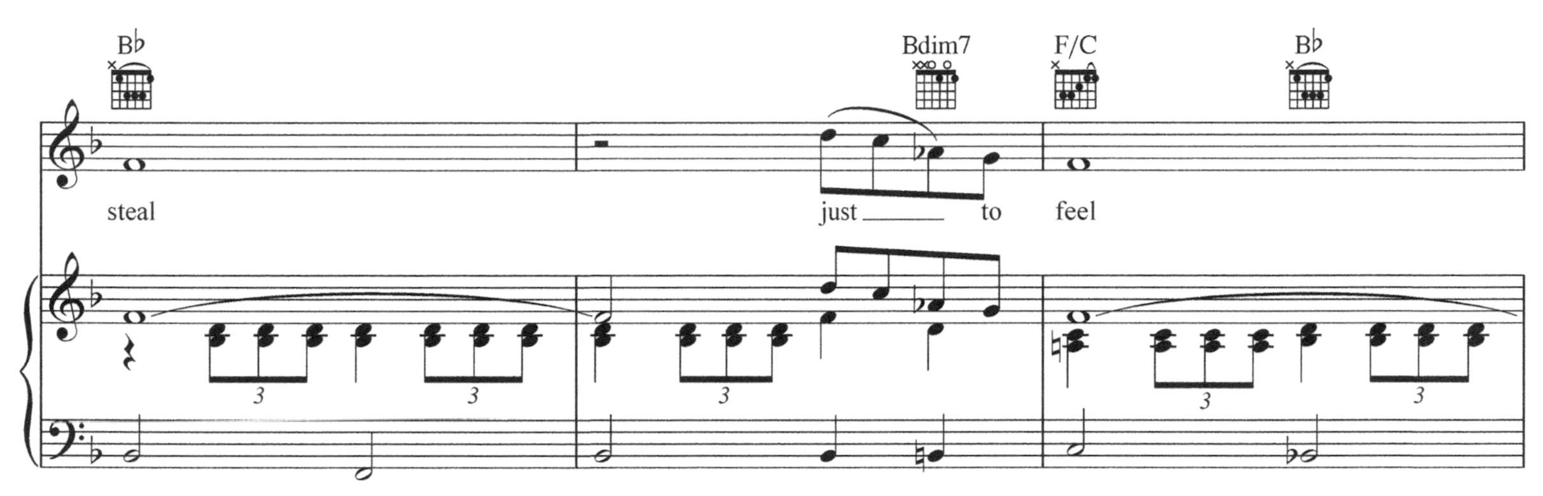

B♭
Bdim7
F/C
B♭
steal just to feel

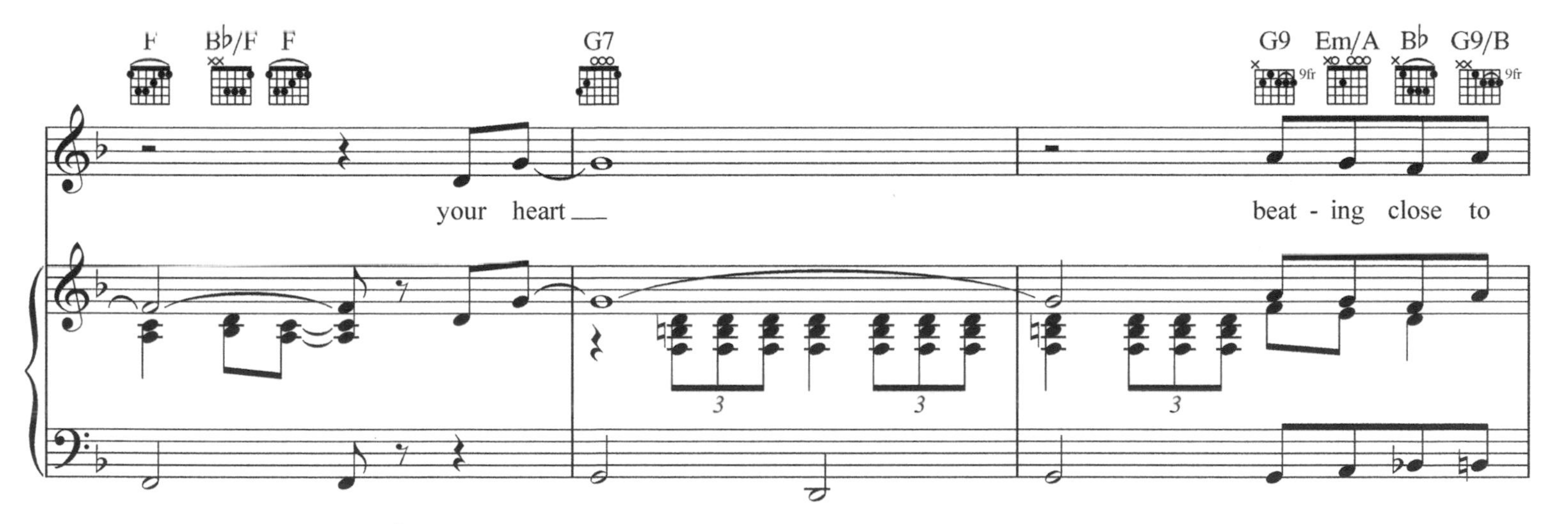

F
B♭/F
F
G7
G9
Em/A
B♭
G9/B
9fr
your heart beat - ing close to

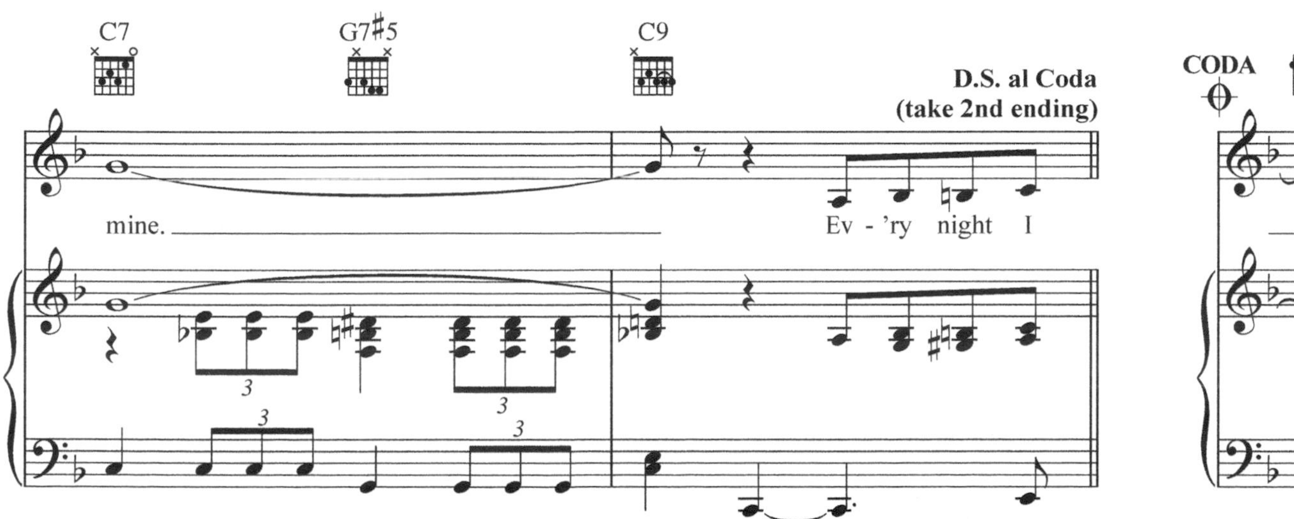

C7
G7♯5
C9
D.S. al Coda
(take 2nd ending)
mine. Ev - 'ry night I

CODA
F

IT'S OVER

Words and Music by
JIMMIE RODGERS

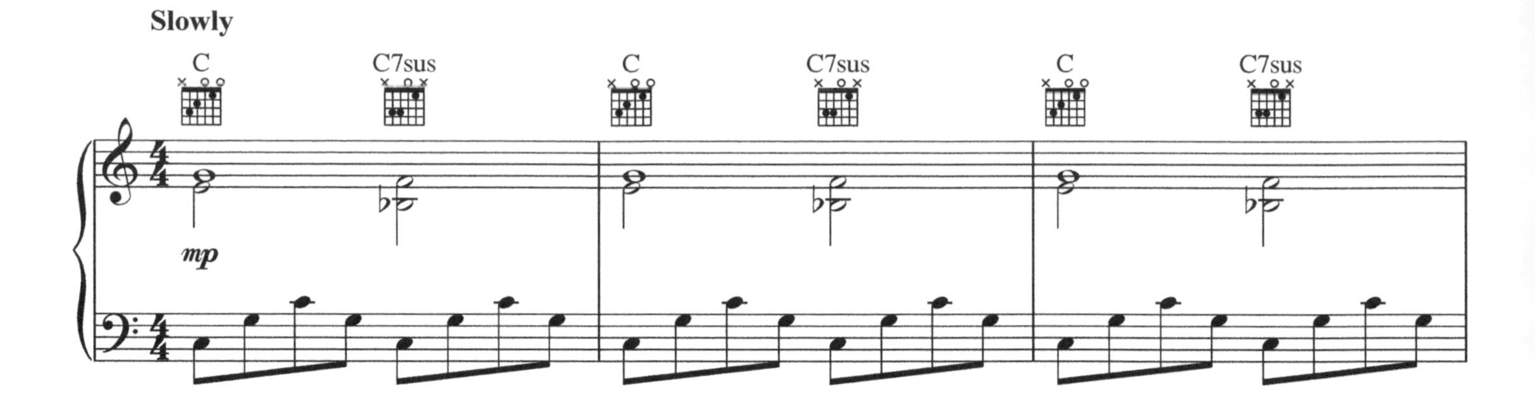

Fm
C(add9)
C
There'd be no com-ing day to shine a morn-ing light, and make us re - al - ize
sun that ris - es o'er the land and I watch you walk a - way, some - how I

B♭(add9)
6fr
B♭
C
C7sus
our night is o - ver.
have to let you go. Now it's o - ver.

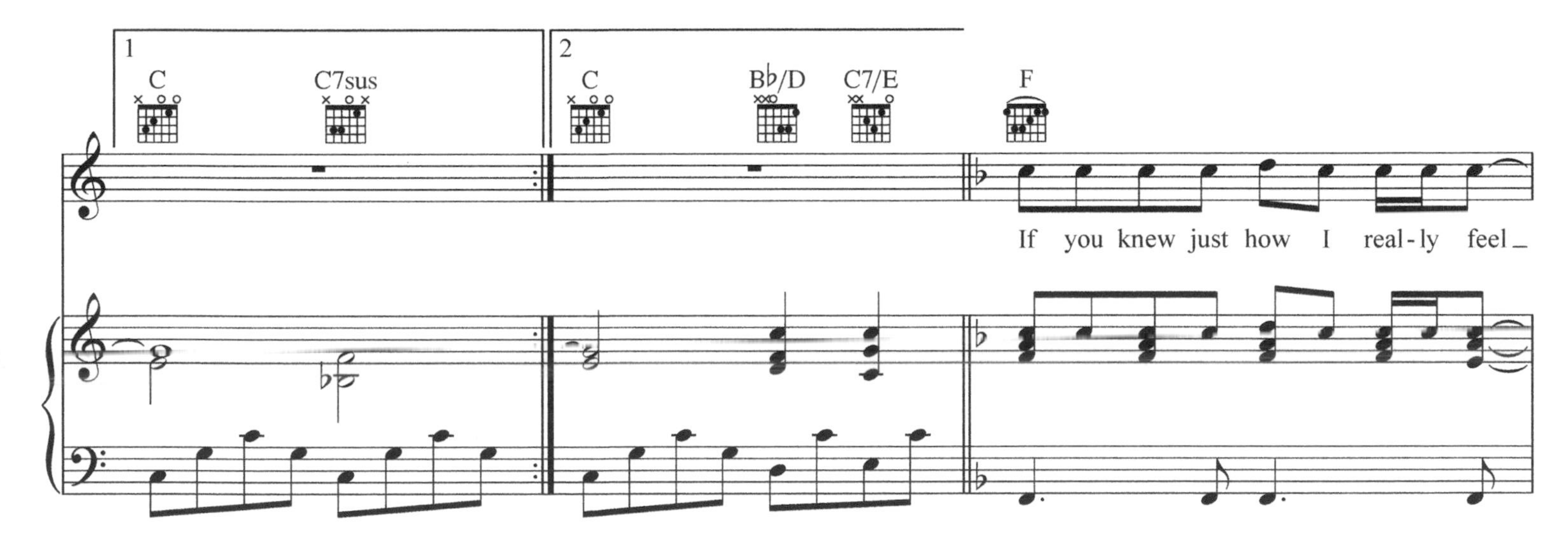
1
C
C7sus
2
C
B♭/D
C7/E
F
If you knew just how I real-ly feel

Am
F7
you might re - turn, and yet there are so man - y times that peo - ple

B♭
F
have to love and then for - get. Though there might have been a way, I

C
F
have to force my - self to say it's o - ver.

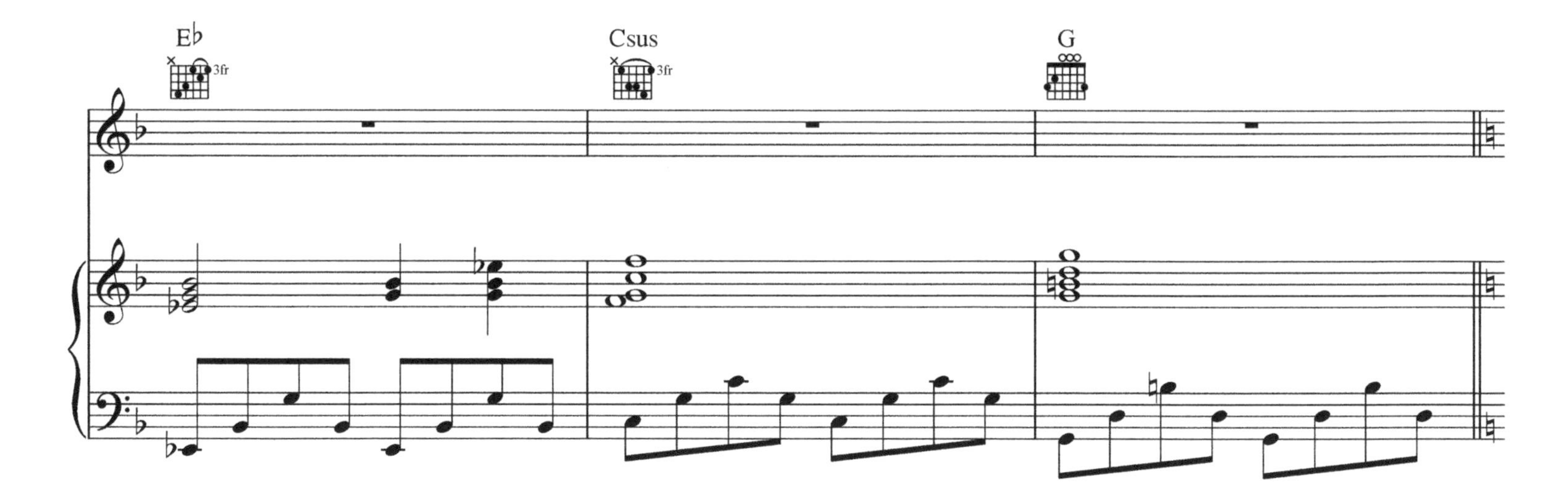
E♭
3fr
Csus
3fr
G

C
Em/B
So I turn my back and turn my col - lar to the wind, move a -

C/B♭
Fm
long in si - lence try - ing not ___ to think at all. ___ I send my

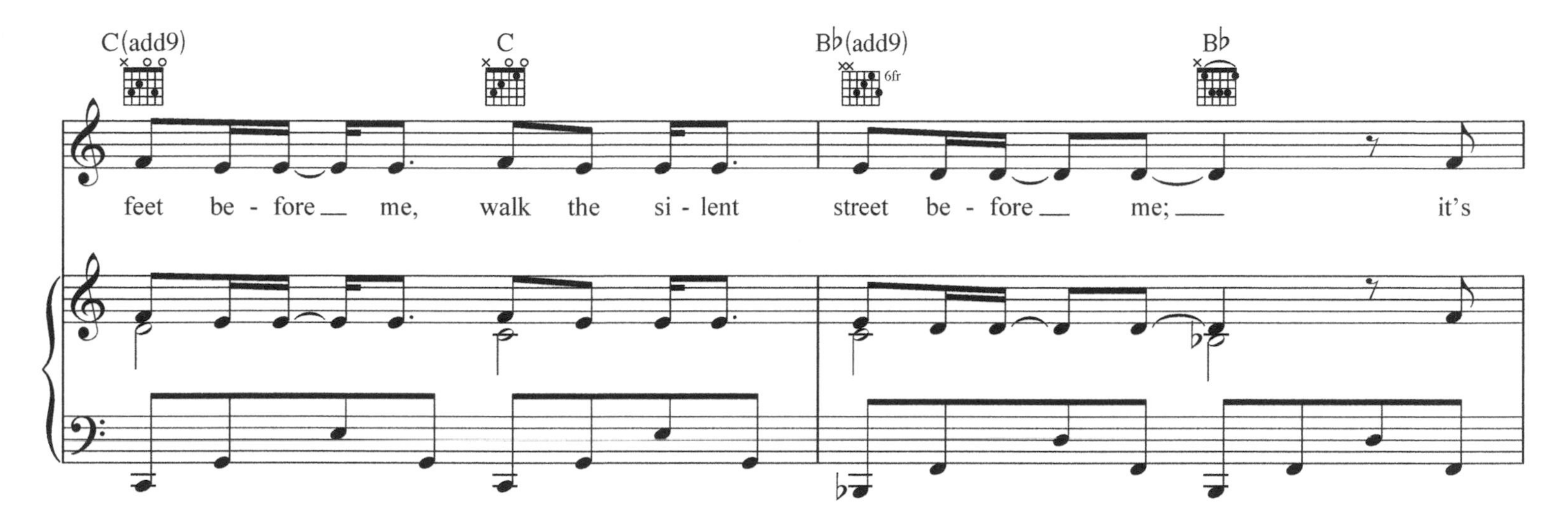
C(add9)
C
B♭(add9)
6fr
B♭
feet be - fore ___ me, walk the si - lent street be - fore ___ me; ___ it's

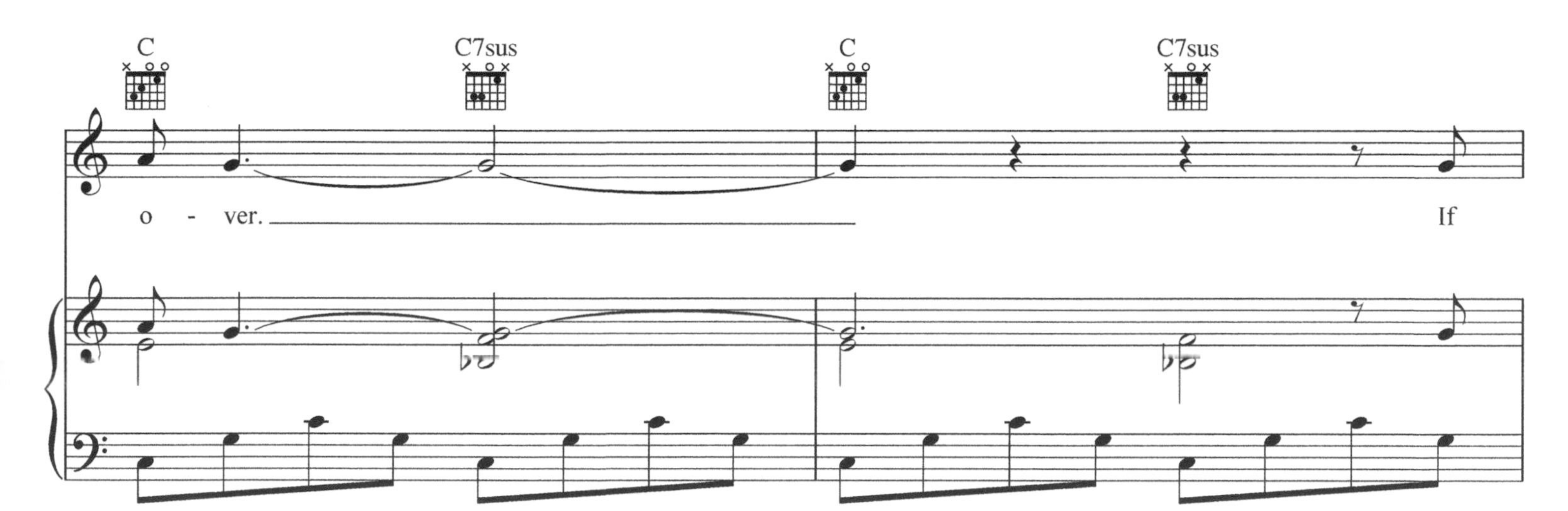
C
C7sus
C
C7sus
o - ver. ___ If

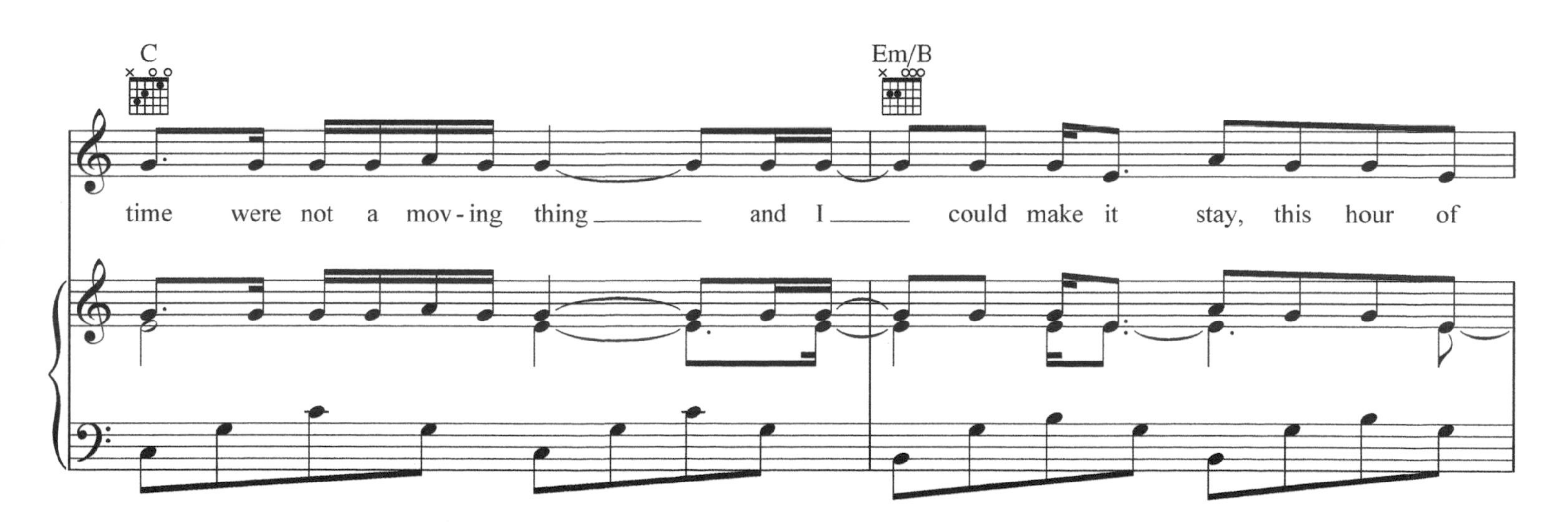
C
Em/B
time were not a mov - ing thing ___ and I ___ could make it stay, this hour of

C/B♭
Fm
love we share would al - ways be.
There'd be no com-ing day to shine a

C(add9)
C
B♭(add9)
6fr
B♭
morn-ing light,
and make us re-al-ize
our night
is

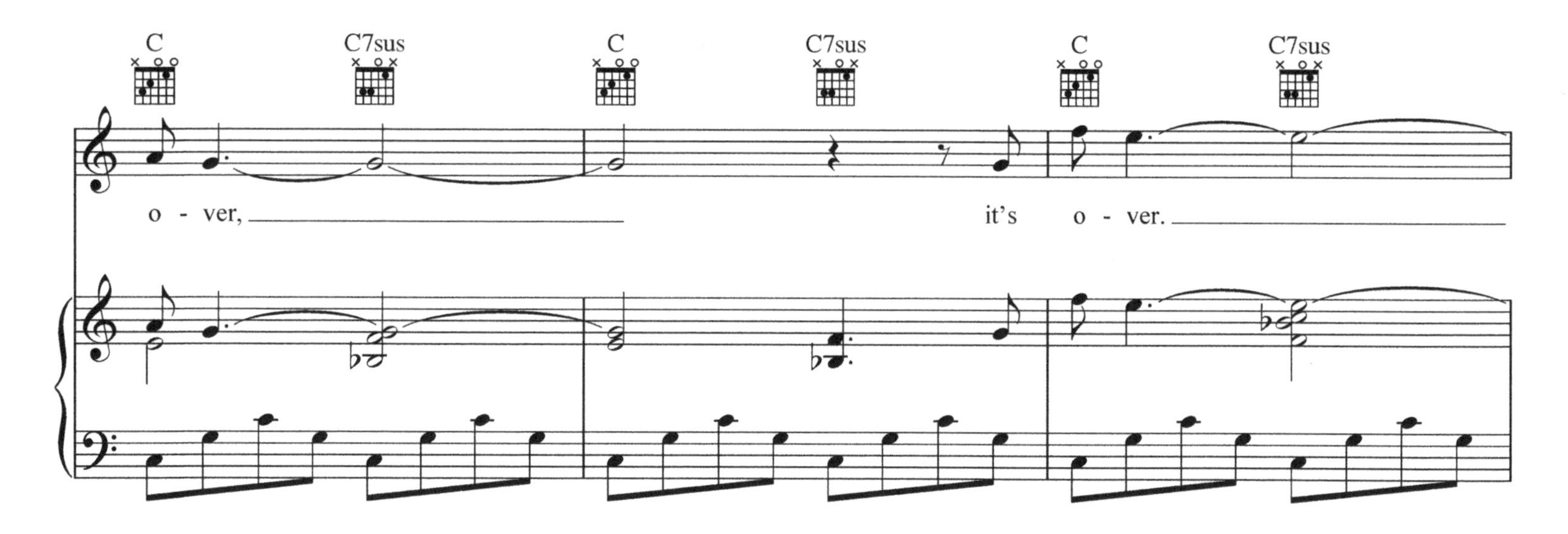
C
C7sus
C
C7sus
C
C7sus
o - ver,
it's o - ver.

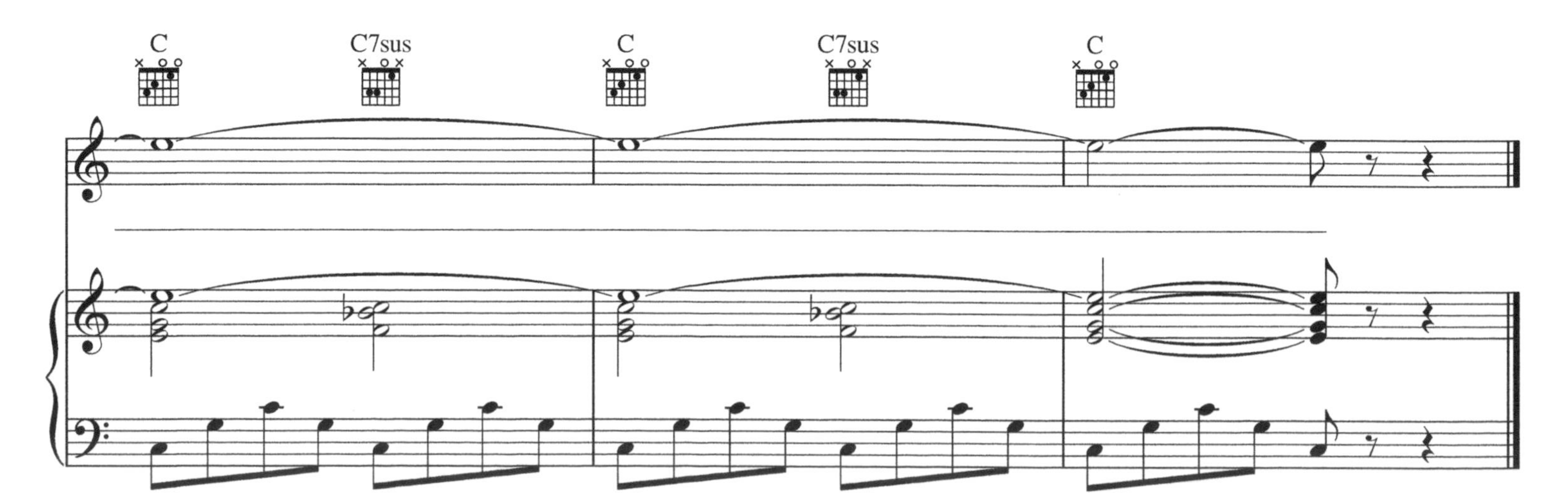
C
C7sus
C
C7sus
C

BLUE SUEDE SHOES

Words and Music by
CARL LEE PERKINS

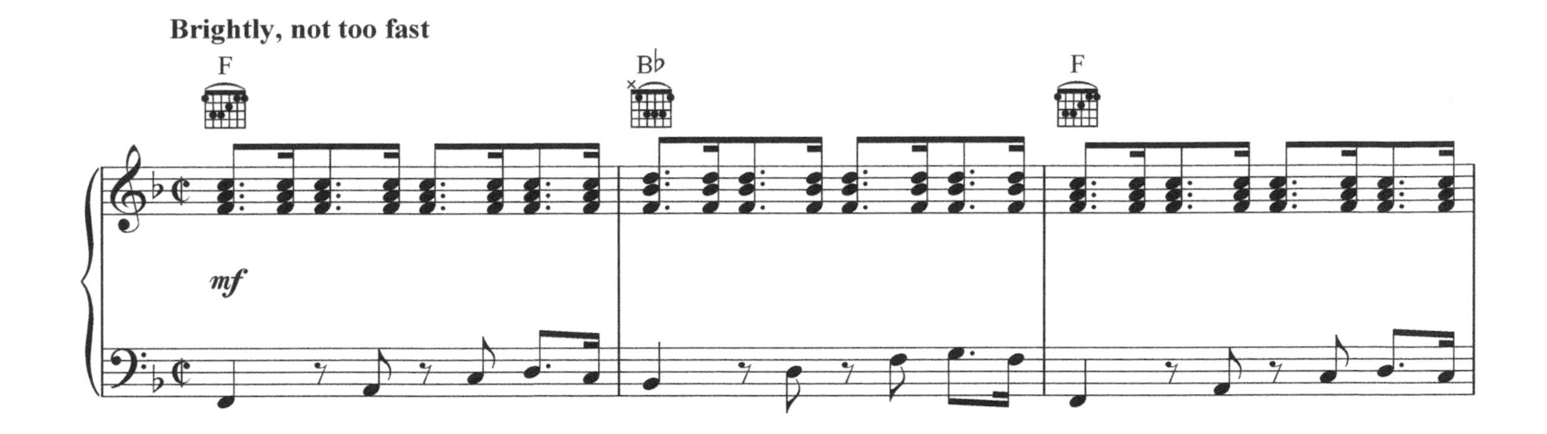

F
step on my blue suede shoes. You can

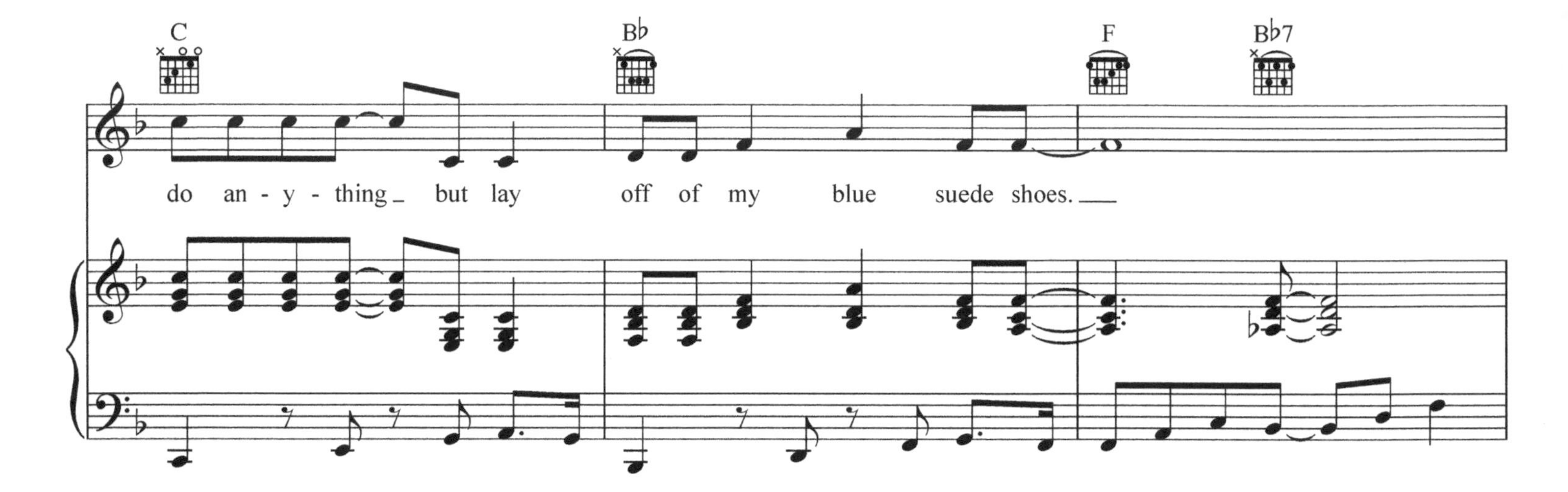
C
B♭
F
B♭7
do an - y - thing but lay off of my blue suede shoes.

F
C
N.C.
F7
N.C.
F7
Well, you can knock me down, step on my face,
burn my house, steal my car,

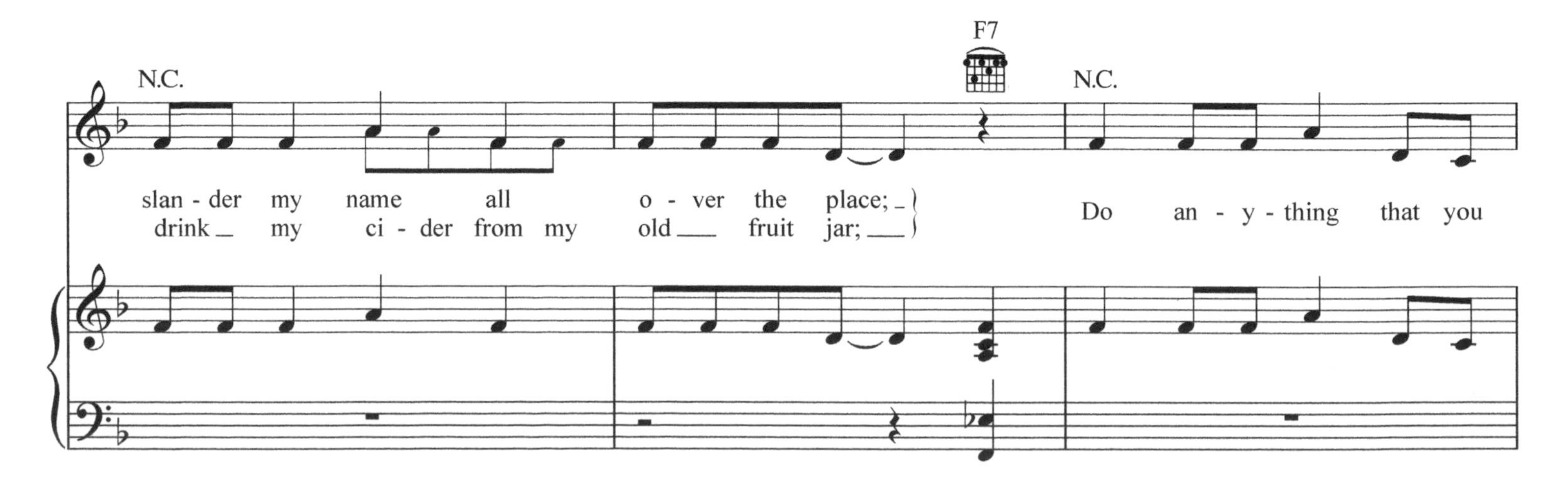
N.C.
F7
N.C.
slan - der my name all o - ver the place;
drink my ci - der from my old fruit jar;
Do an - y - thing that you

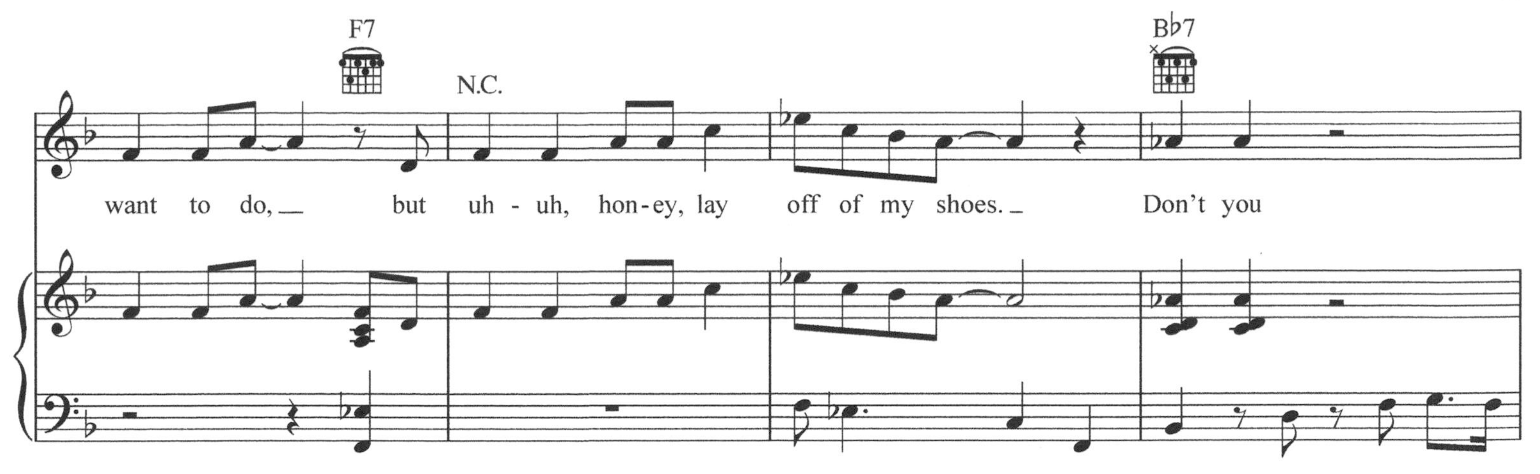
F7
N.C.
B♭7
want to do, but uh - uh, hon-ey, lay off of my shoes. Don't you

F
3
step on my blue suede shoes. You can
3

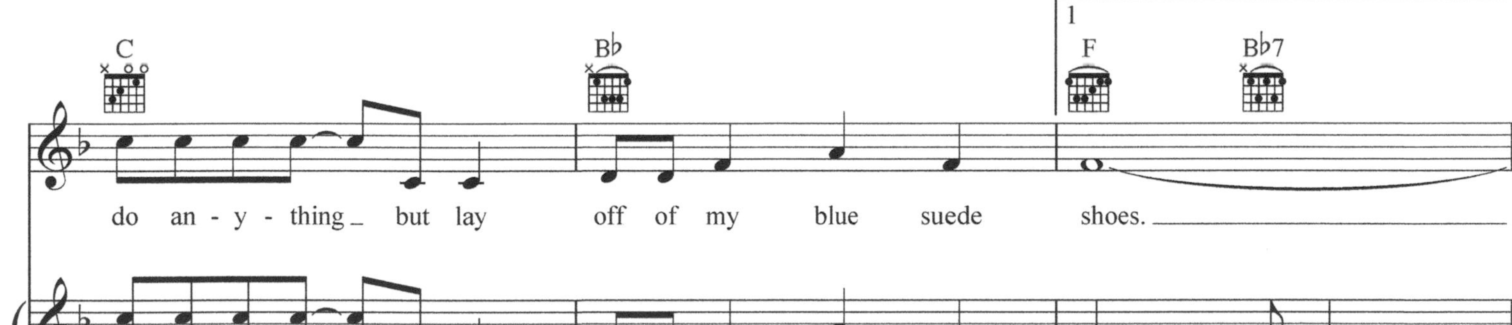
1
C
B♭
F
B♭7
do an - y - thing but lay off of my blue suede shoes.

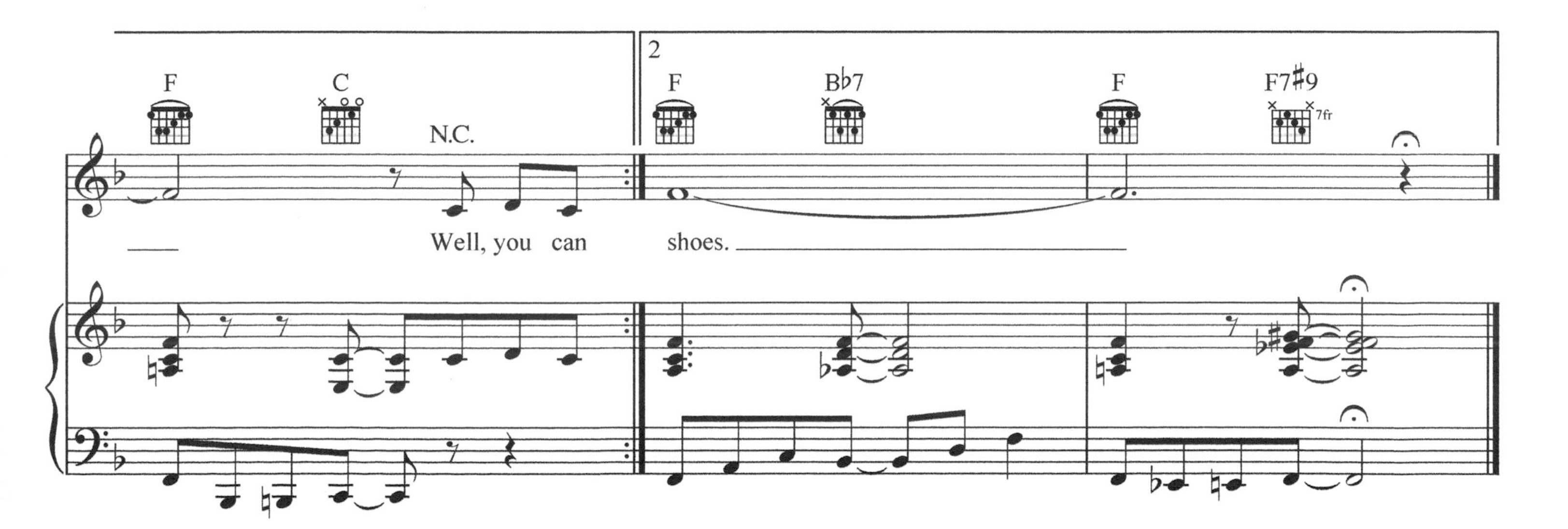
F
C
N.C.
2
F
B♭7
F
F7♯9
7fr
Well, you can shoes.

I'M SO LONESOME I COULD CRY

Words and Music by
HANK WILLIAMS

Moderately (♩♩ = ♩♪ triplet)

F

mf

I've nev - er seen a night so long, when
The si - lence of a fall - ing star lights

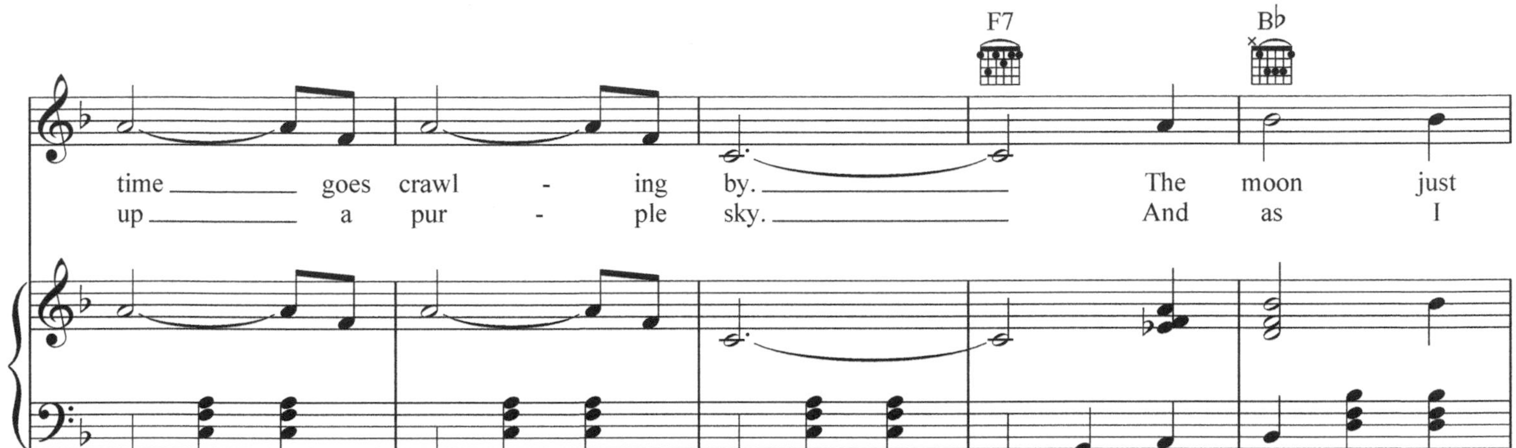
F7
B♭
time goes crawl - ing by. The moon just
up a pur - ple sky. And as I

F
C7
went be - hind a cloud to hide its face and
won - der where you are I'm so lone - some I could

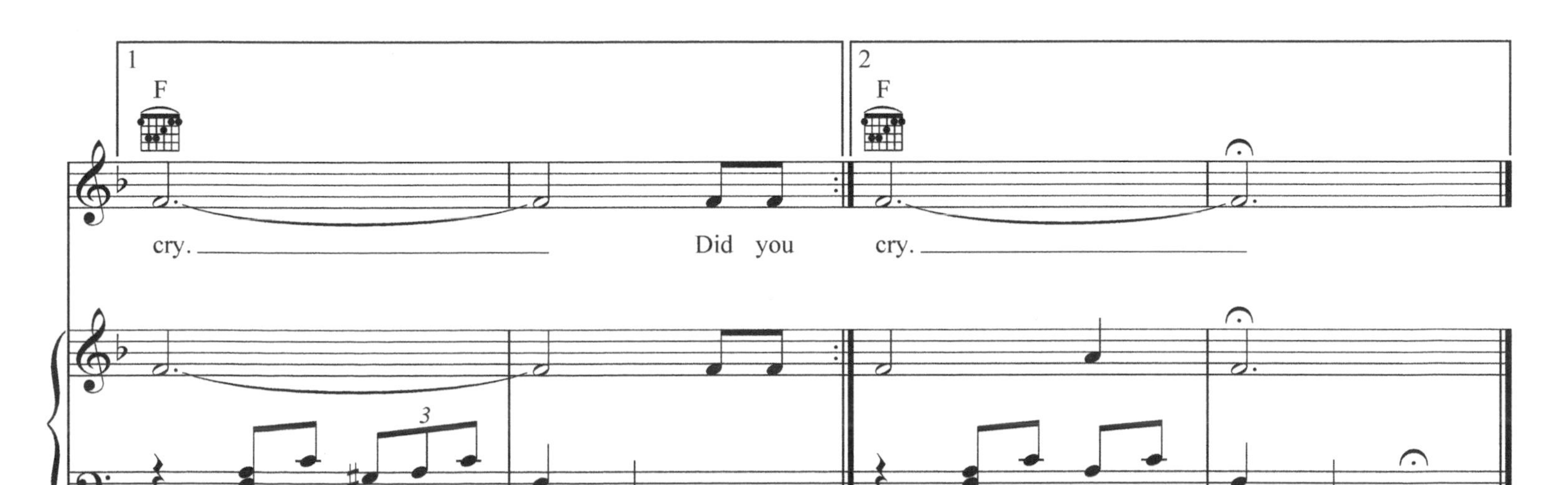
1
F
2
F
cry. Did you cry.

I CAN'T STOP LOVING YOU

Words and Music by
DON GIBSON

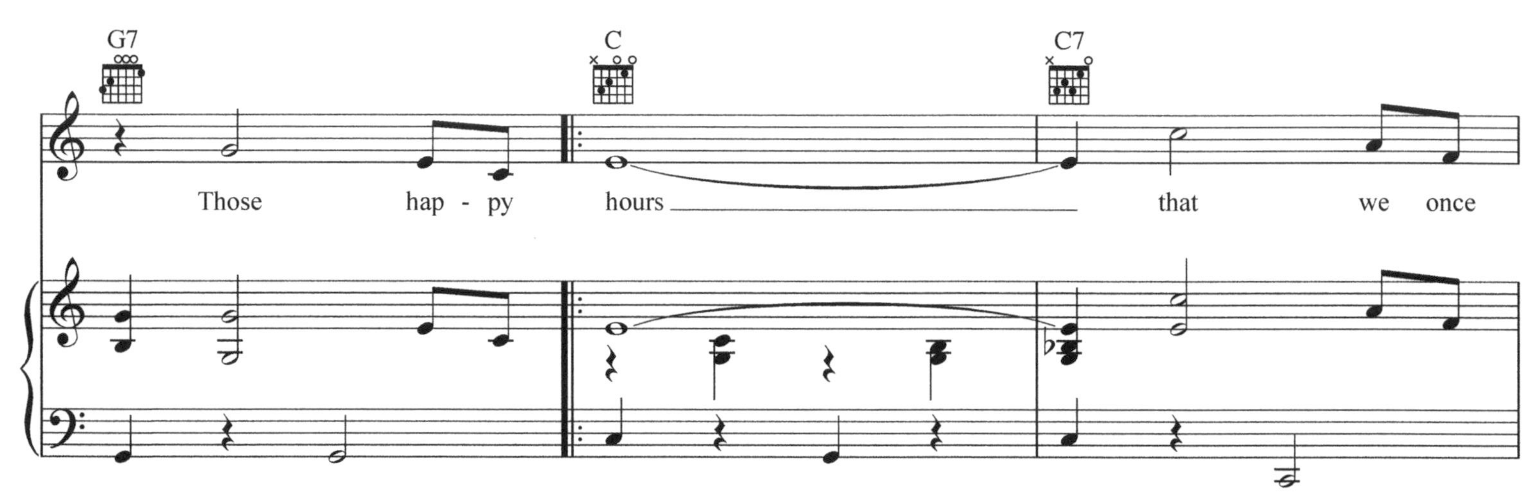

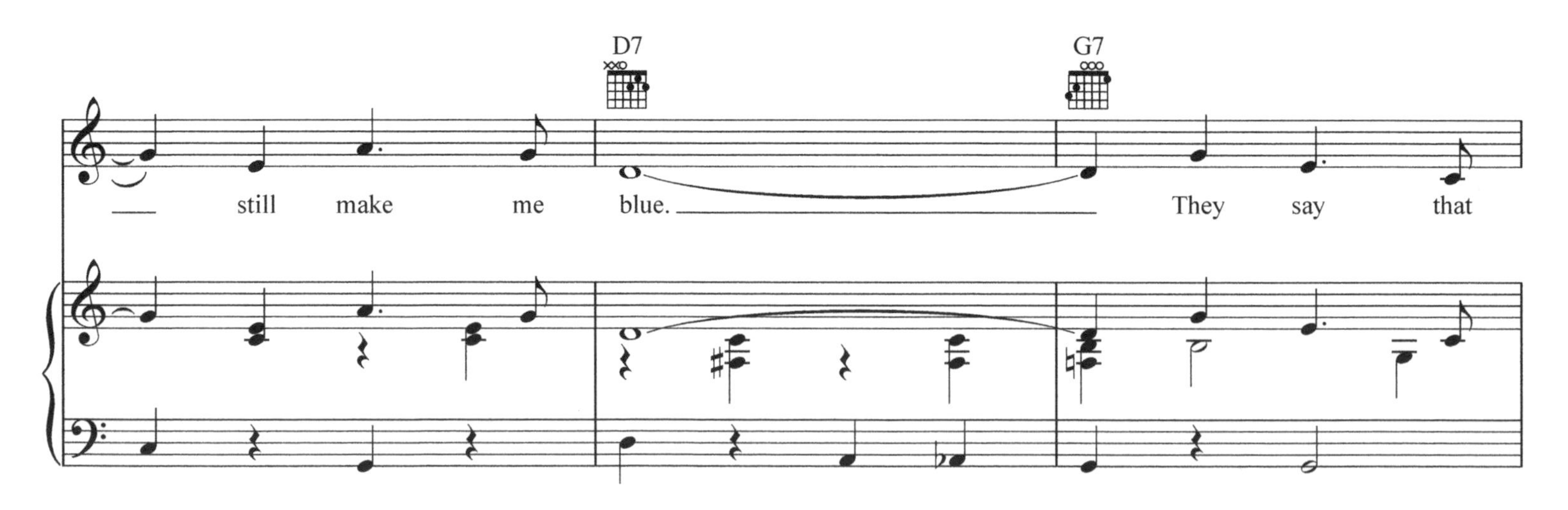

C
C7
F
time heals a bro - ken heart,

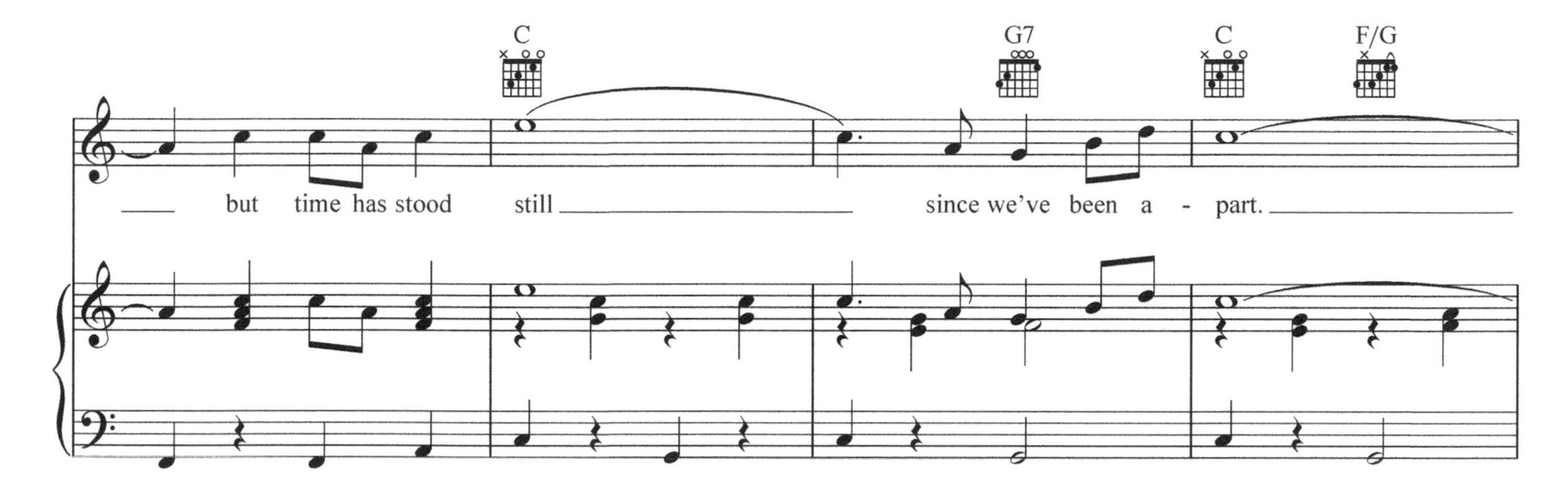
C
G7
C
F/G
but time has stood still since we've been a - part.

C
C7
F
3
I can't stop lov - ing you, so I've made up my
I can't stop lov - ing you, there's no use to

C
G7
mind to live in mem - o - ry
try. Pre - tend there's some - one new;

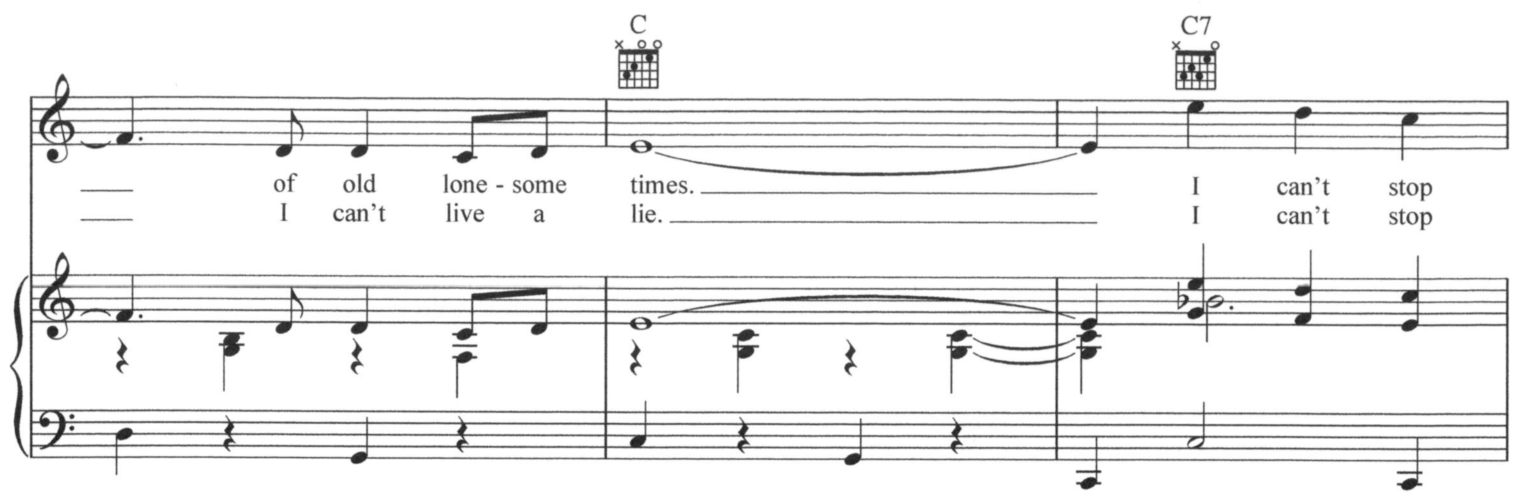
C
C7
of old lone - some times. I can't stop
I can't live a lie. I can't stop

F
C
3
want - ing you, it's use - less to say,
want - ing you the way that I do.

G7
so I'll just live my life in dreams of yes - ter -
There's on - ly been one love for me, that one love is

1
2
C
F/G
C
G7
C
F
C
3
day. Those hap - py
you.

HOUND DOG

Words and Music by JERRY LEIBER
and MIKE STOLLER

G7
F7
C
nev - er caught a rab - bit and you ain't no friend of mine.
C
Well, they said you was high - classed,
but, that was just a
lie.
Yeah, they said you was high - classed,
F7
but, that was just a lie.
C
Yeah, you ain't

G7
F7
C
nev - er caught a rab - bit and you ain't no friend of mine.

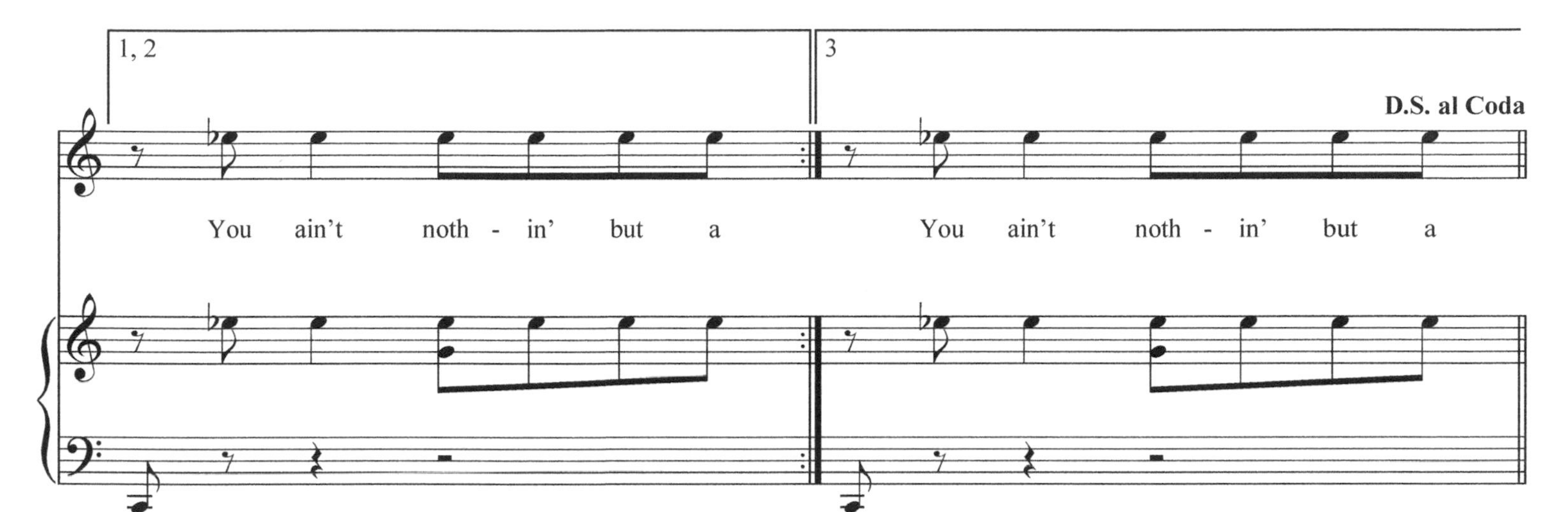
1, 2
3
D.S. al Coda
You ain't noth - in' but a
You ain't noth - in' but a

CODA
G7
F7
nev - er caught a rab - bit, and you ain't no friend of mine.

C
C7

WHAT NOW MY LOVE
(Original French Title: "Et Maintenant")

Original French Lyric by PIERRE DELANO
Music by GILBERT BECAUD
English Adaptation by CARL SIGMAN

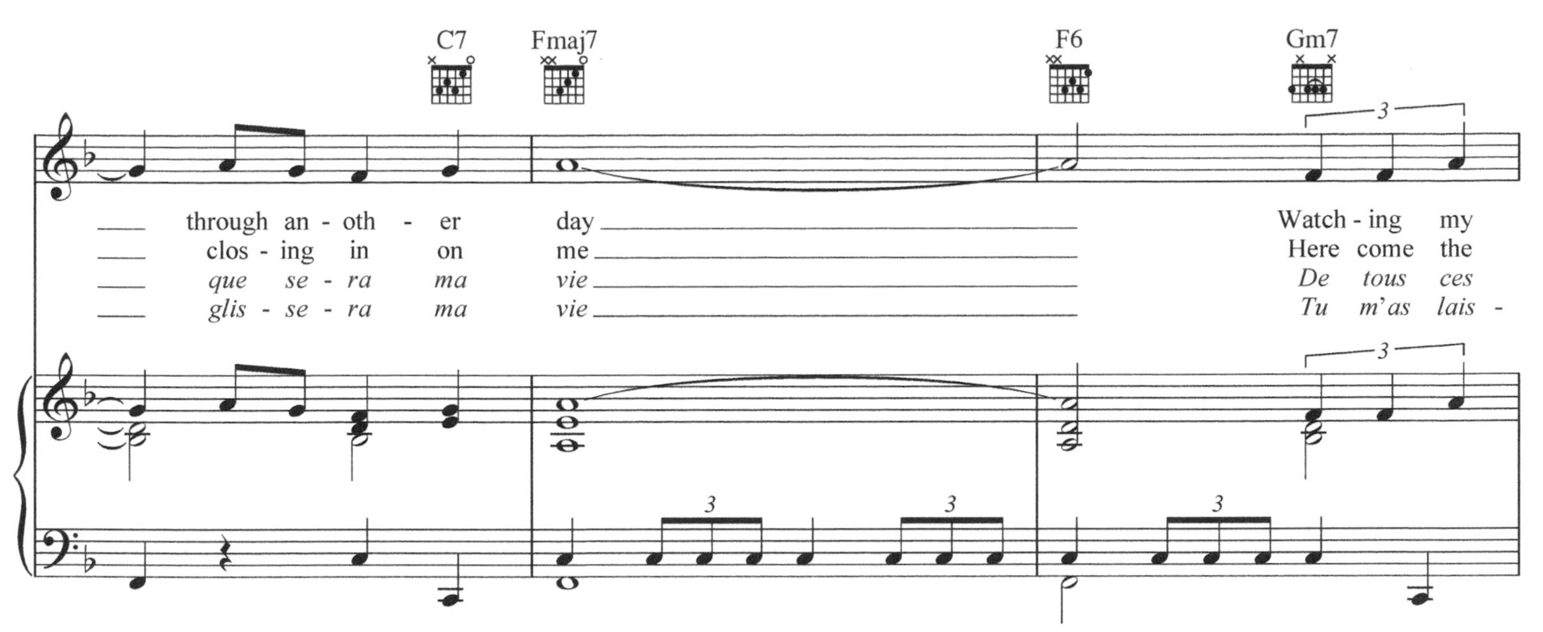
C7
Fmaj7
F6
Gm7
3
through an - oth - er day Watch - ing my
clos - ing in on me Here come the
que se - ra ma vie De tous ces
glis - se - ra ma vie Tu m'as lais -

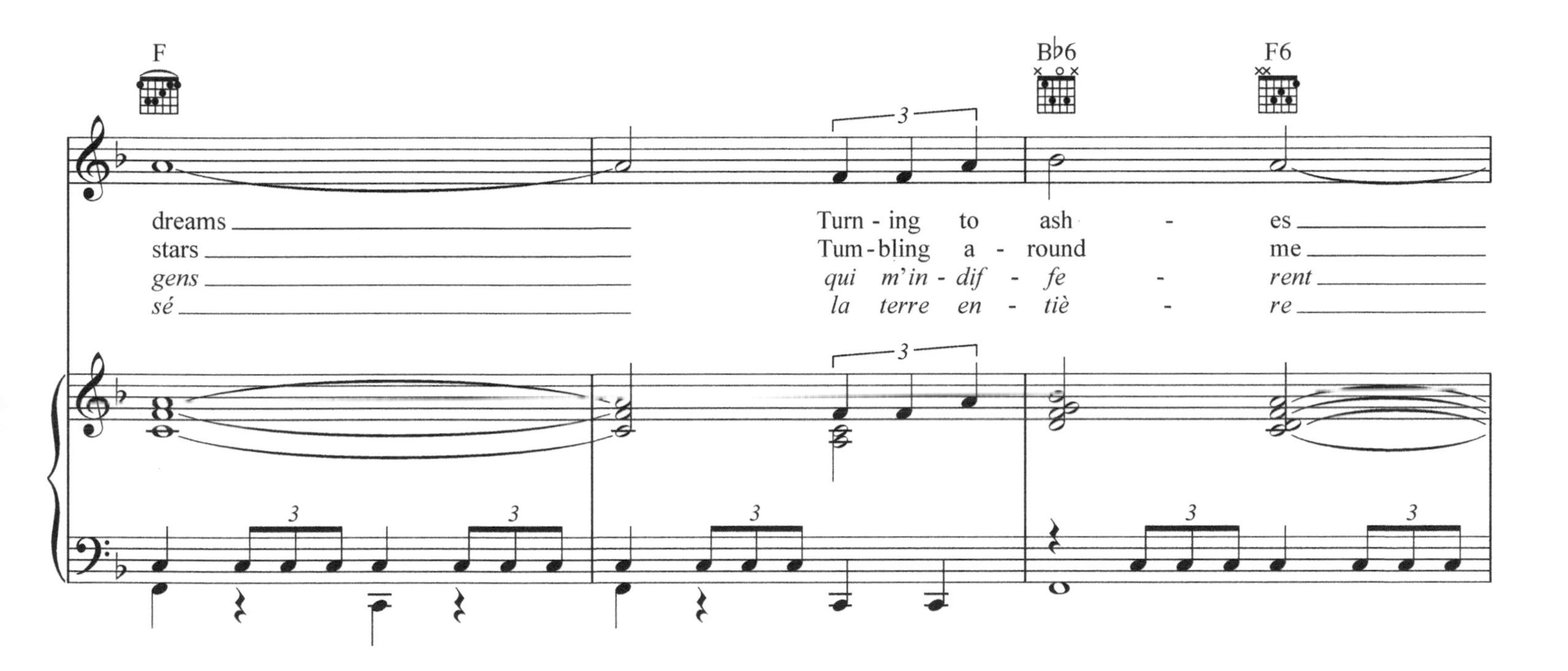
F
B♭6
F6
3
dreams Turn - ing to ash - es
stars Tum - bling a - round me
gens qui m'in - dif - fe - rent
sé la terre en - tiè - re

Gm7
C7
3
And my hopes in - to bits of
There's the sky where the sea should
Main - te - nant que tu es par -
Mais la terre sans toi c'est pe -

F
Fmaj7
F7
Gm7
clay Once I could see
be What now my love
tie Tou - tes ces nuits
tit Vous mes a - mis

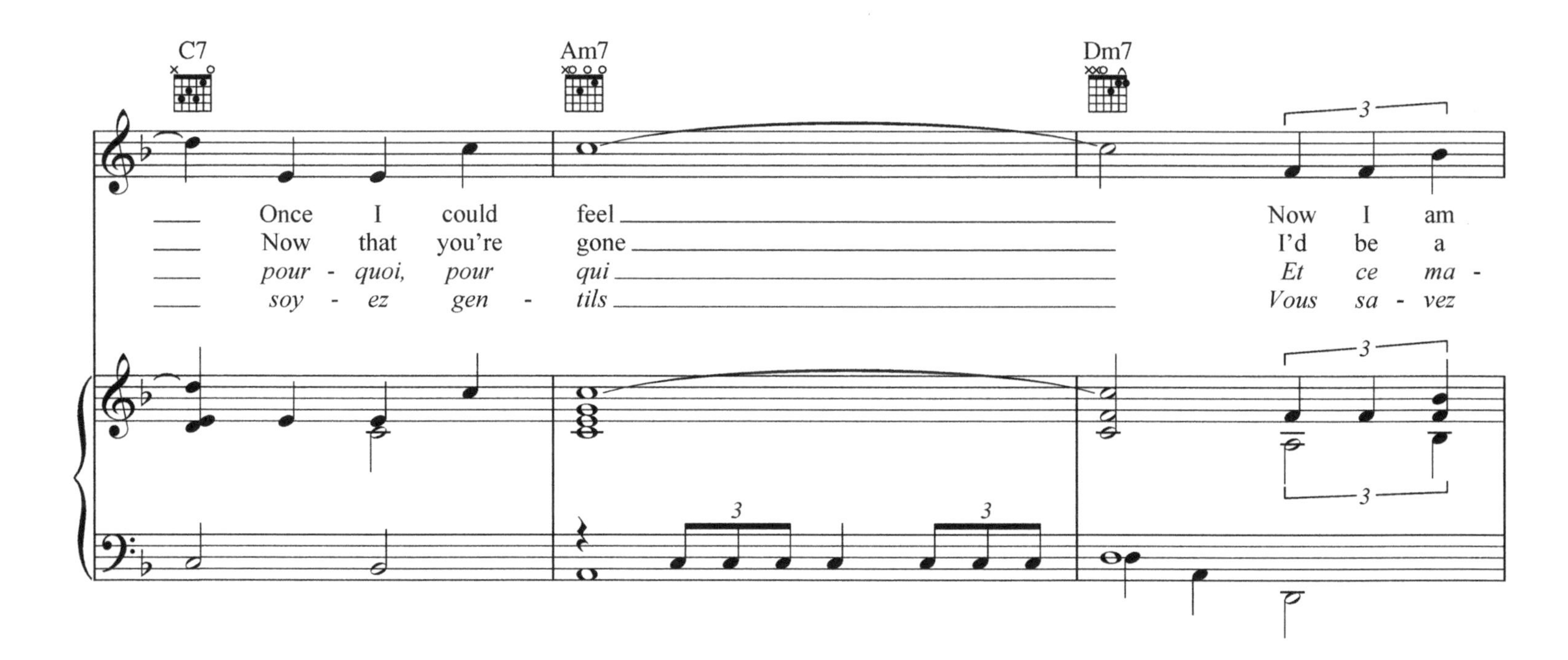
C7
Am7
Dm7
Once I could feel Now I am
Now that you're gone I'd be a
pour - quoi, pour qui Et ce ma -
soy - ez gen - tils Vous sa - vez

Gm7
C7
Gm7
C7
F
numb I've be - come un - real
fool to go on and on
tin qui re - vient pour rien
bien que l'on n'y peut rien

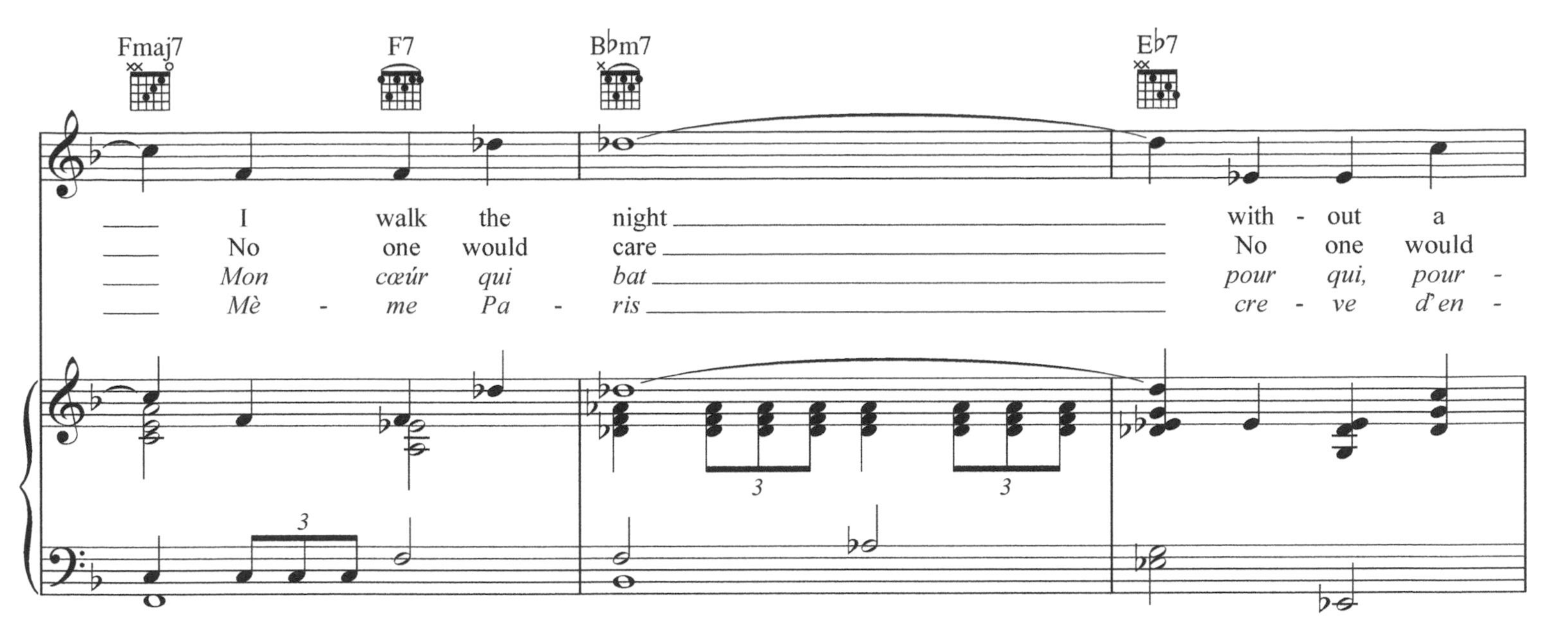
Fmaj7
F7
B♭m7
E♭7
I walk the night with - out a
No one would care No one would
Mon cœúr qui bat pour qui, pour -
Mè - me Pa - ris cre - ve d'en -
3
3
3

A♭maj7
D♭maj7
D♭6
B♭m6
6fr
goal Stripped of my heart,
cry If I should live
quoi Qui bat trop fort,
nui Tou - tes ces rues
3
3
3
3
3
3
3
3

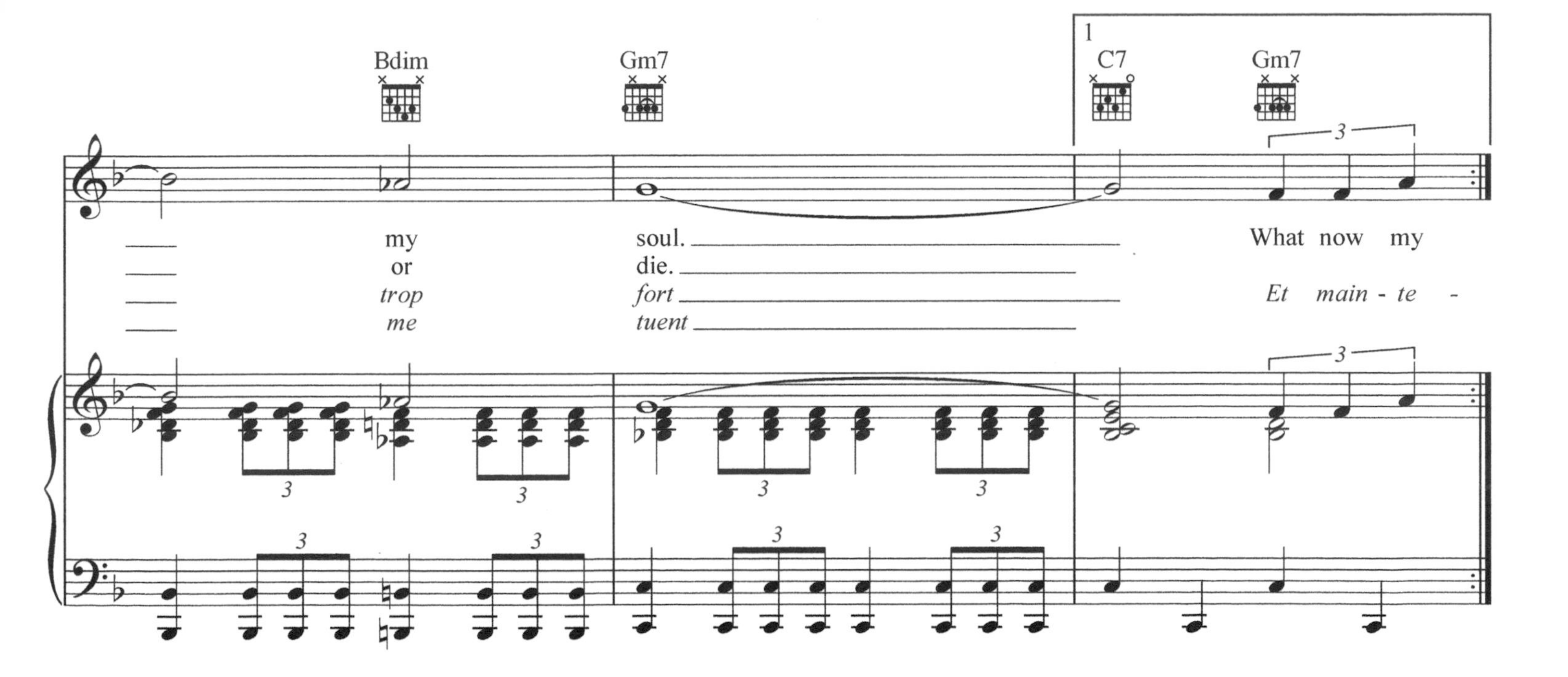
1
Bdim
Gm7
C7
Gm7
my soul. What now my
or die.
trop fort Et mainte -
me tuent
3
3
3
3
3
3
3
3
3
3
3

2
C7
Gm7
F
what now my love
Je n'ai vrai - ment
Now there is
plus rien a
B♭6
F6
Gm7
noth - ing
fai - re
On - ly my last
Je n'ai vrai - ment
C9
Fmaj7
F6
good - bye.
plus rien.
Fmaj7
F6

FEVER

Words and Music by JOHN DAVENPORT
and EDDIE COOLEY

Moderately, with a beat

E7
Am
fe - ver that's so hard to bear. You give me fe - ver
know I'm gon - na treat you right. You give me fe - ver
"Ju - lie, ba - by, you're my flame. Thou giv - est fe - ver
"Dad - dy - o, don't you dare. Give me fe - ver
Fahr - en - heit or cen - ti - grade. They give you fe - ver

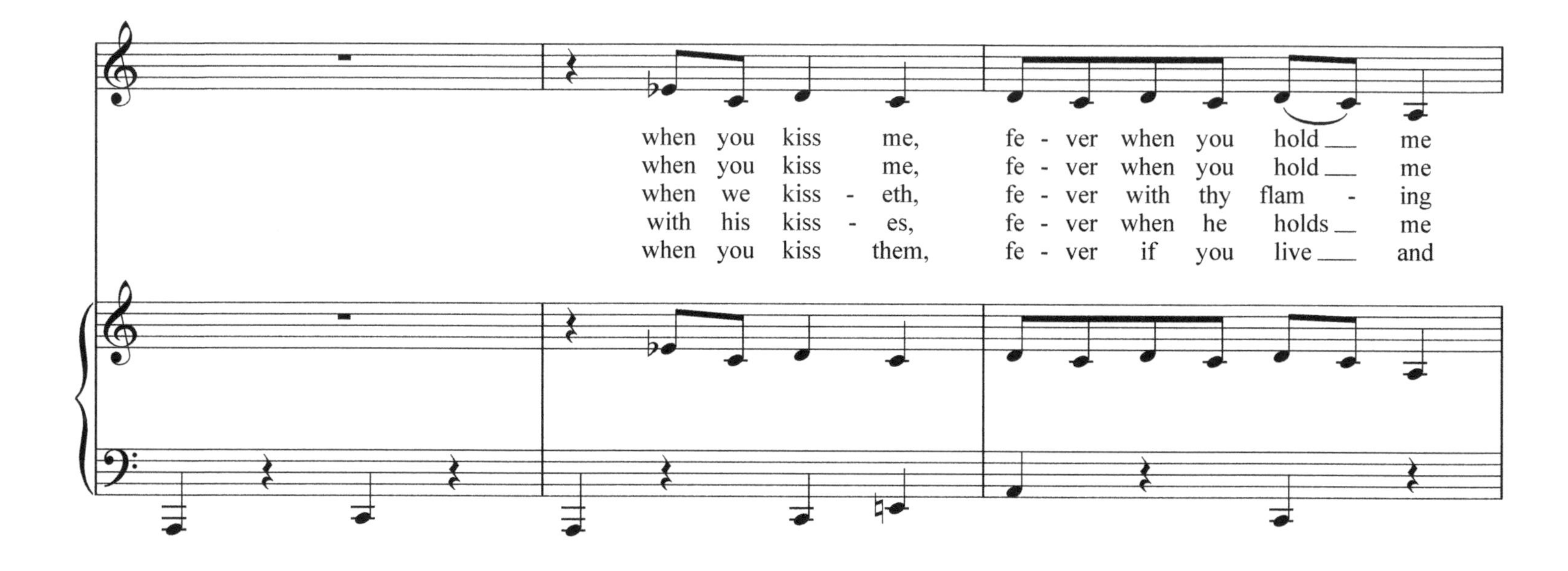
when you kiss me, fe - ver when you hold me
when you kiss me, fe - ver when you hold me
when we kiss - eth, fe - ver with thy flam - ing
with his kiss - es, fe - ver when he holds me
when you kiss them, fe - ver if you live and

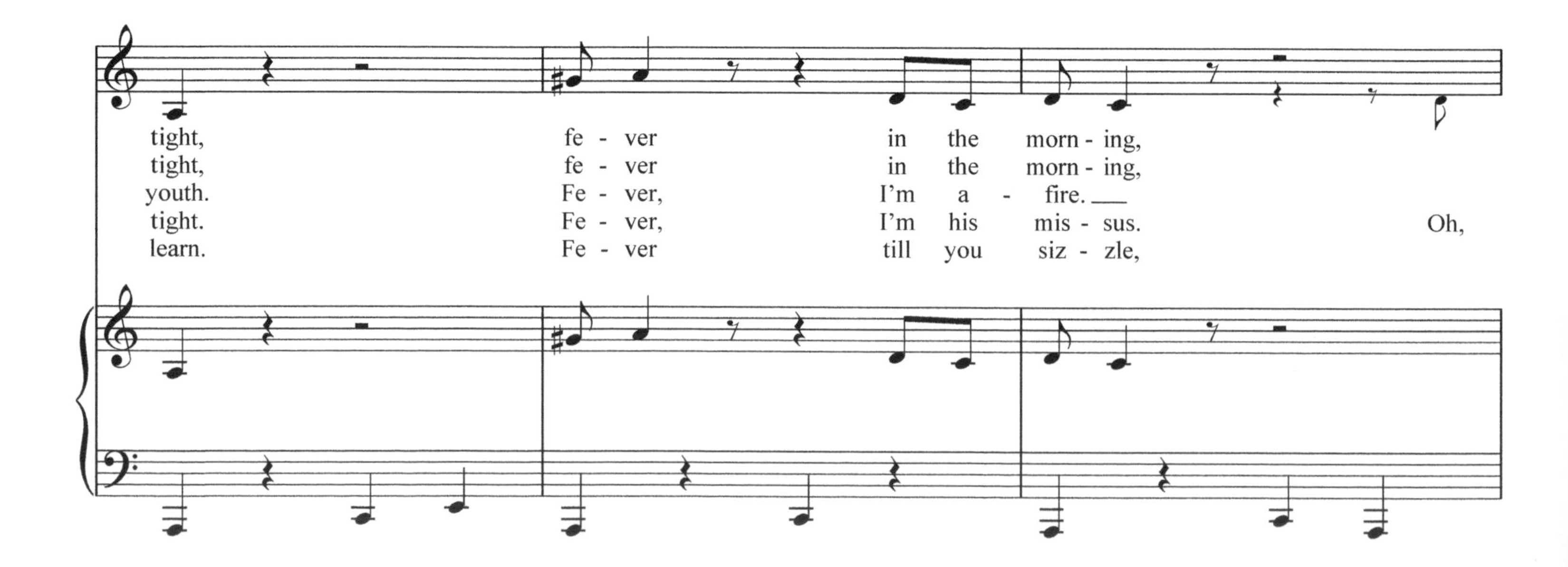
tight, fe - ver in the morn - ing,
tight, fe - ver in the morn - ing,
youth. Fe - ver, I'm a - fire.
tight. Fe - ver, I'm his mis - sus. Oh,
learn. Fe - ver till you siz - zle,

E7
1, 3, 4
Am
fe - ver all through the night.
fe - ver all through the
Fe - ver, yeah, I burn for - sooth."
Dad - dy, won't you treat him right?"
what a love - ly way to
2
Am
night. Ev - 'ry - bod - y's got the fe - ver; that is some - thing
you all know. Fe - ver is - n't such a new thing;

E7
Am
5
Am
fe - ver start - ed long a - go.
burn.

WELCOME TO MY WORLD

Words and Music by RAY WINKLER
and JOHN HATHCOCK

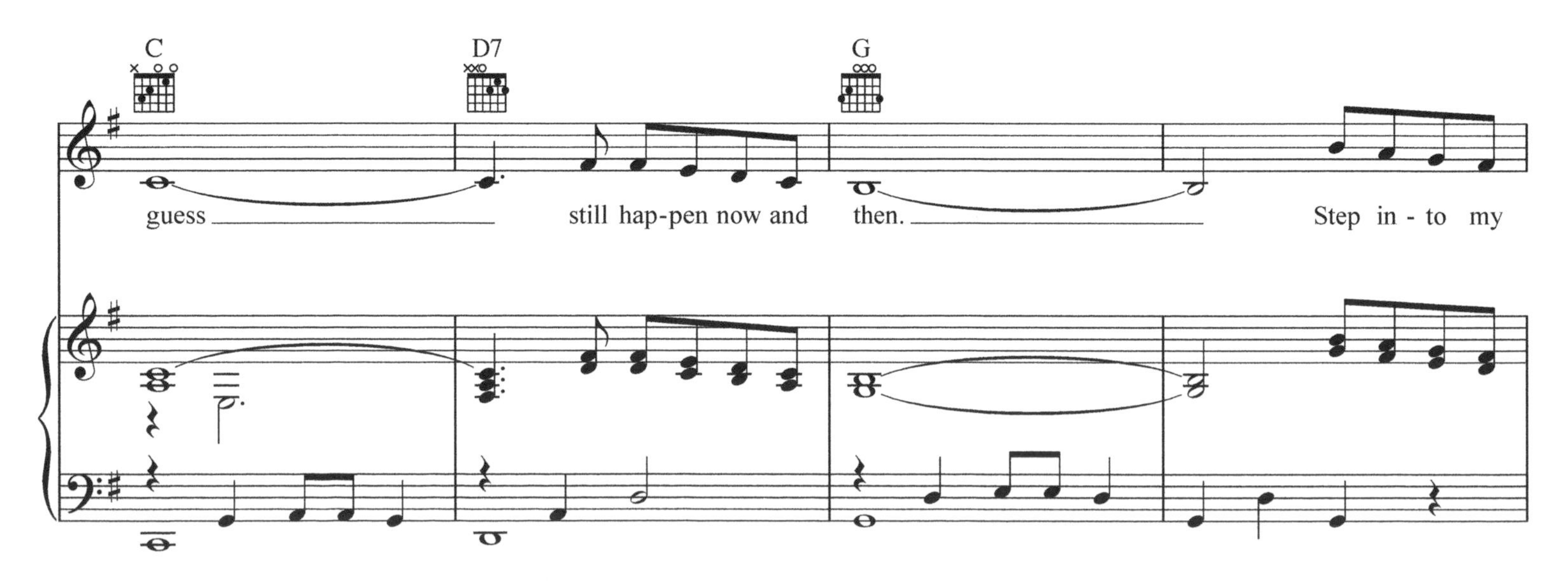

C
D9
4fr
G
heart, leave your cares be - hind, wel-come to my
C
D7
G
C
G
world built with you in mind.
D7
G
D7
Knock and the door will o - pen, seek and you will
G
D7
G
find, ask and you'll be giv - en the

A7
D
G
key to this world of mine.
I'll be wait - ing
C
D9
4fr
G
here
with my arms un - furled,
wait-ing just for
C
D7
1
G
Am7
you,
wel-come to my world.
D7♯5
G
2
G
C
G
Wel-come to my world.

SUSPICIOUS MINDS

Words and Music by
FRANCIS ZAMBON

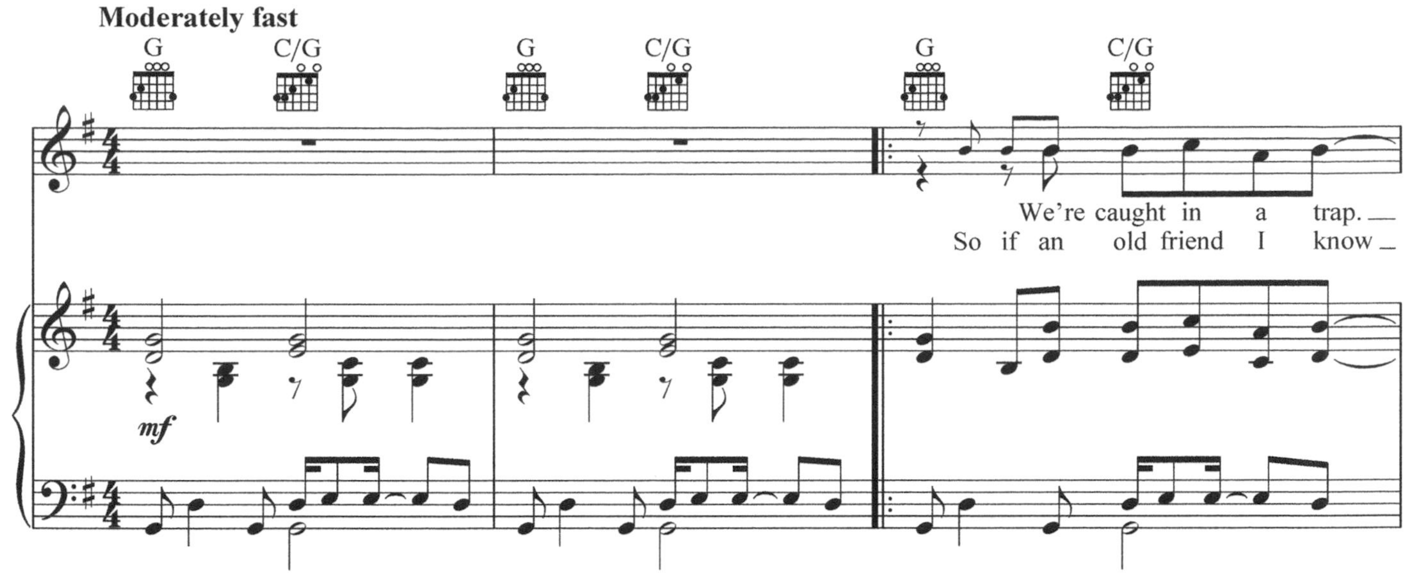

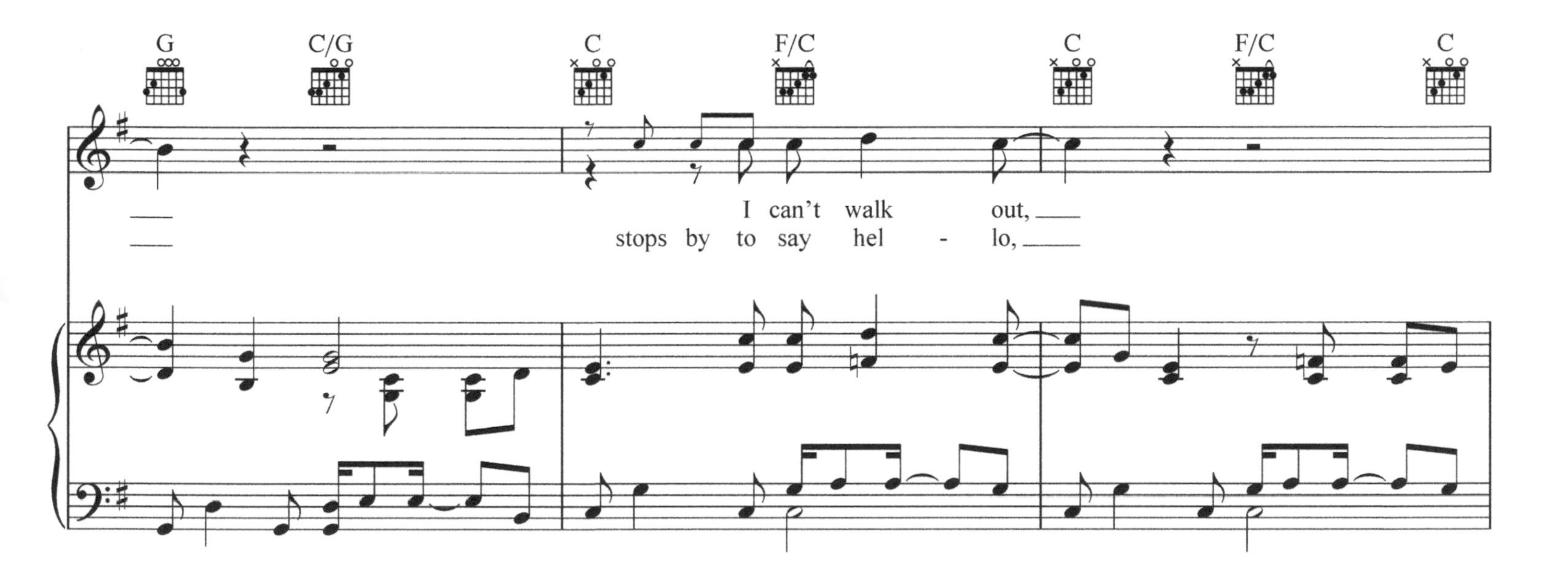

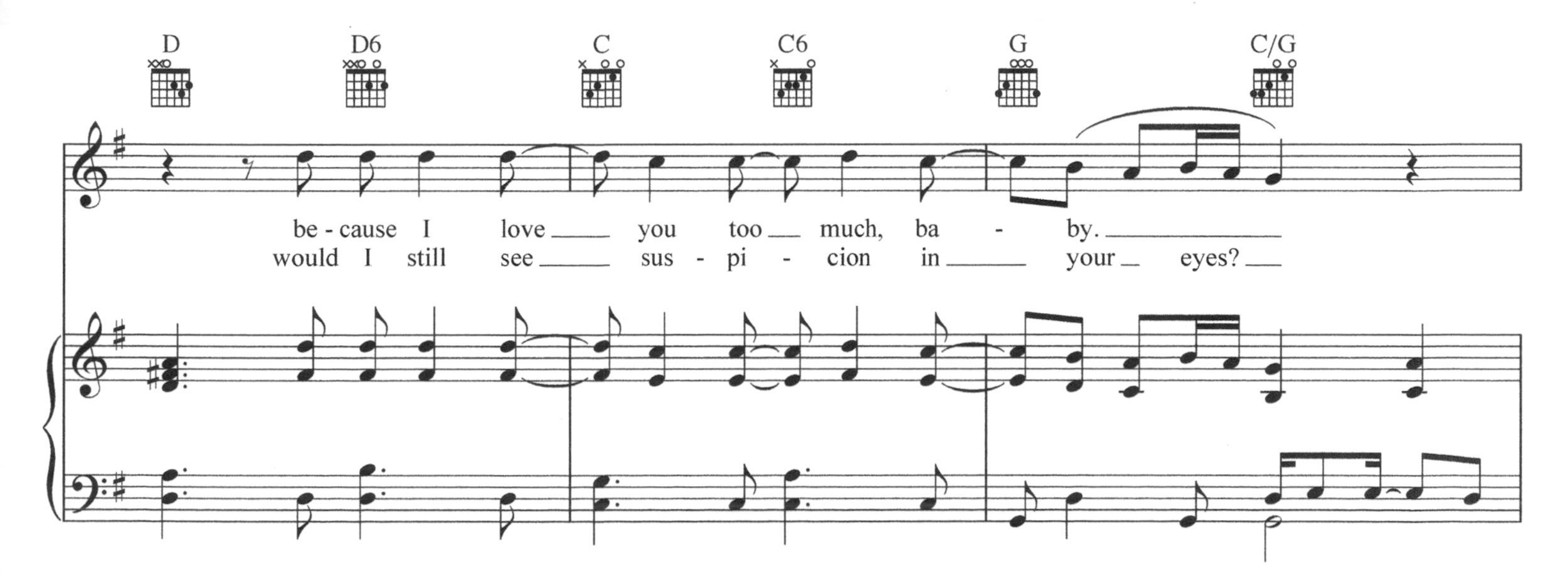

G
C/G
G
C/G
G
C/G
Why can't you see
But here we go a - gain,

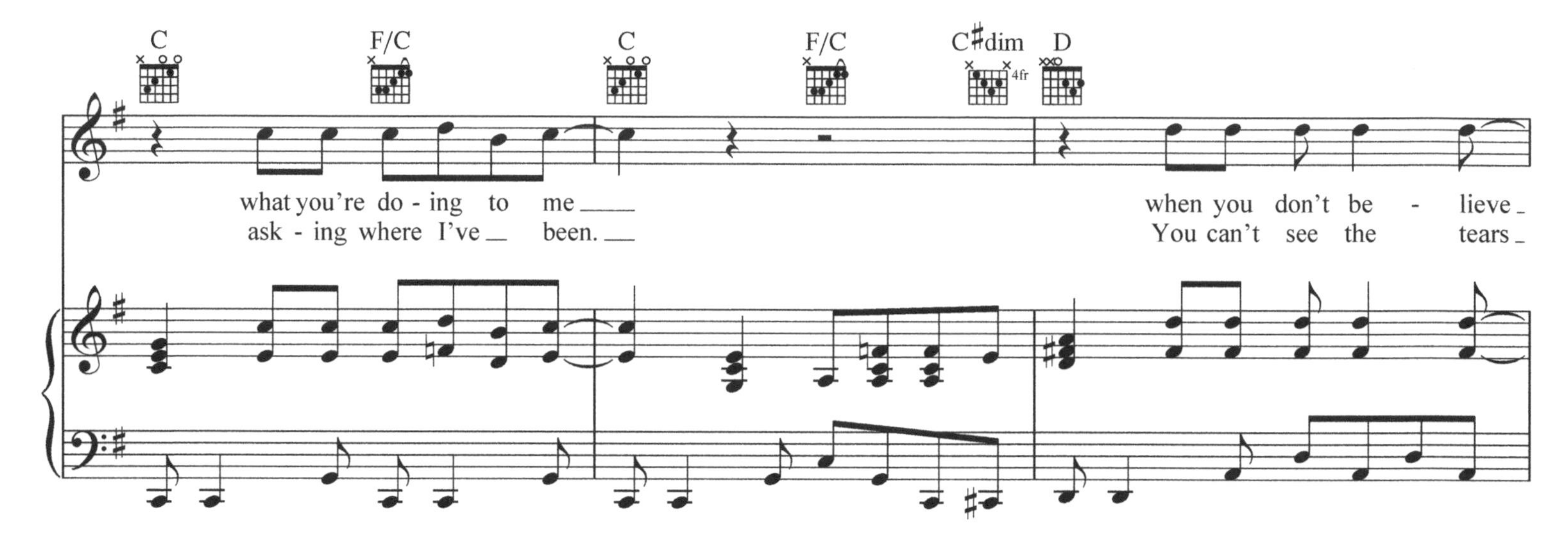
C
F/C
C
F/C
C♯dim
D
4fr
what you're do - ing to me
ask - ing where I've been.
when you don't be - lieve
You can't see the tears

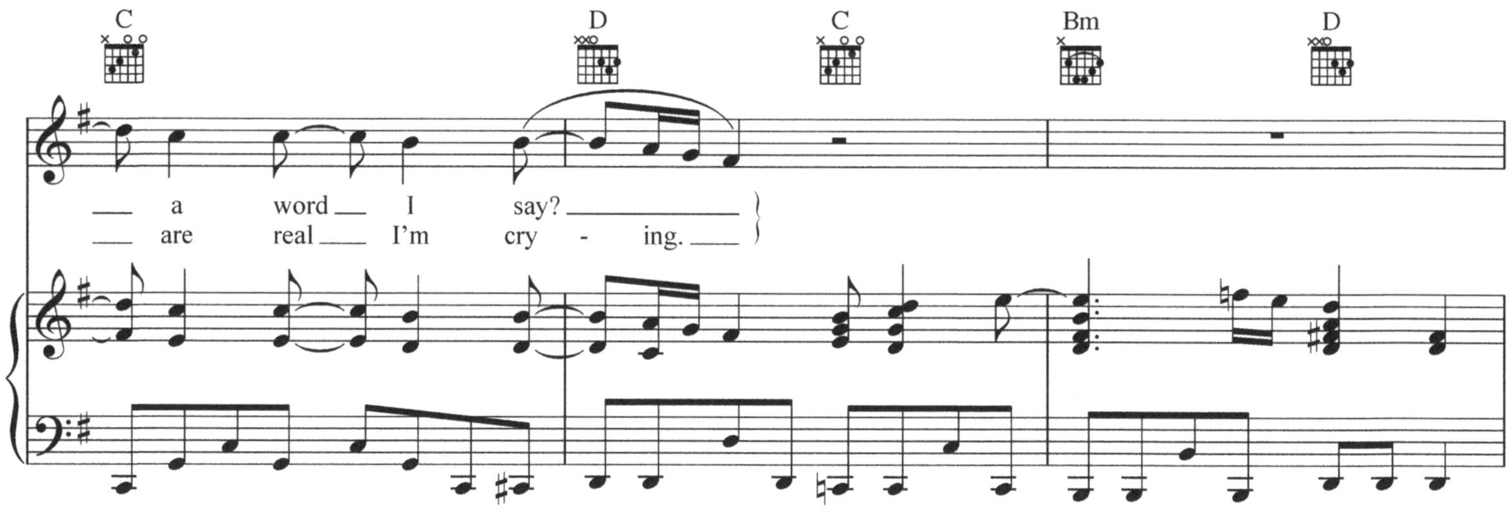
C
D
C
Bm
D
a word I say?
are real I'm cry - ing.

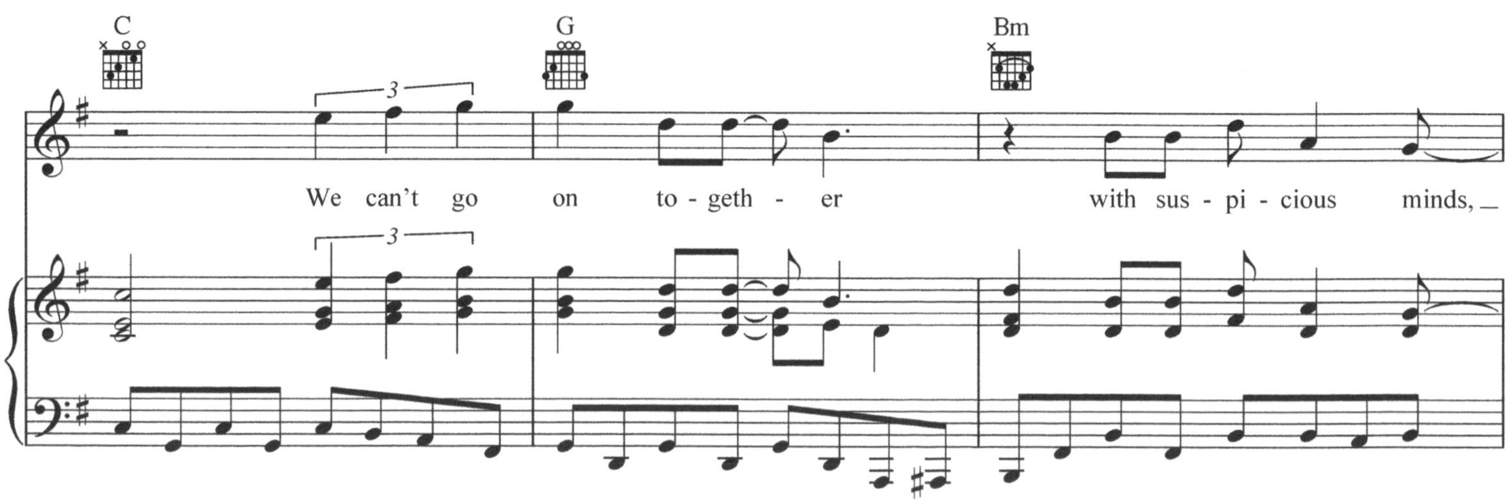
C
G
Bm
3
We can't go on to - geth - er with sus - pi - cious minds,

C
D
Em
Bm
and we can't build our dreams

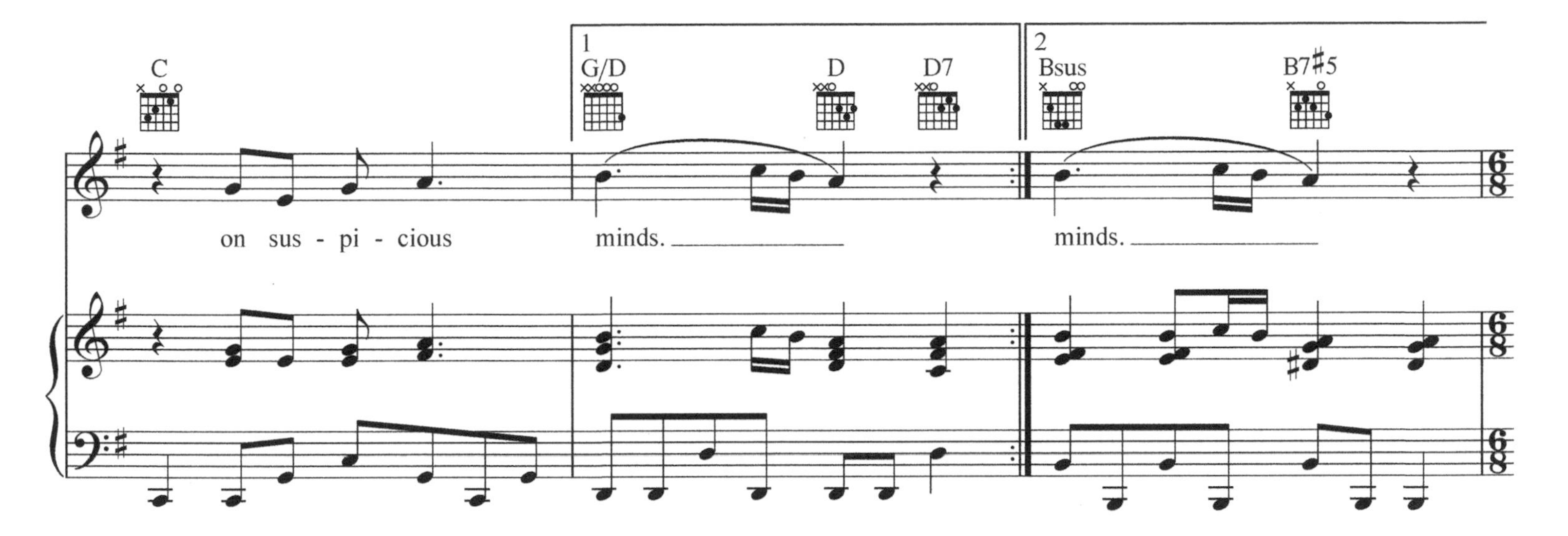
C
1
G/D
D
D7
2
Bsus
B7♯5
on sus - pi - cious minds.
minds.

(♩ = ♪)
Em
Bm7
C
Oh, let our love sur - vive,
or drive the

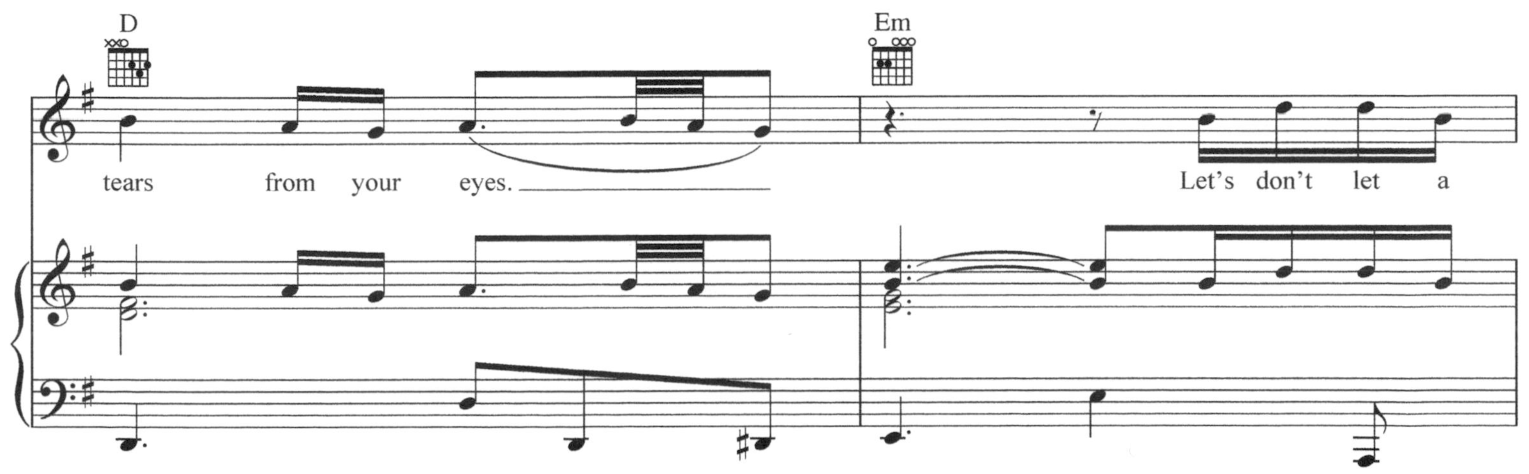
D
Em
tears from your eyes.
Let's don't let a

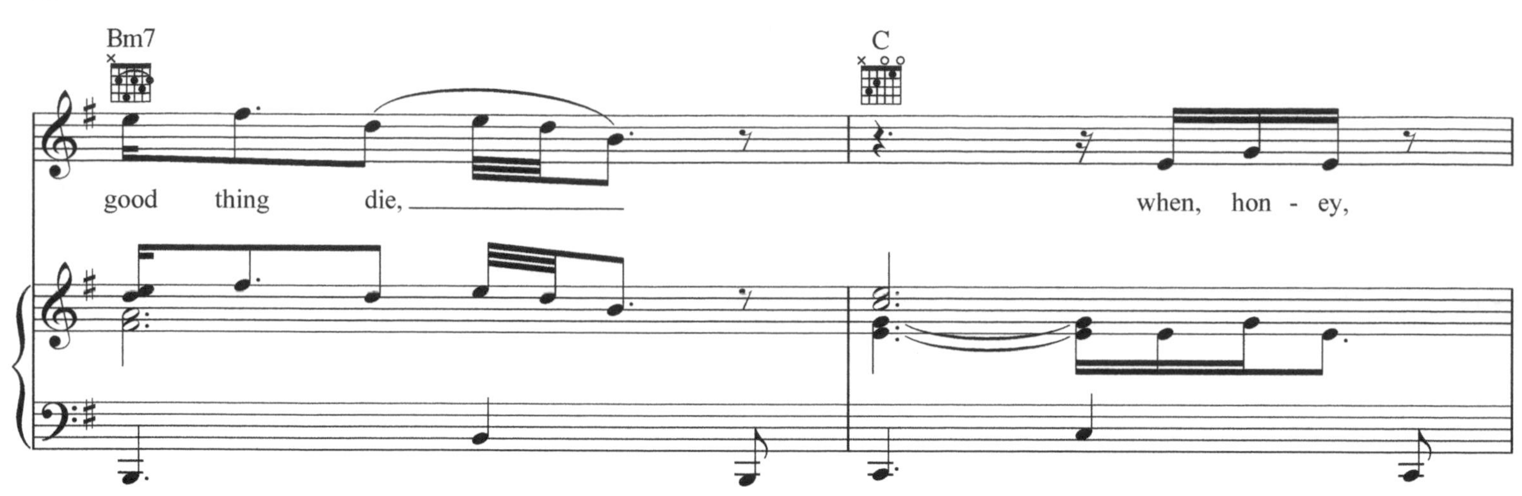
Bm7
C
good thing die,
when, honey,

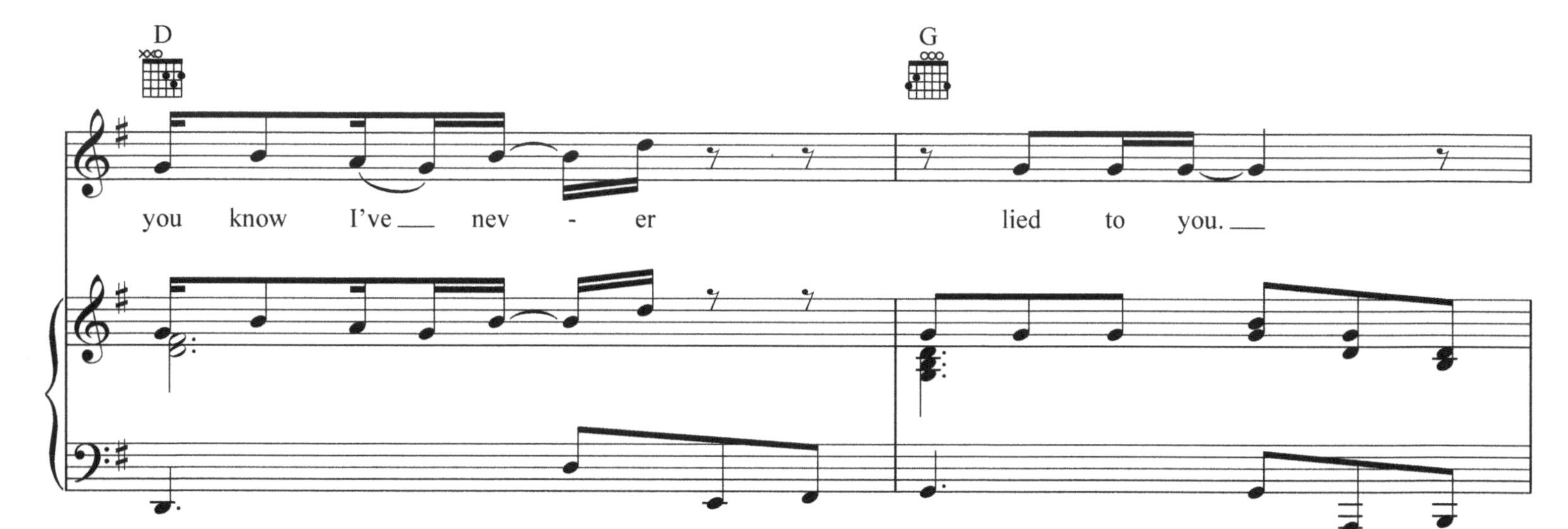
D
G
you know I've never
lied to you.

C
G
D
Mm,
yeah,
yeah.

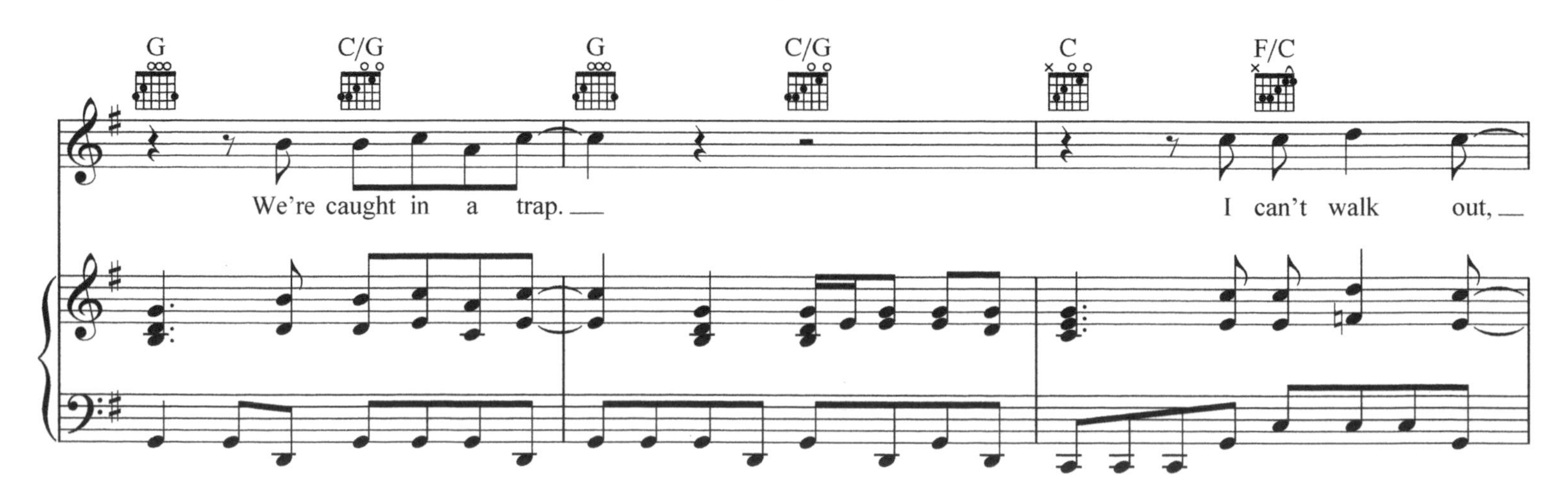
G
C/G
G
C/G
C
F/C
We're caught in a trap.
I can't walk out,

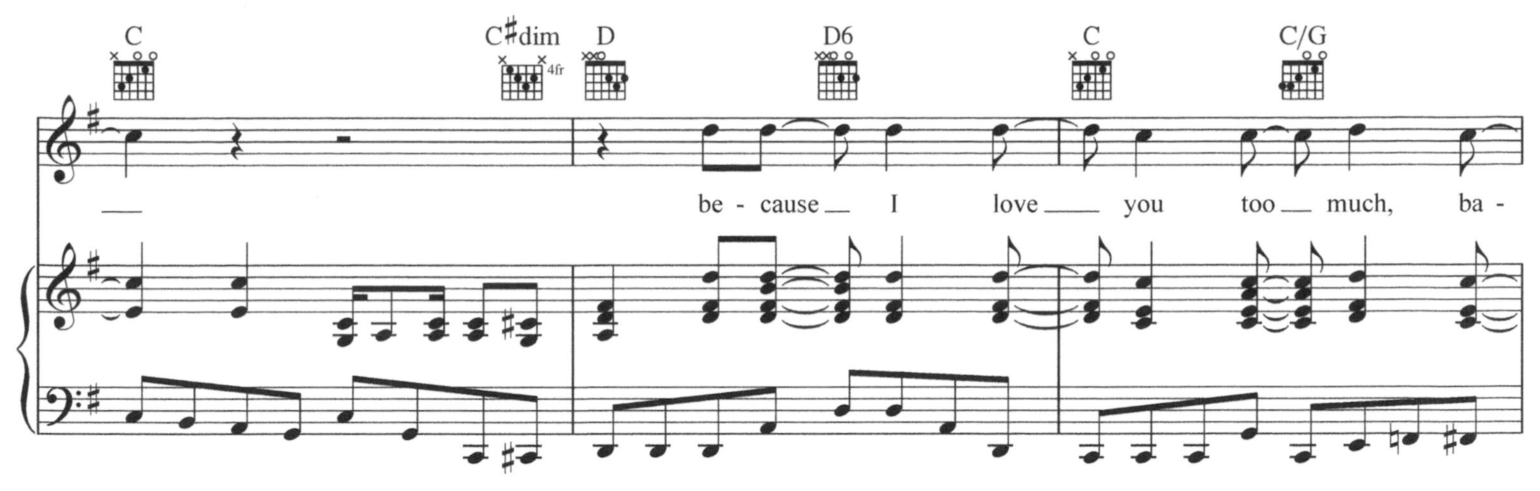
C
C♯dim
4fr
D
D6
C
C/G
because I love you too much, ba-

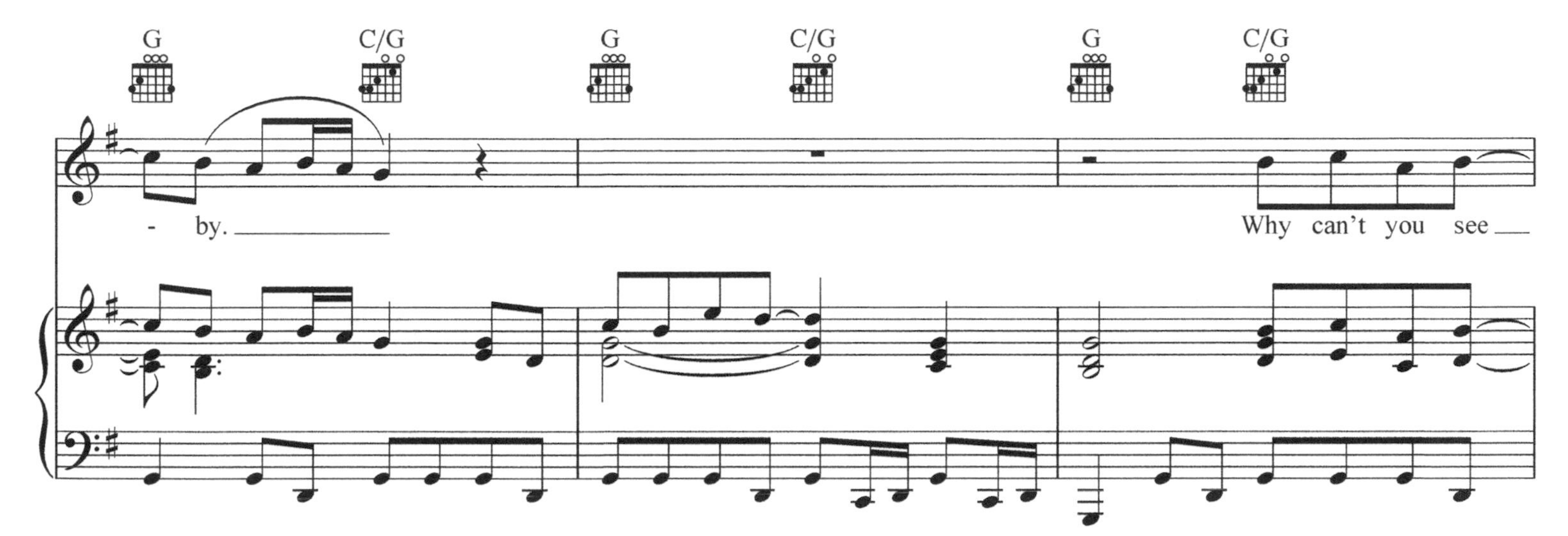
G
C/G
G
C/G
G
C/G
by.
Why can't you see

G
C/G
C
F
C♯dim
4fr
what you're do-ing to me

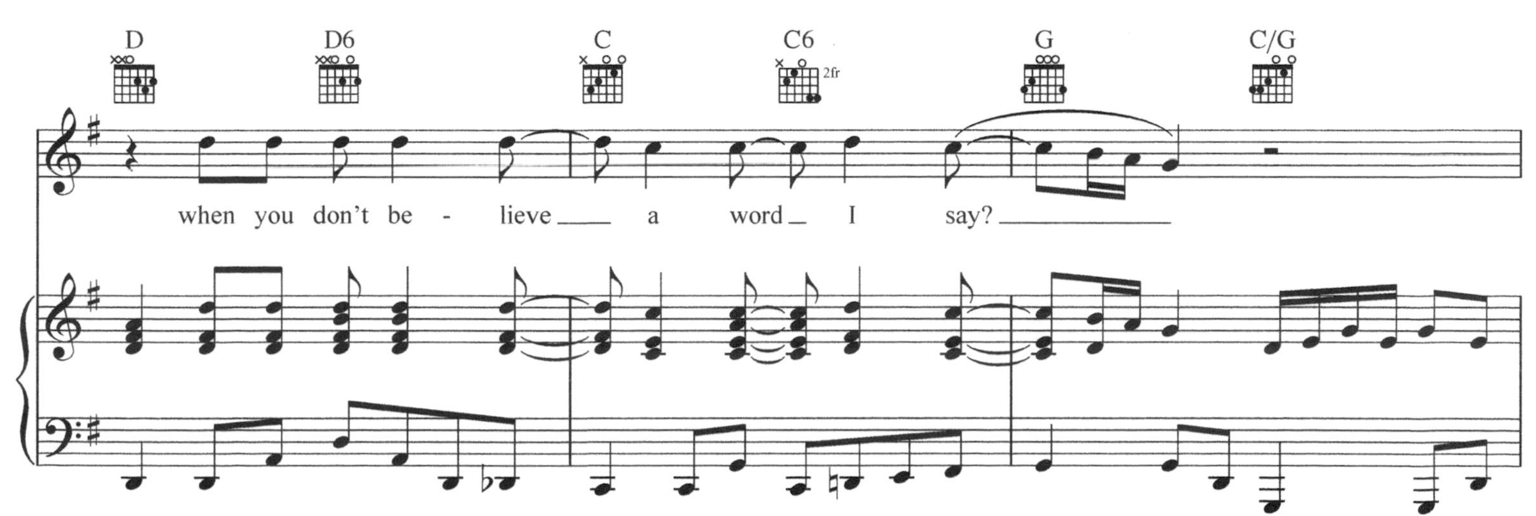
D
D6
C
C6
2fr
G
C/G
when you don't be-lieve a word I say?

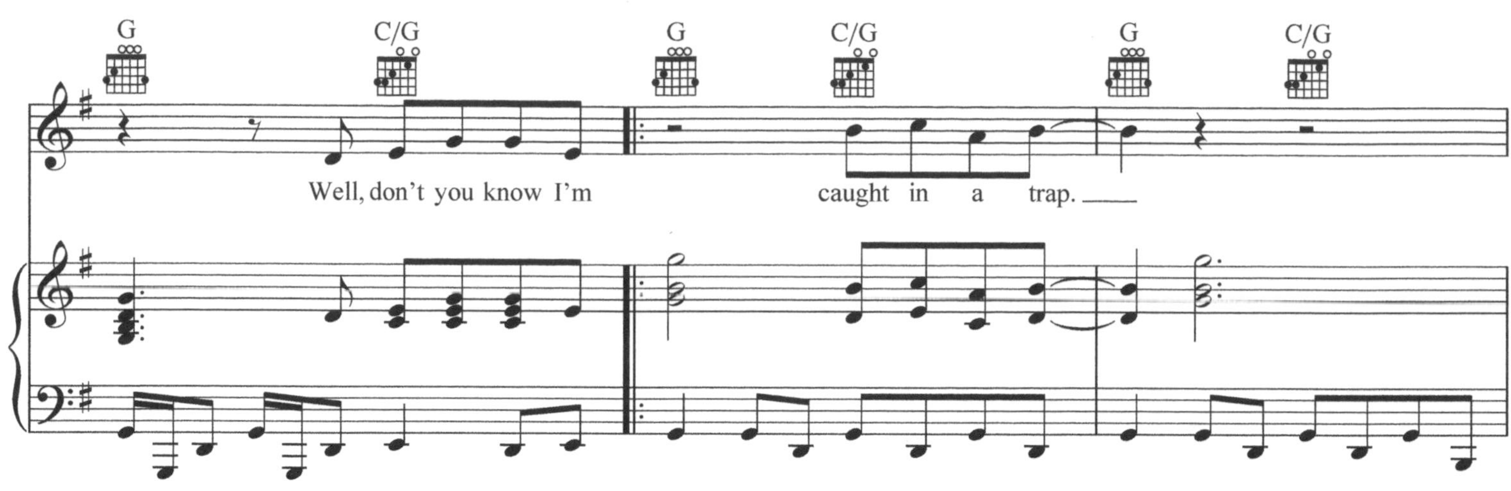
G
C/G
G
C/G
G
C/G
Well, don't you know I'm
caught in a trap.

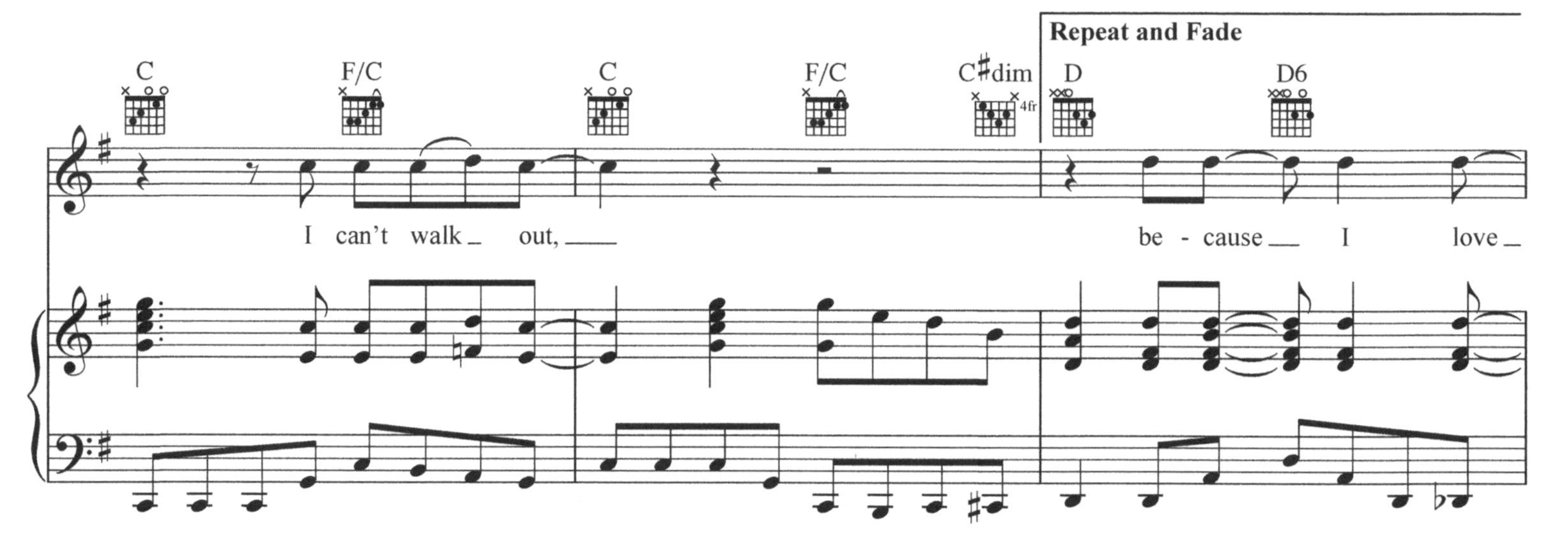
Repeat and Fade
C
F/C
C
F/C
C♯dim
4fr
D
D6
I can't walk out,
be - cause I love

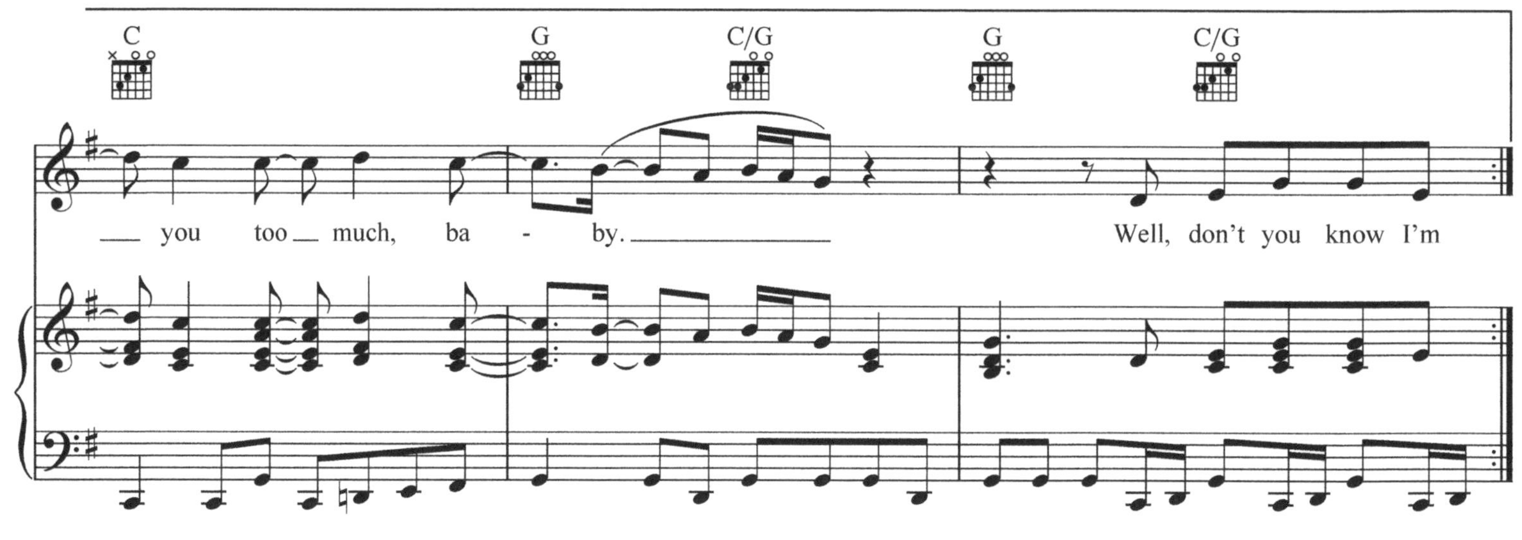
C
G
C/G
G
C/G
you too much, ba - by.
Well, don't you know I'm

Optional Ending
D
D6
C
G
be - cause I love you too much, ba - by.

I'LL REMEMBER YOU

Words and Music by
KUIOKALANI LEE

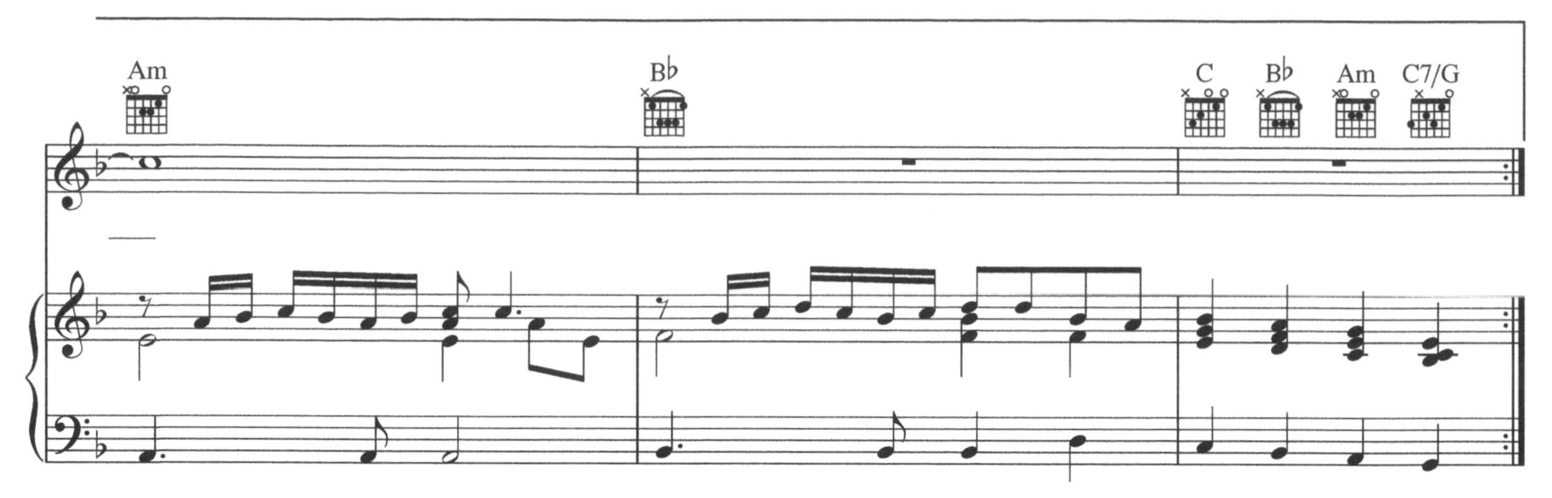
Am
Bb
C
Bb
Am
C7/G

2
F
F7
Bb
you.
To your arms some - day,

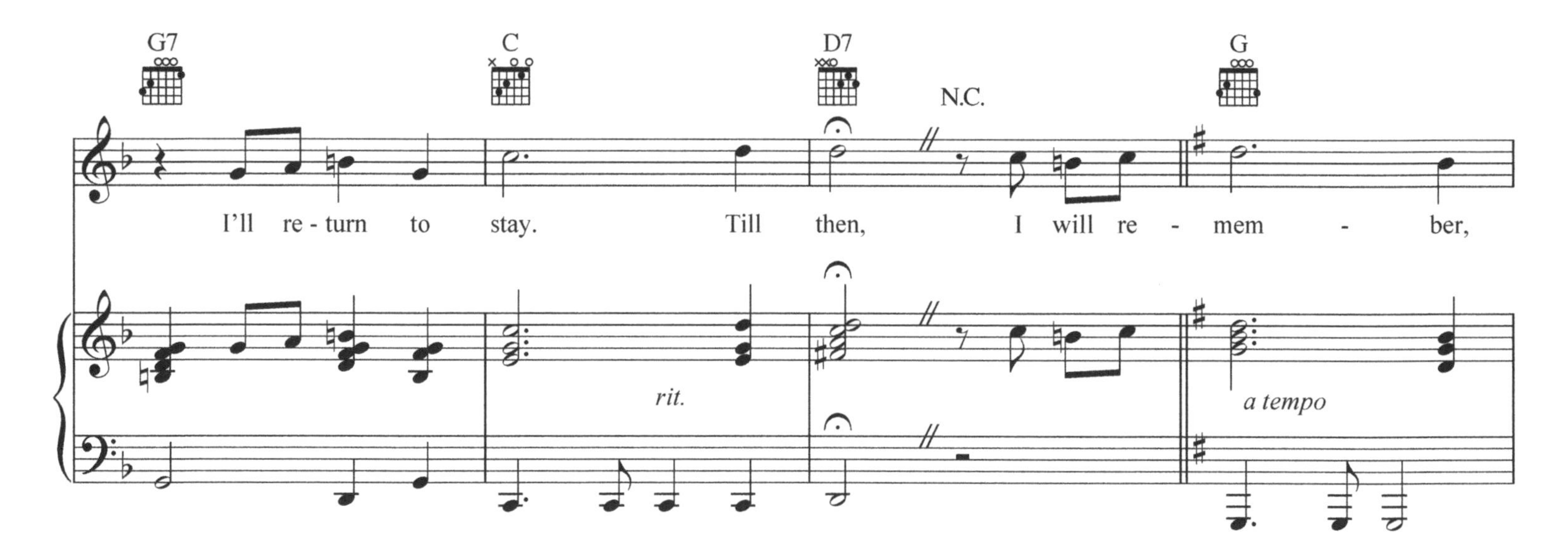
G7
C
D7
N.C.
G
I'll re - turn to stay.
Till then,
I will re - mem - ber,
rit.
a tempo

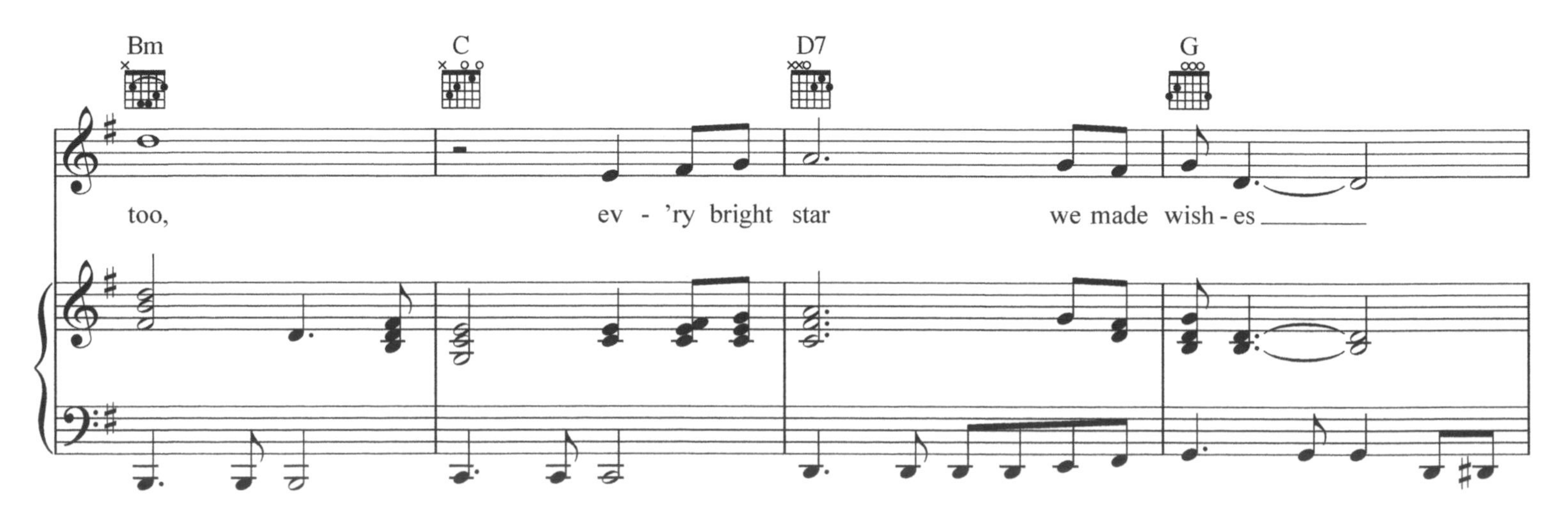
Bm
C
D7
G
too,
ev - 'ry bright star
we made wish - es

E7
Am
Cm
3fr
up - on.
Love me al - ways,
prom - ise al - ways,

Am
D
F9
ooh,
you'll re - mem - ber,
too.

G
I'll re - mem - ber

Gmaj7
you.
rit.

WHOLE LOTTA SHAKIN' GOIN' ON

Words and Music by
DAVID WILLIAMS

Moderately, with a solid beat

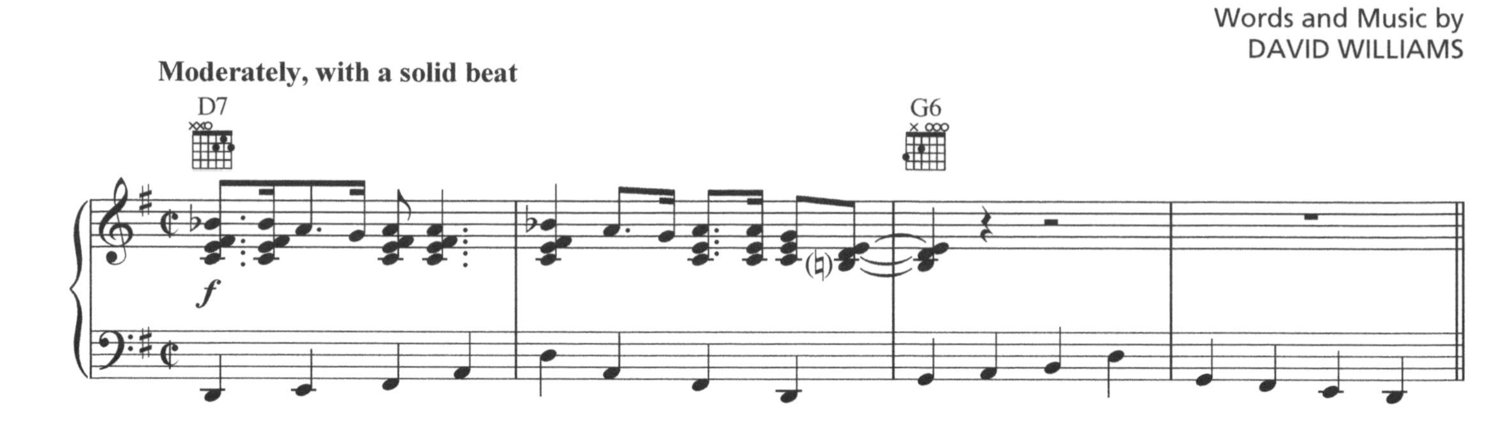

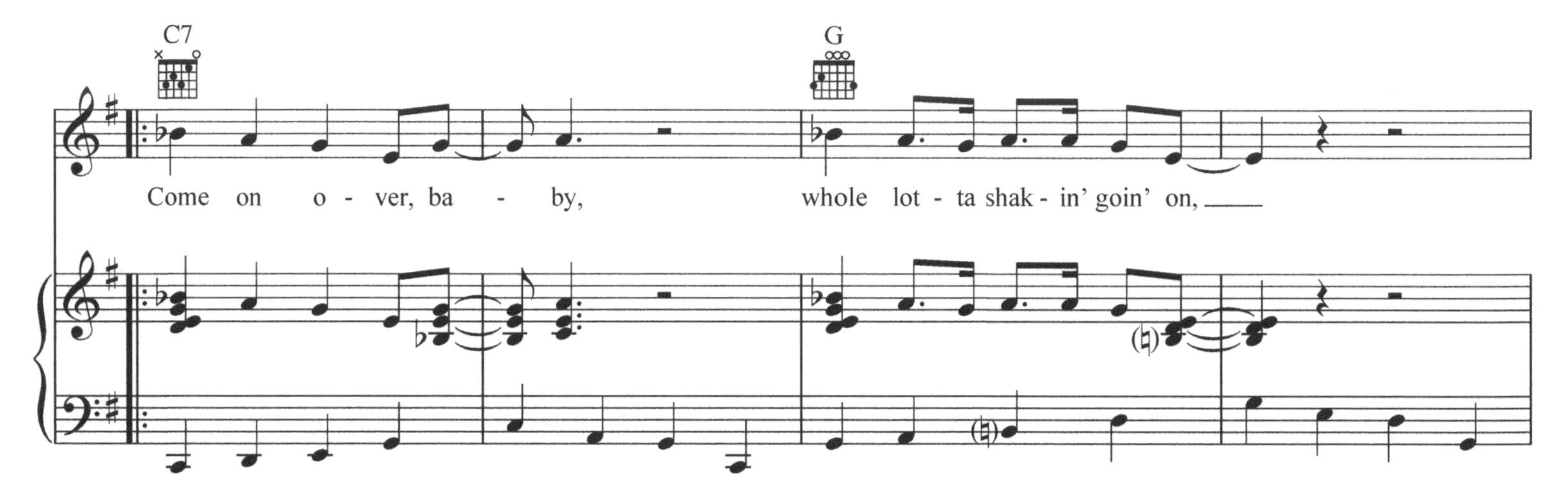

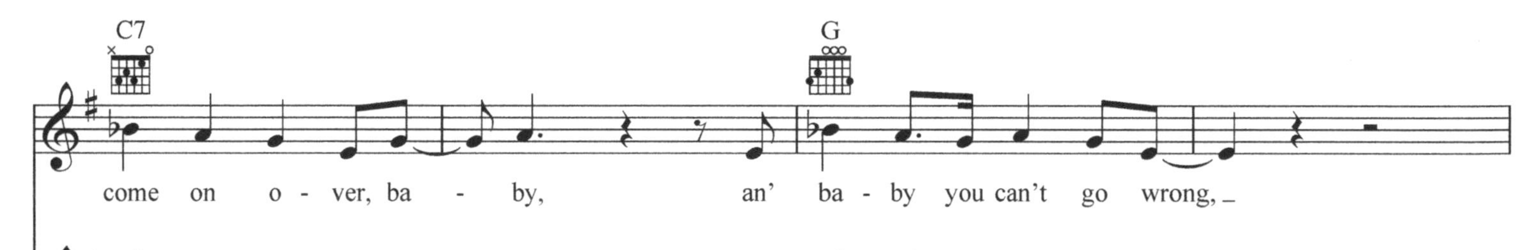

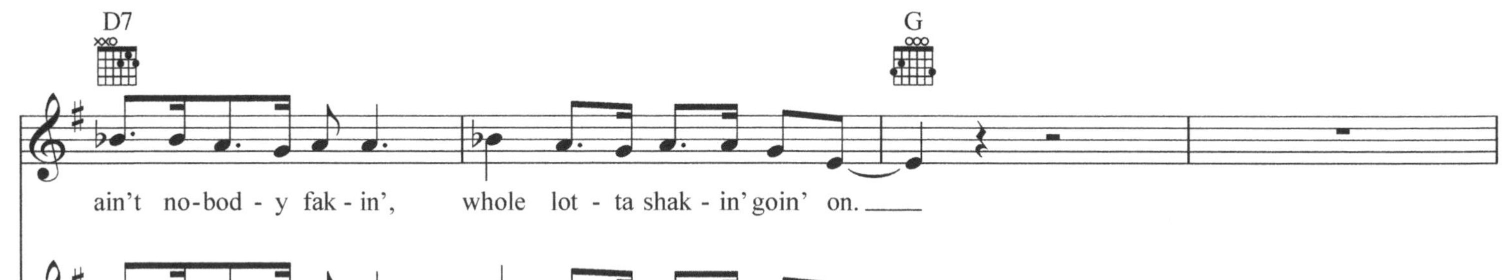

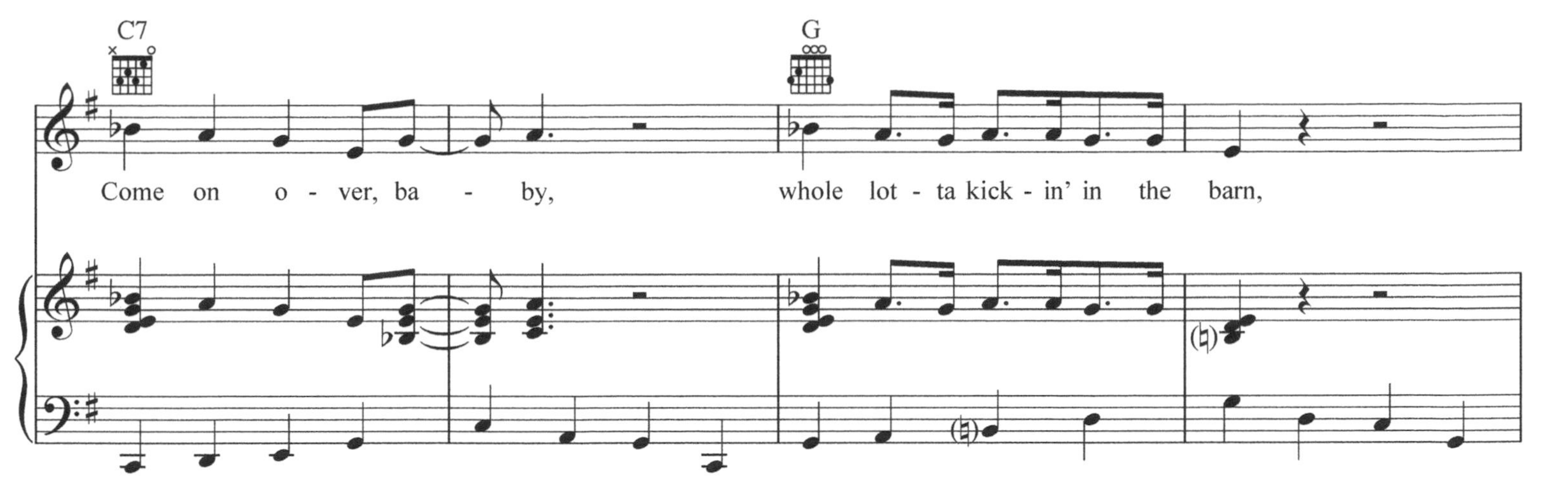
C7
G
Come on o - ver, ba - by, whole lot - ta kick - in' in the barn,

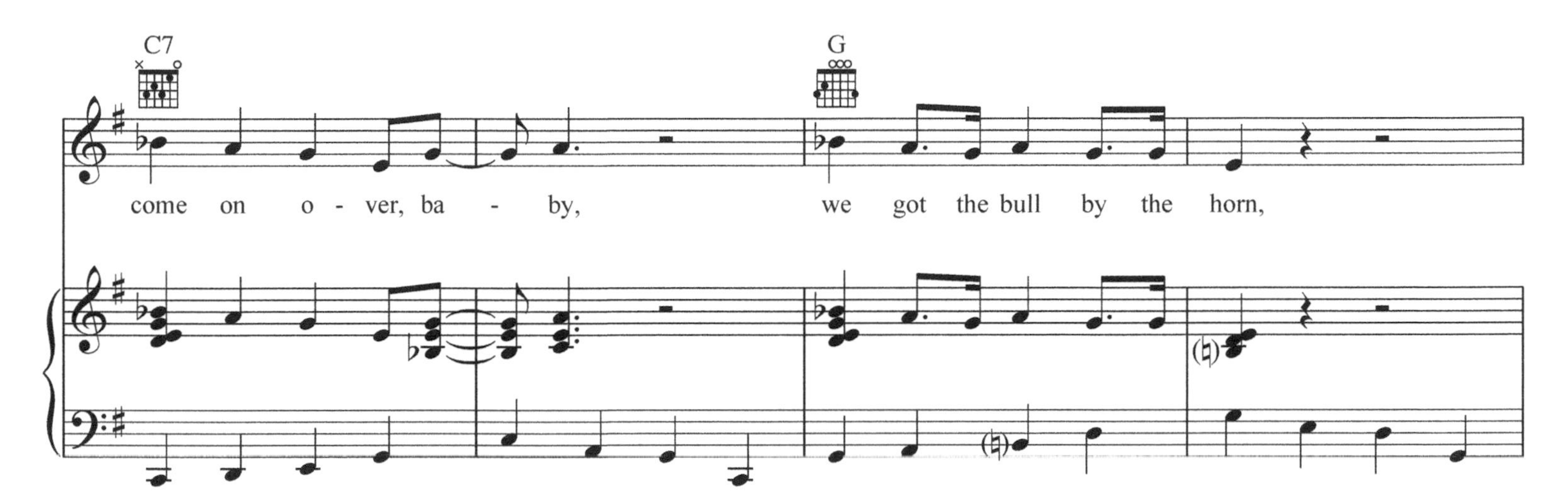
C7
G
come on o - ver, ba - by, we got the bull by the horn,

D7
1
G
ev - 'ry-thing is tak - in', whole lot - ta shak - in' goin' on.

2
G
D7
Em7
D7
G6

ff

LONG TALL SALLY

Words and Music by ENOTRIS JOHNSON,
RICHARD PENNIMAN and ROBERT BLACKWELL

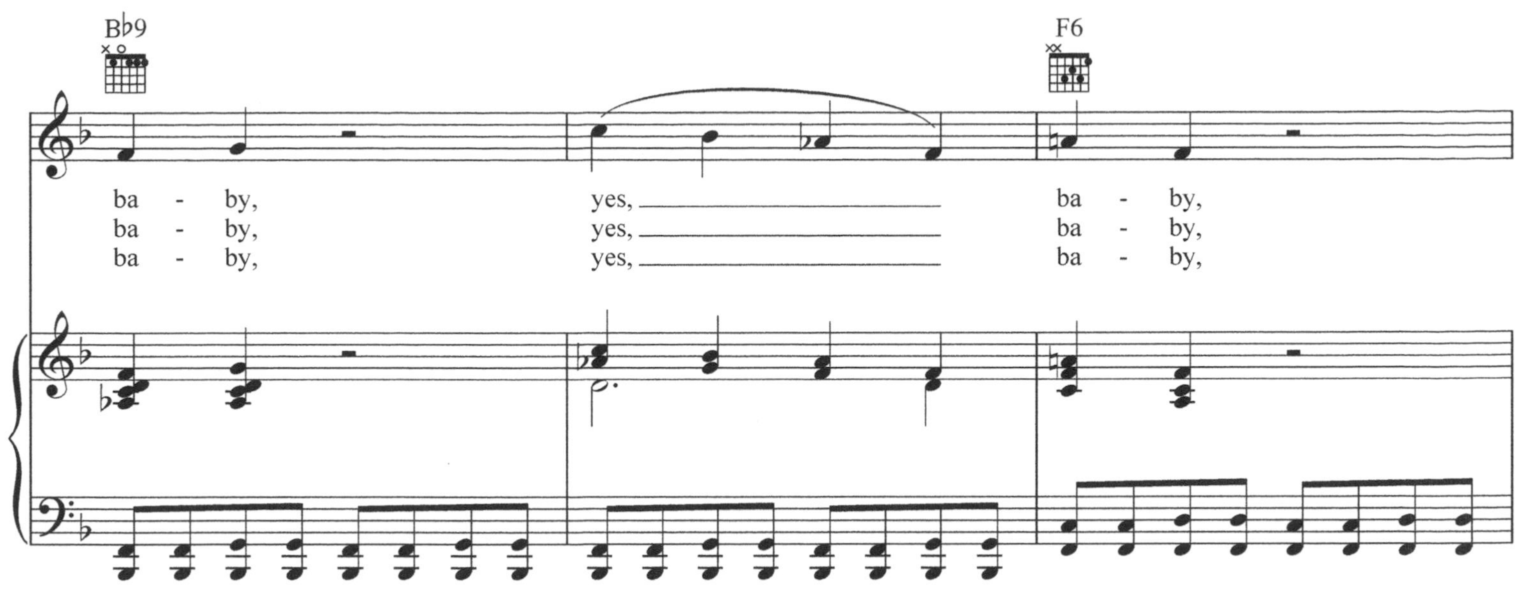
B♭9
F6
ba - by,
yes,
ba - by,
ba - by,
yes,
ba - by,
ba - by,
yes,
ba - by,

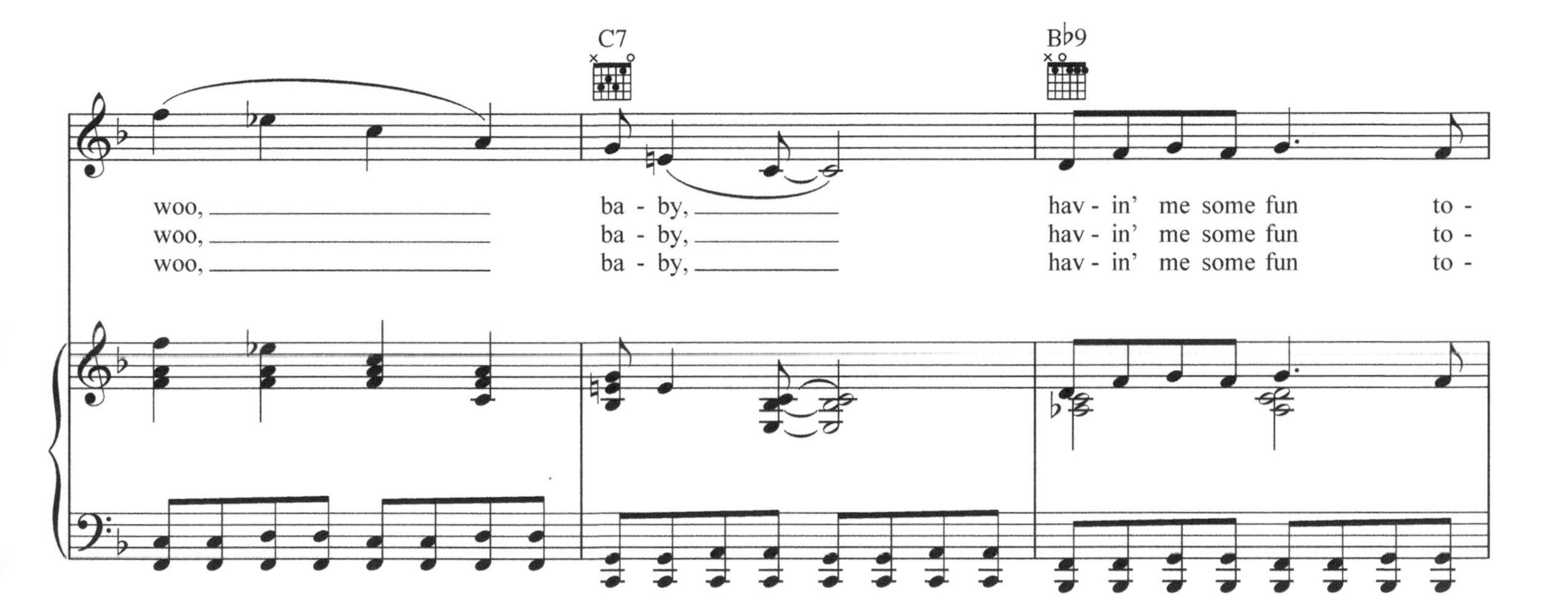
C7
B♭9
woo,
ba - by,
hav - in' me some fun to -
woo,
ba - by,
hav - in' me some fun to -
woo,
ba - by,
hav - in' me some fun to -

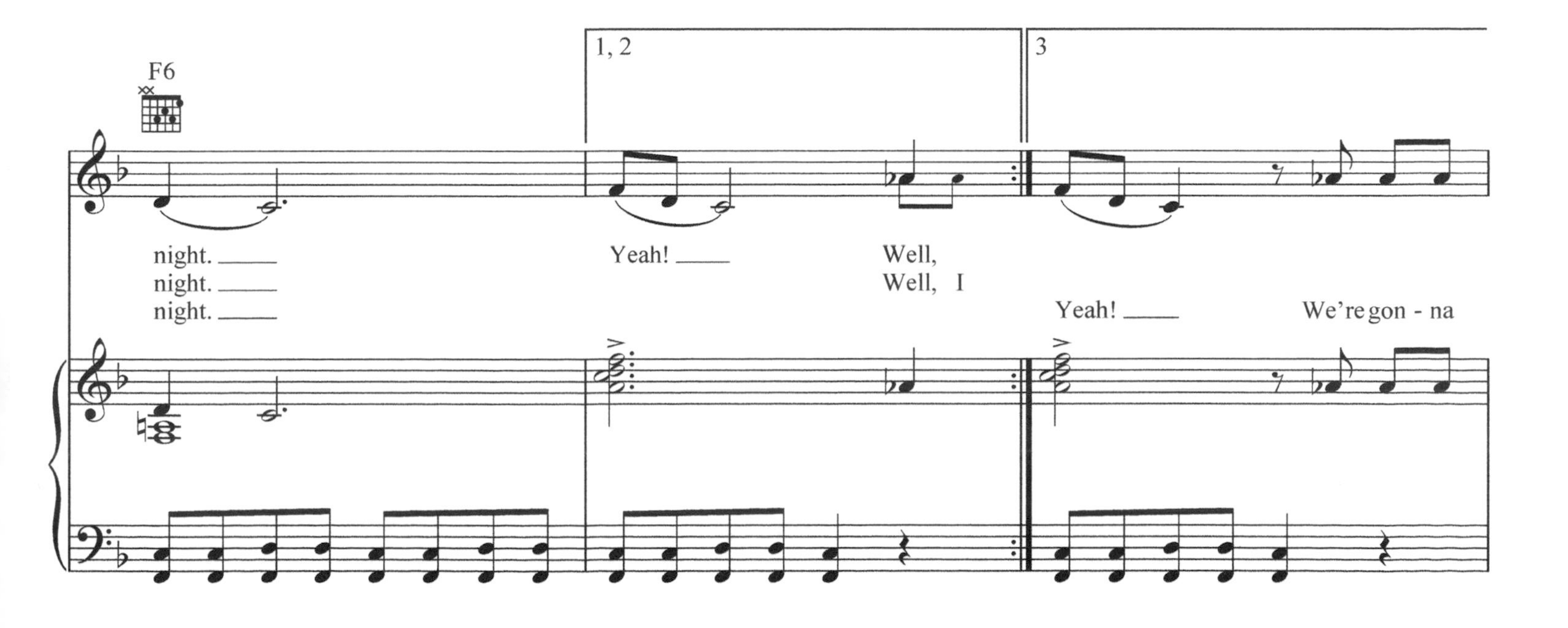
F6
1, 2
3
night.
Yeah!
Well,
night.
Well, I
night.
Yeah!
We're gon - na

have some fun to - night,
gon - na have some fun to - night,

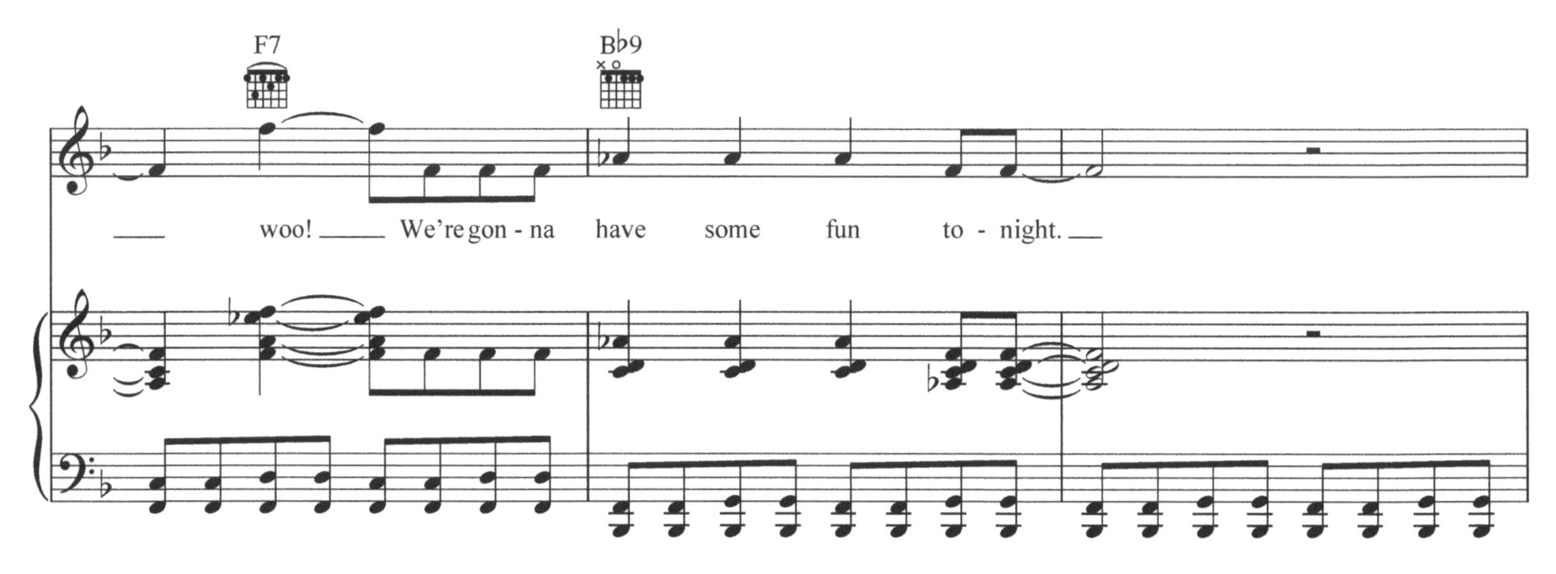
F7
B♭9
woo! We're gon - na have some fun to - night.

F6
C7
Ev - 'ry - thing will be all right.
We're gon - na have some fun, gon - na

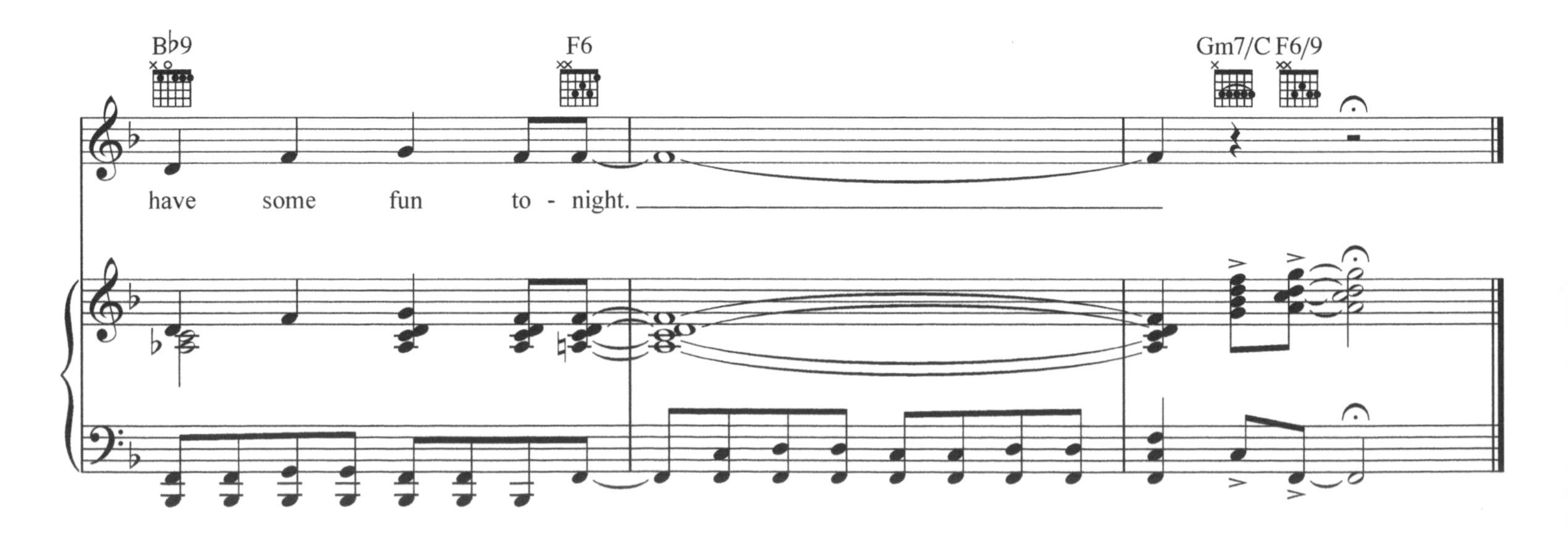
B♭9
F6
Gm7/C
F6/9
have some fun to - night.

AN AMERICAN TRILOGY

Words and Music by
MICKEY NEWBURY

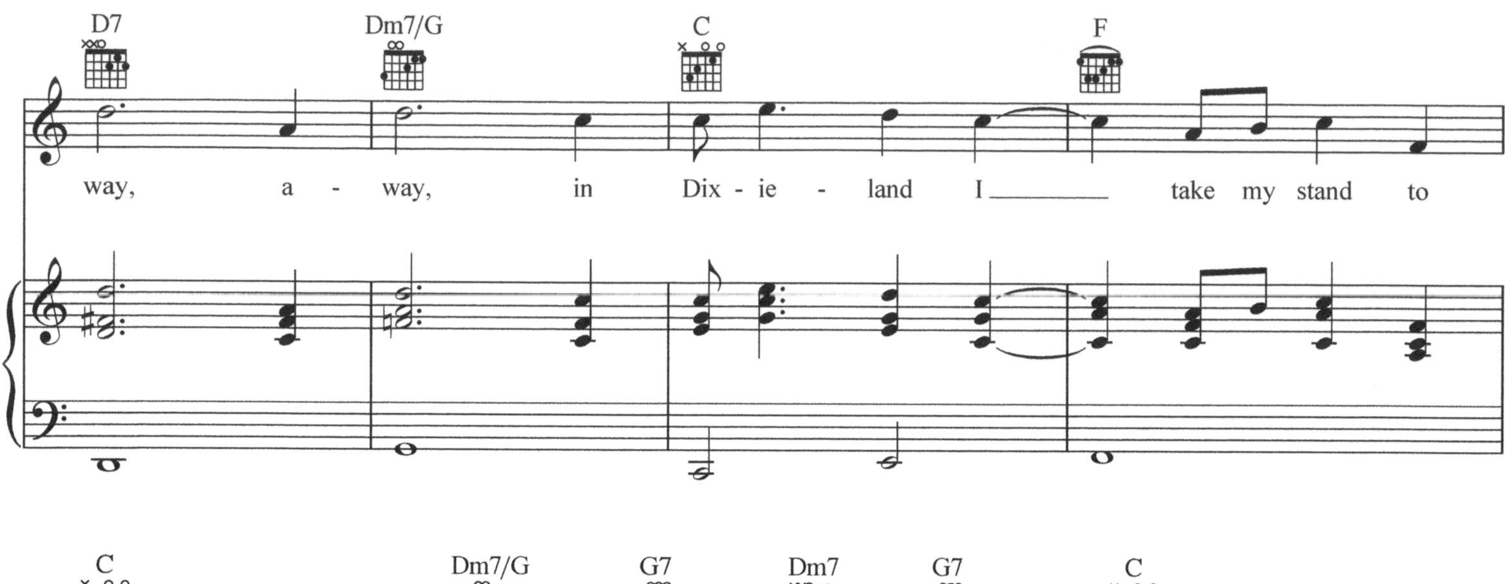
D7
Dm7/G
C
F
way, a - way, in Dix - ie - land I take my stand to

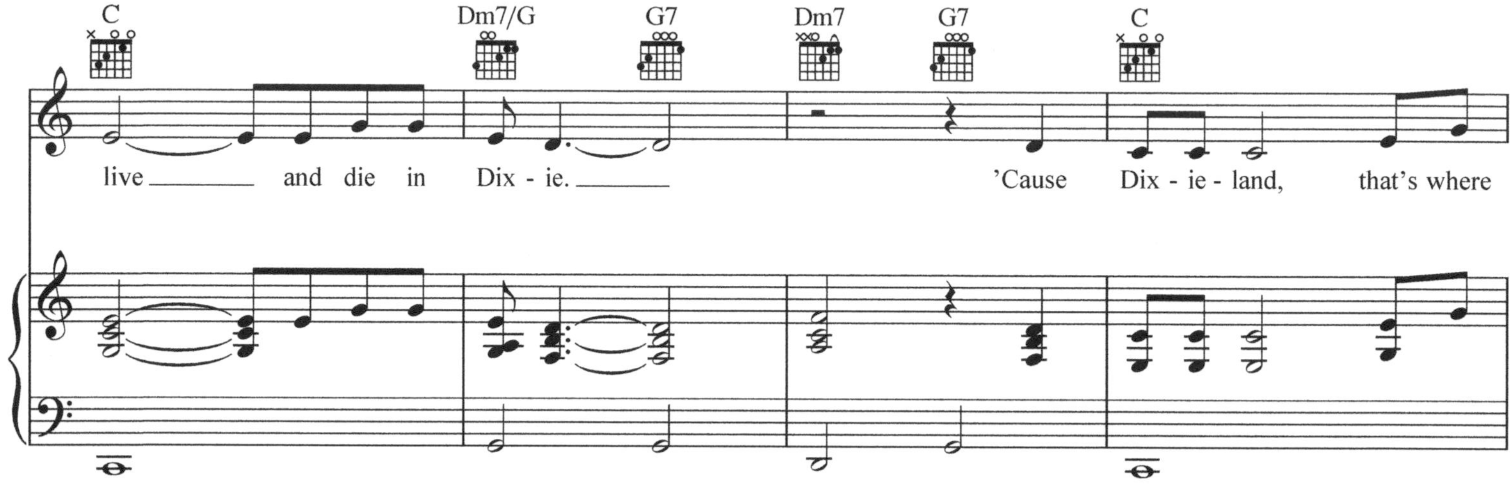
C
Dm7/G
G7
Dm7
G7
C
live and die in Dix - ie. 'Cause Dix - ie - land, that's where

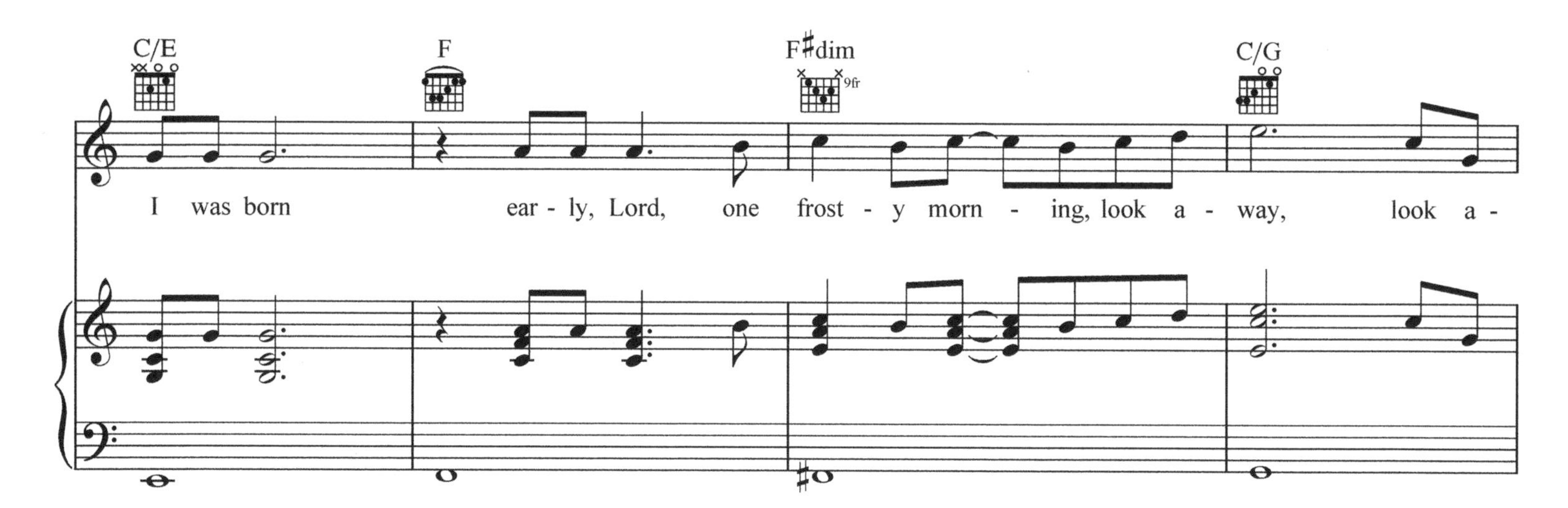
C/E
F
F♯dim
9fr
C/G
I was born ear - ly, Lord, one frost - y morn - ing, look a - way, look a -

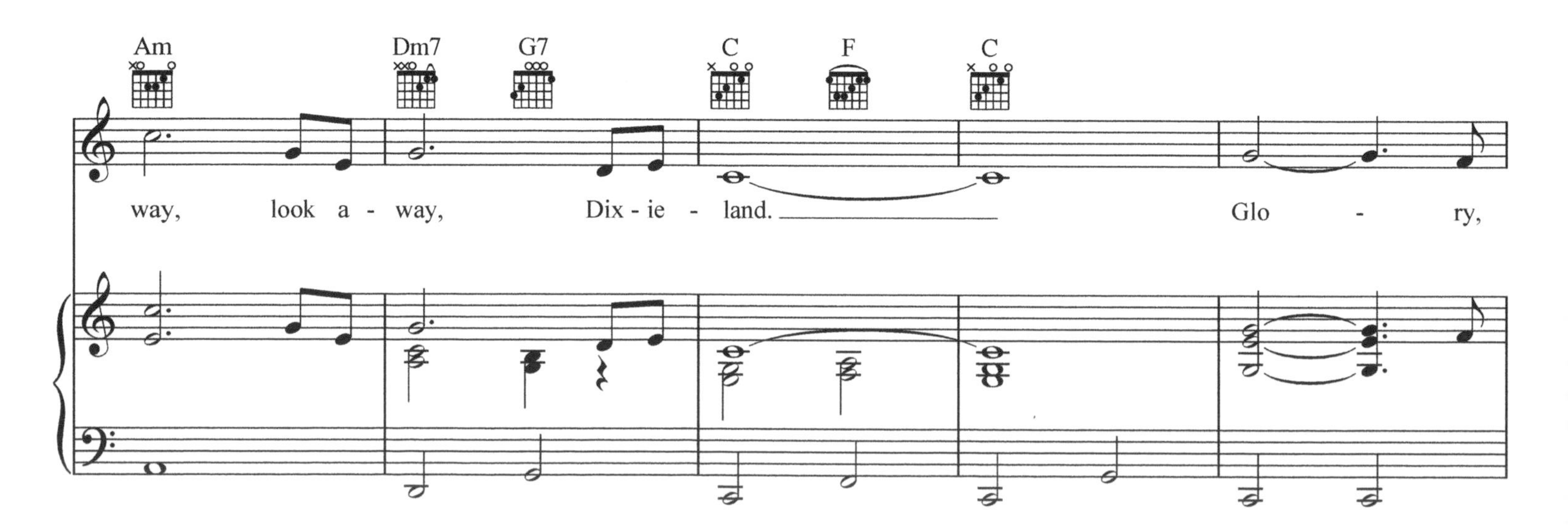
Am
Dm7
G7
C
F
C
way, look a - way, Dix - ie - land. Glo - ry,

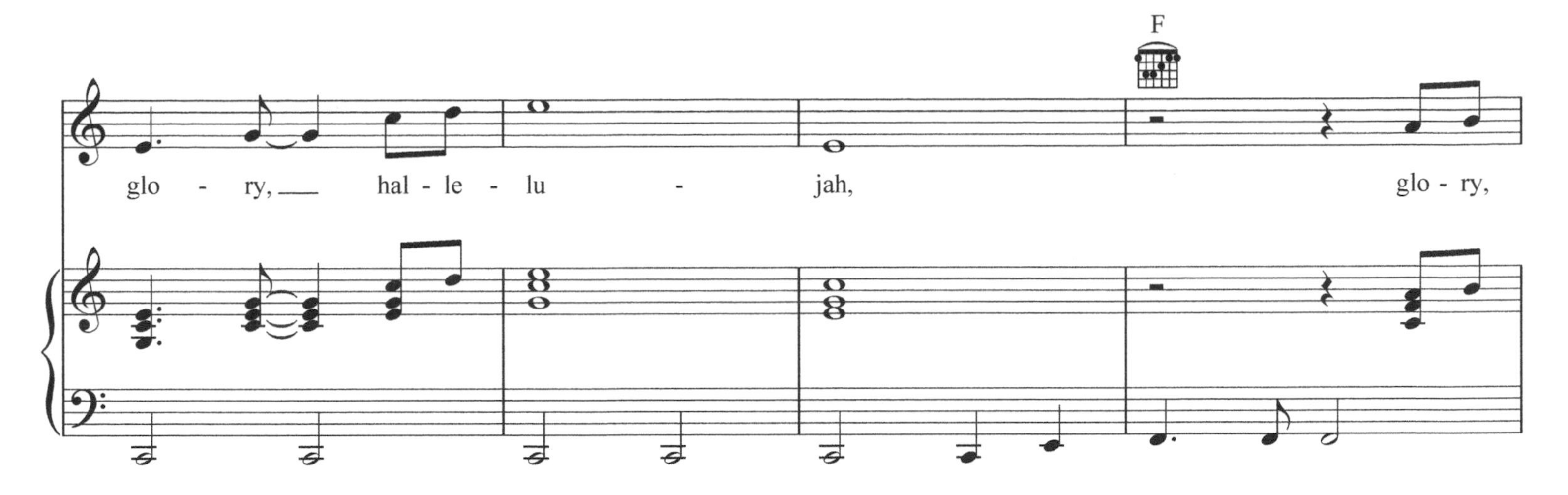
F
glo - ry, hal - le - lu - jah, glo - ry,

C
glo - ry, hal - le - lu - jah. Glo - ry,

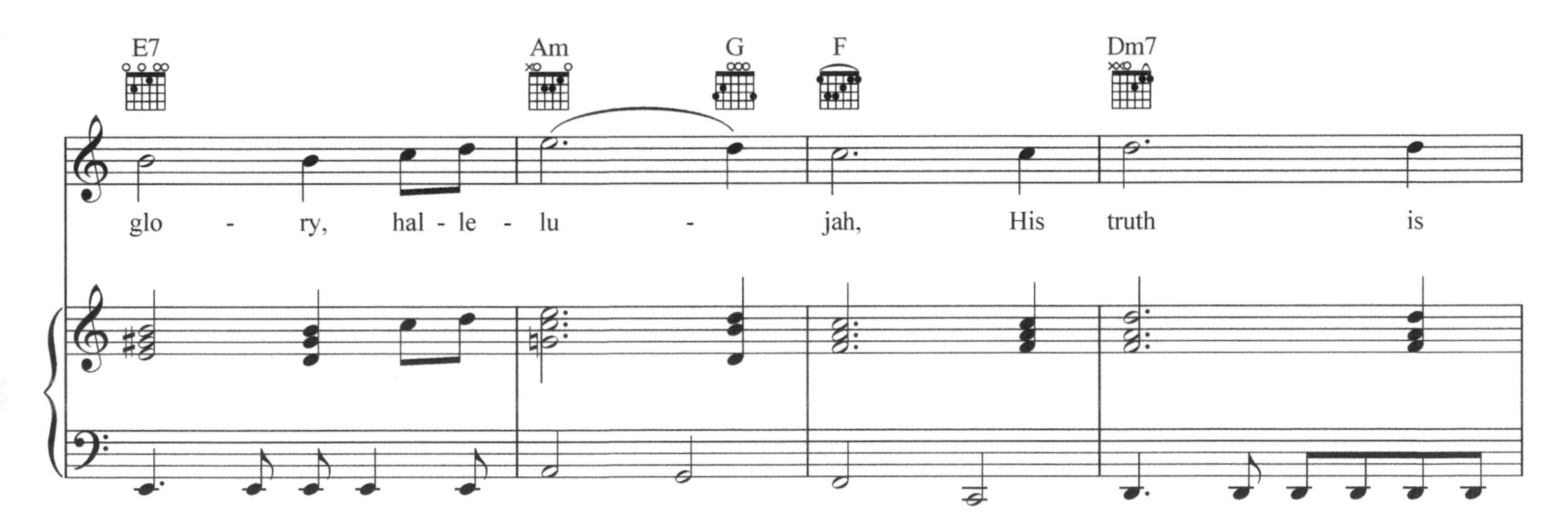
E7
Am
G
F
Dm7
glo - ry, hal - le - lu - jah, His truth is

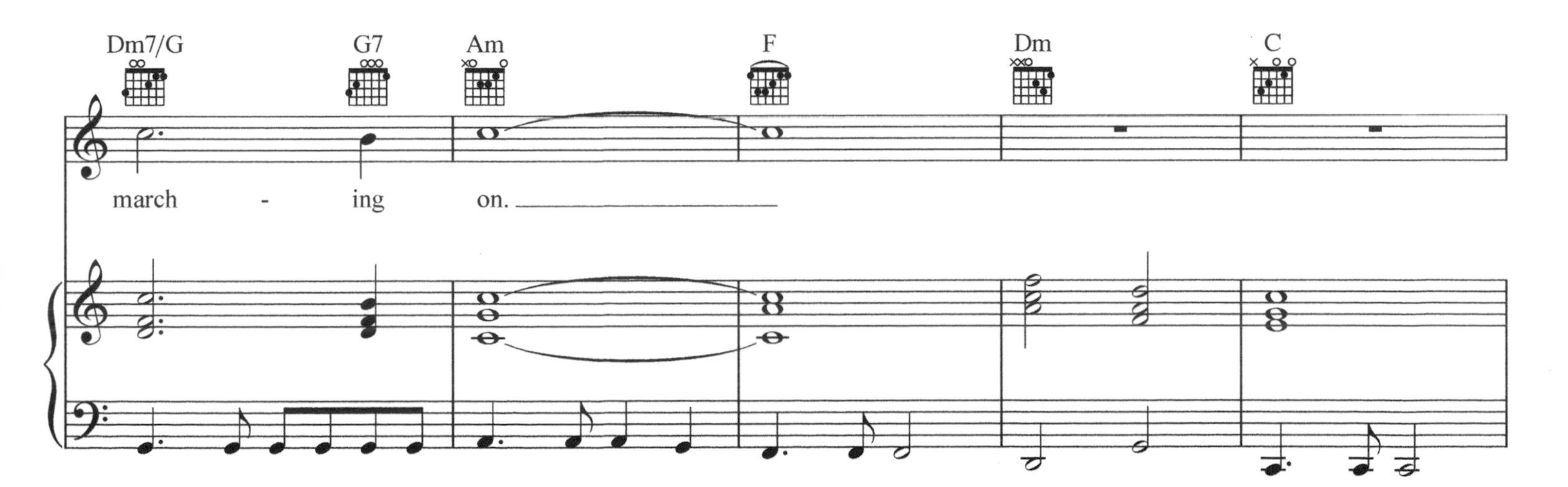
Dm7/G
G7
Am
F
Dm
C
march - ing on.

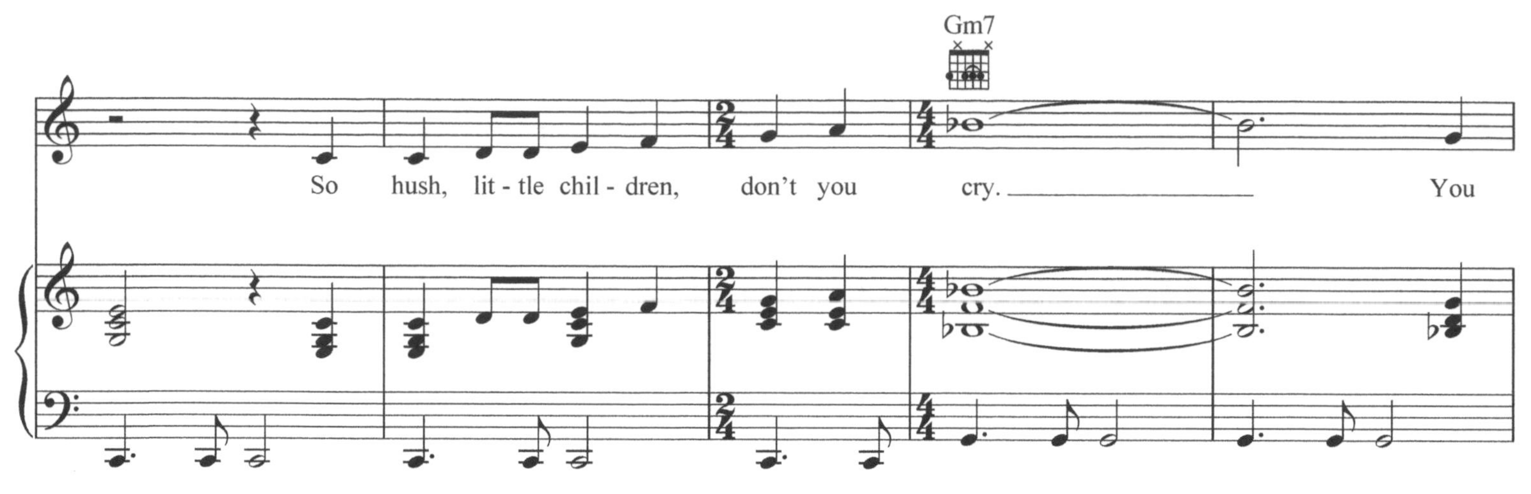
Gm7
So hush, lit - tle chil - dren, don't you cry. You

C
Am
F
know your dad - dy's bound to die.

C
Am7
F
Dm7
But all my trials, Lord,

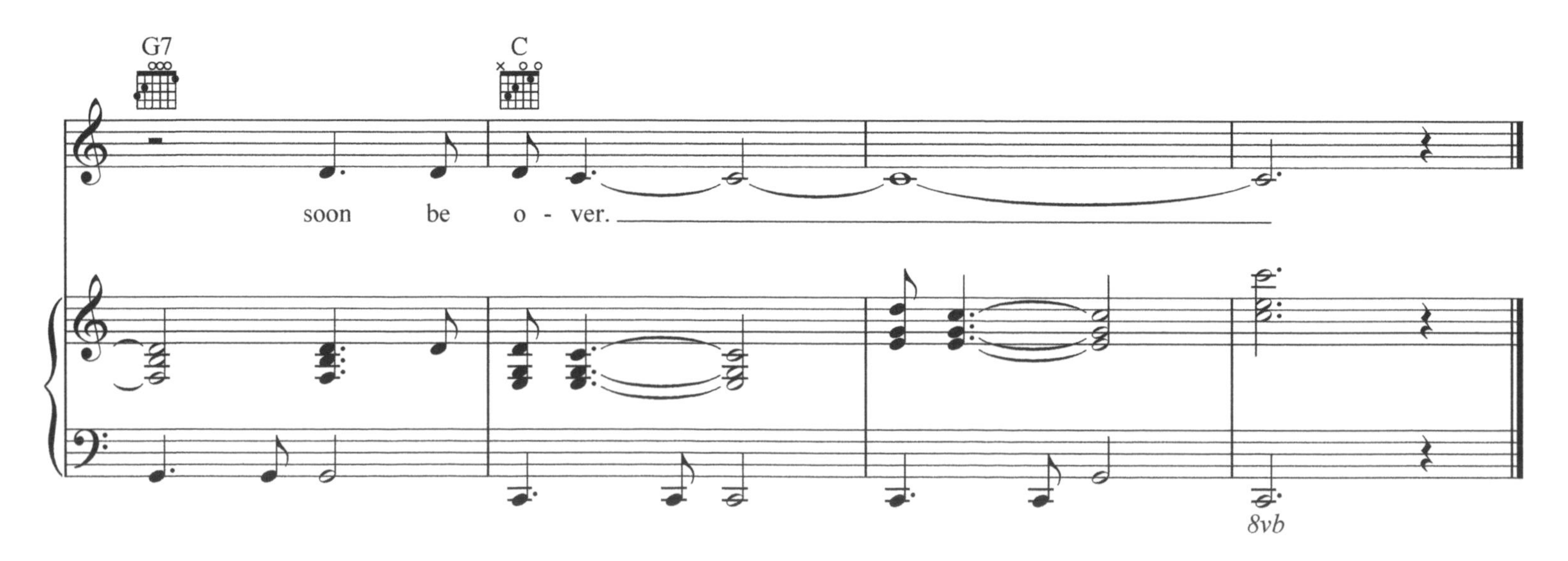
G7
C
soon be o - ver.
8vb

A BIG HUNK O' LOVE

Words and Music by AARON SCHROEDER
and SIDNEY WYCHE

Bright Rock

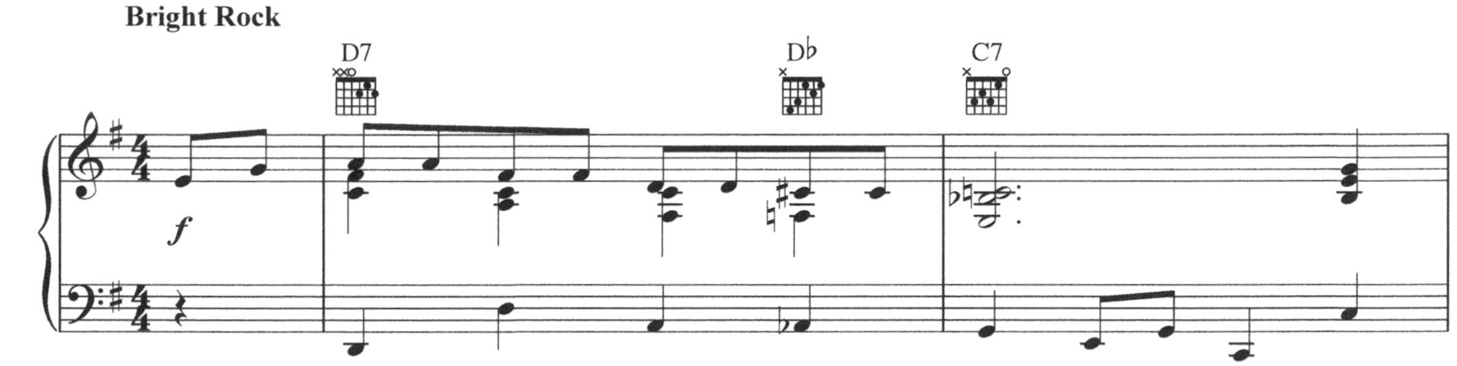

D7
Db7
4fr
C7
Just a big - a big - a big - a hunk o' love will
G
G
N.C.
do.
Don't be a stin - gy lit - tle ma - ma;
nat - 'ral born bee - hive,
G
N.C.
you 'bout to starve me half to death.
filled with hon - ey to the top.
Now
But
G
N.C.
C7
you could spare a kiss or two and still have plen - ty left.
I ain't greed - y, ba - by, all I want is all you got.
Oh, no, no, ba - by,

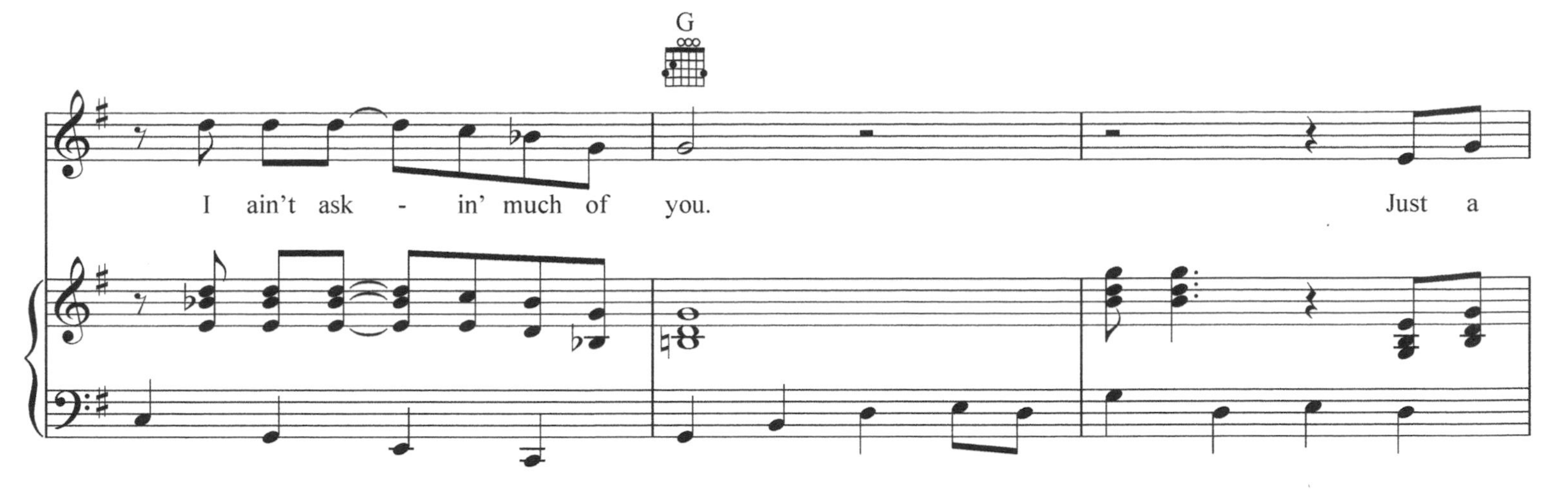
G
I ain't ask - in' much of you. Just a

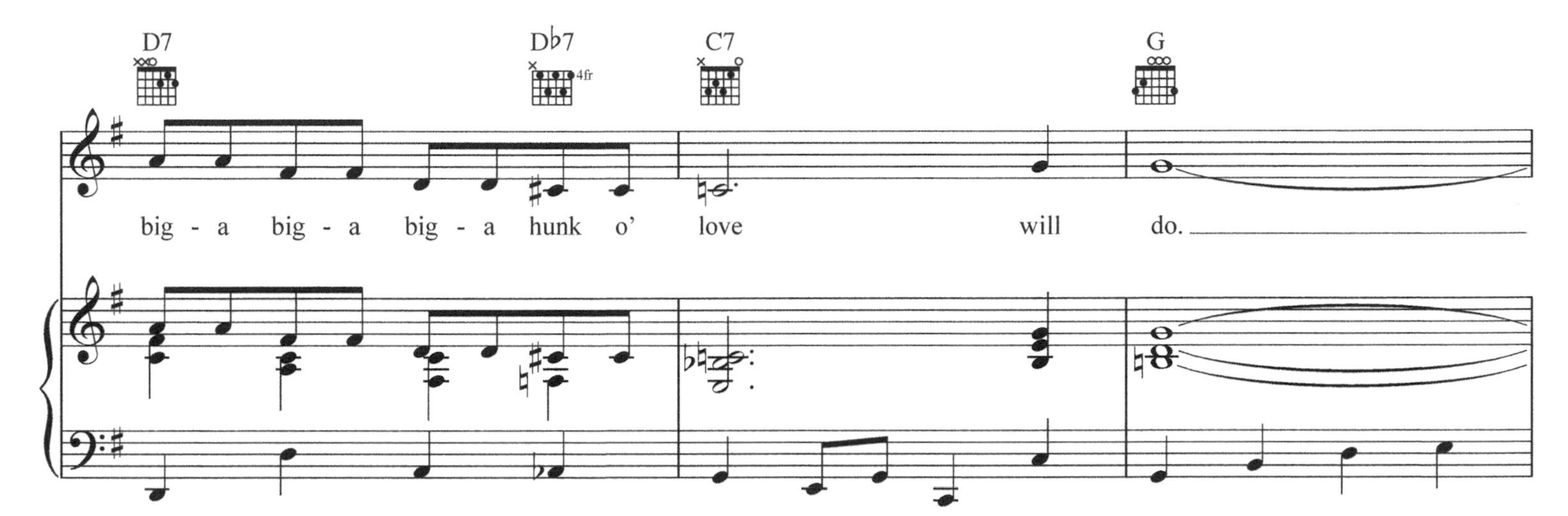
D7
D♭7
4fr
C7
G
big - a big - a big - a hunk o' love will do.

1
2
G
N.C.
You're just a
I got a wish - bone in my

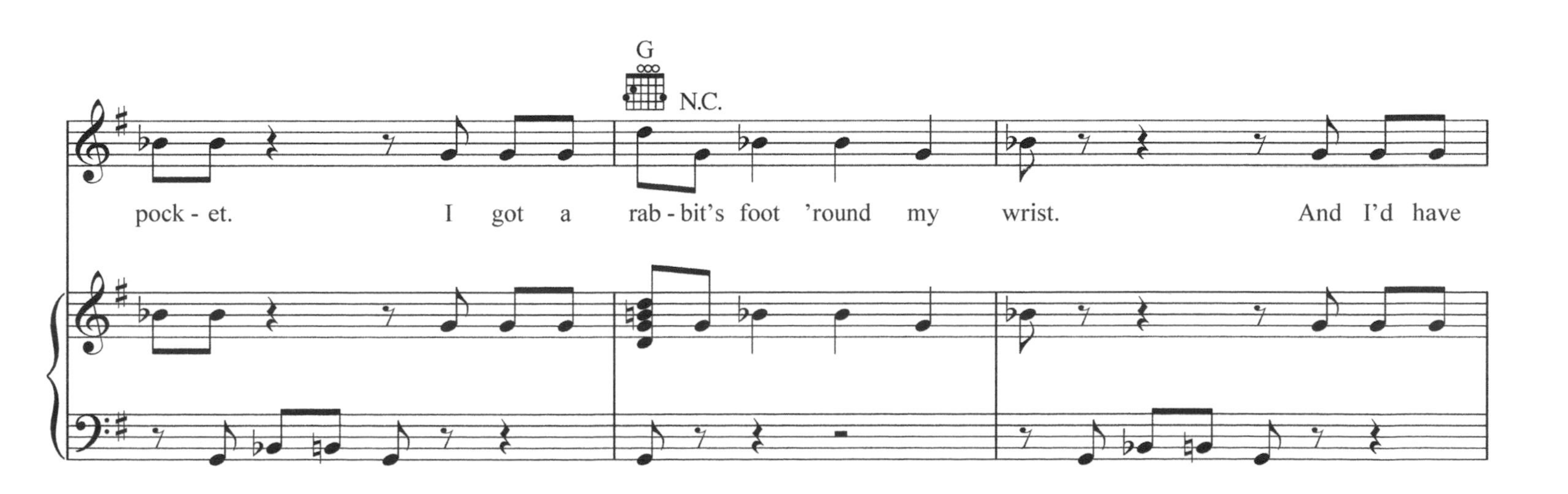
G
N.C.
pock - et. I got a rab - bit's foot 'round my wrist. And I'd have

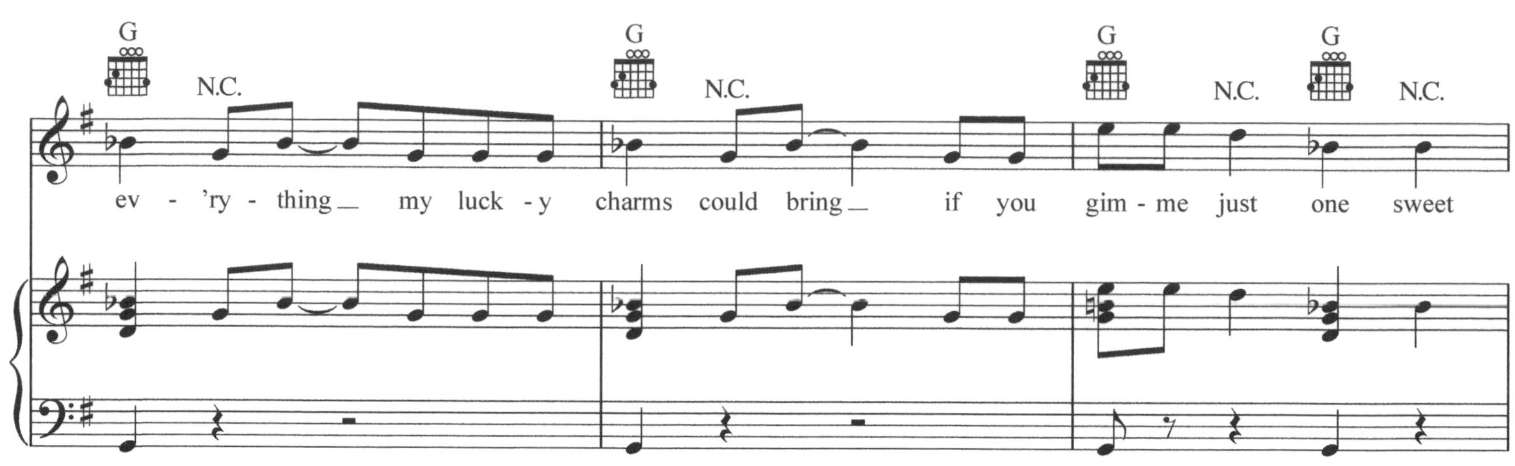
G
N.C.
G
N.C.
G
N.C.
G
N.C.
ev - 'ry - thing my luck - y charms could bring if you gim - me just one sweet

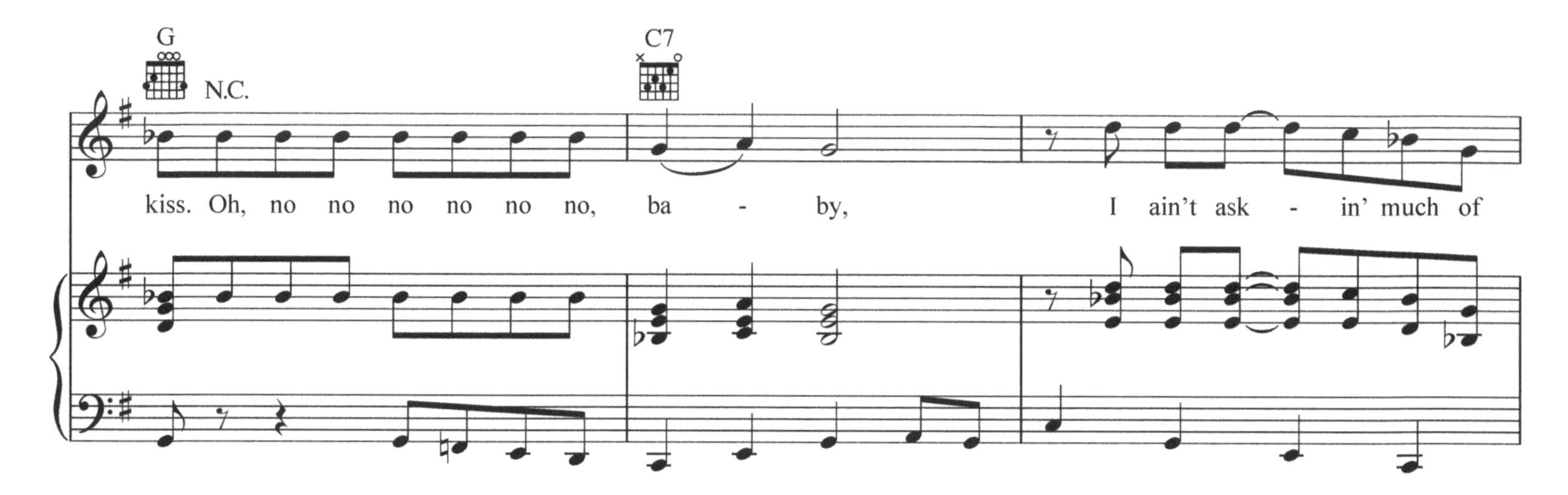
G
N.C.
C7
kiss. Oh, no no no no no no, ba - by, I ain't ask - in' much of

G
D7
D♭7
4fr
you. Just a big - a big - a big - a hunk o'

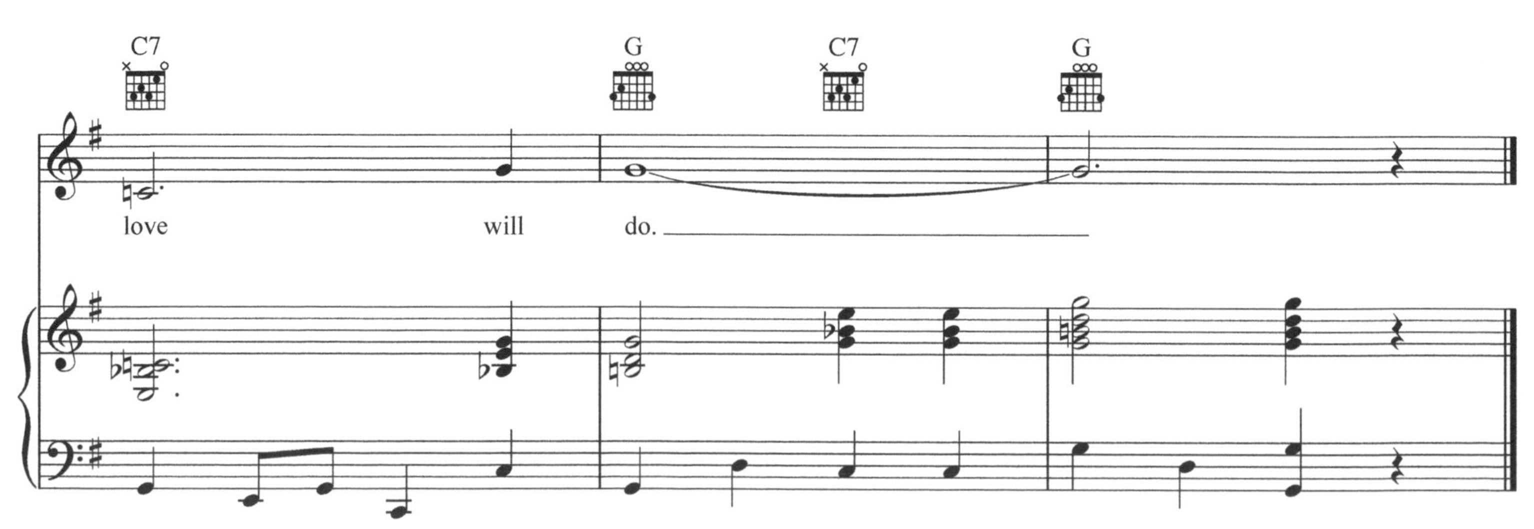
C7
G
C7
G
love will do.

CAN'T HELP FALLING IN LOVE

from the Paramount Picture BLUE HAWAII

Words and Music by GEORGE DAVID WEISS,
HUGO PERETTI and LUIGI CREATORE

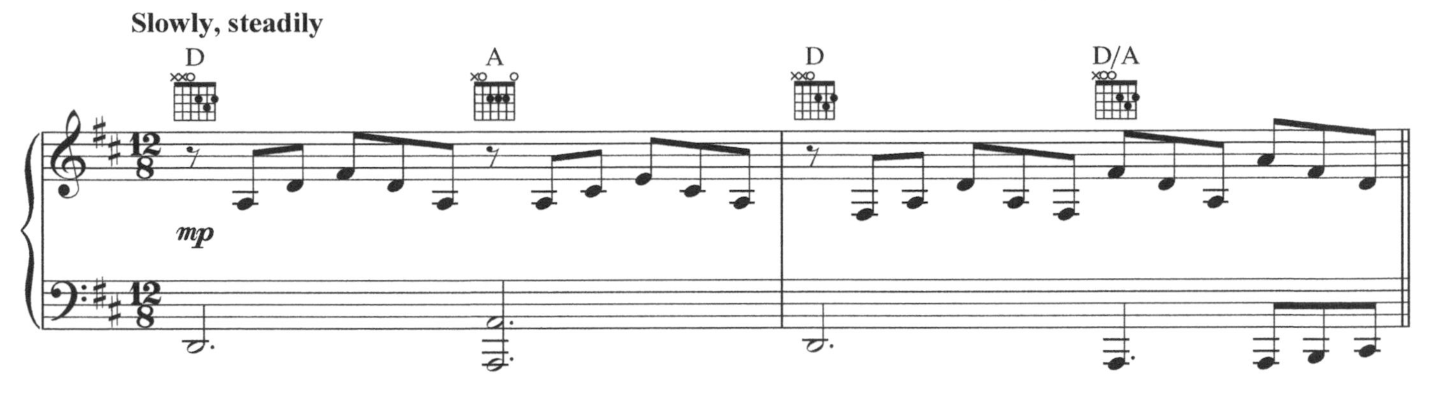

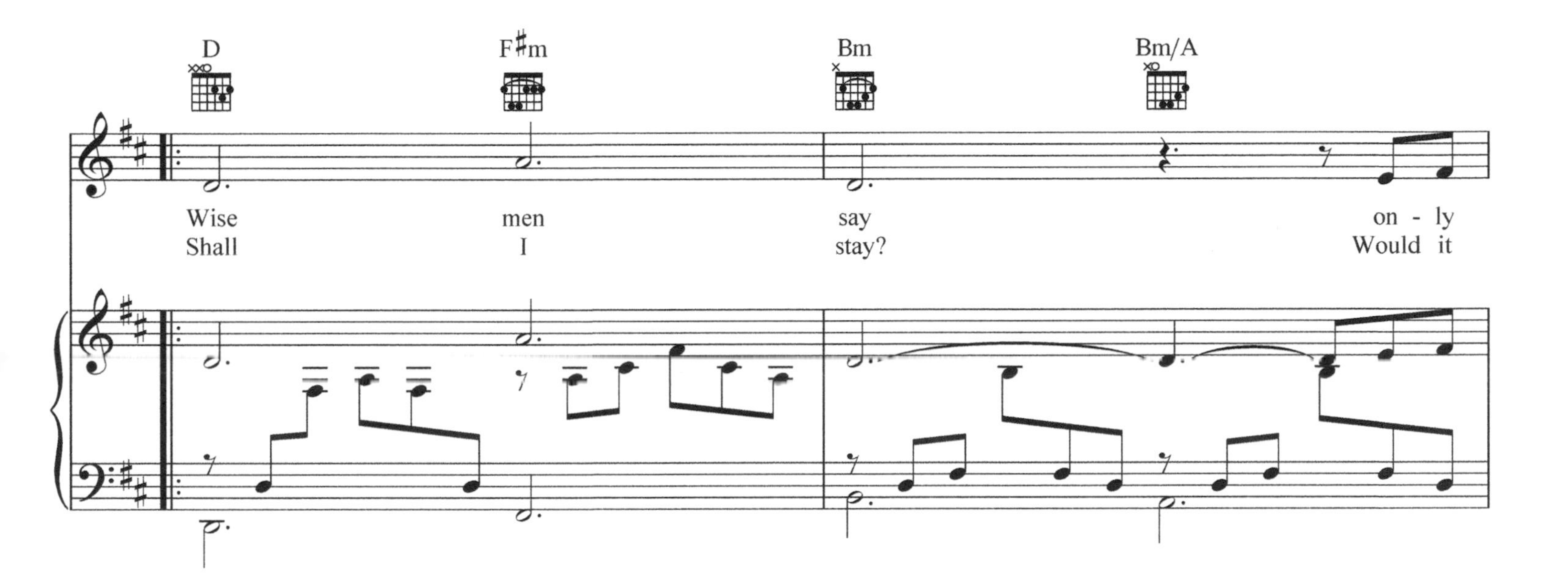

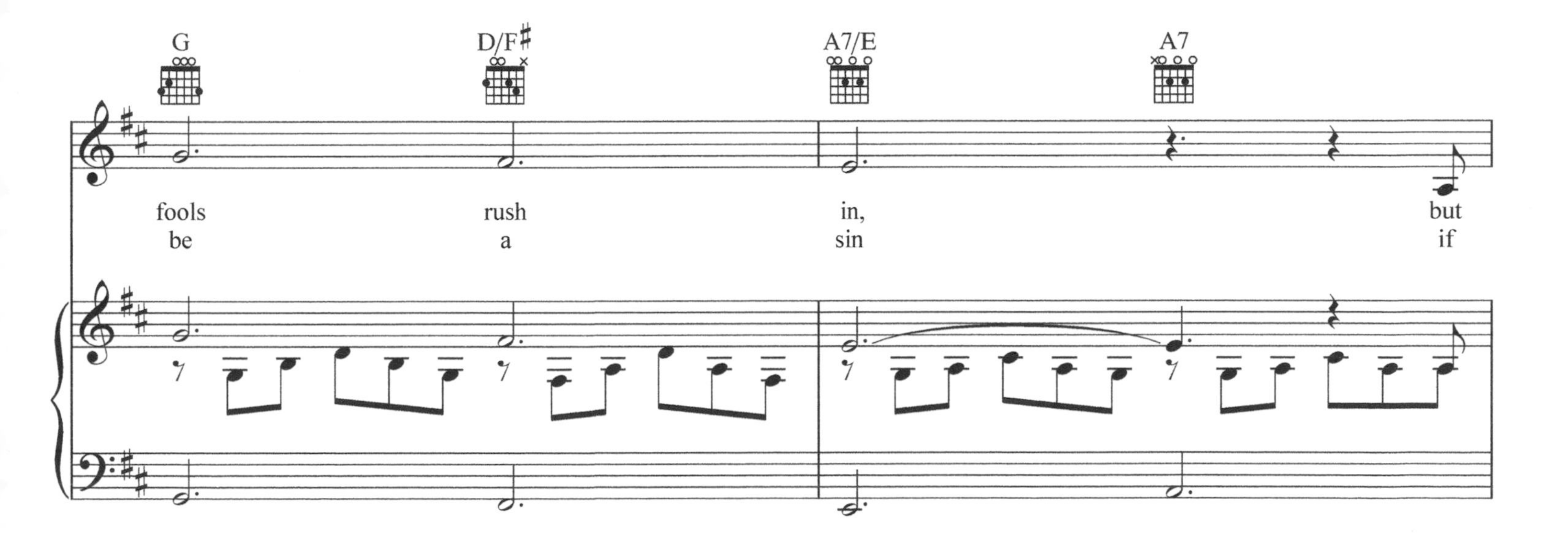

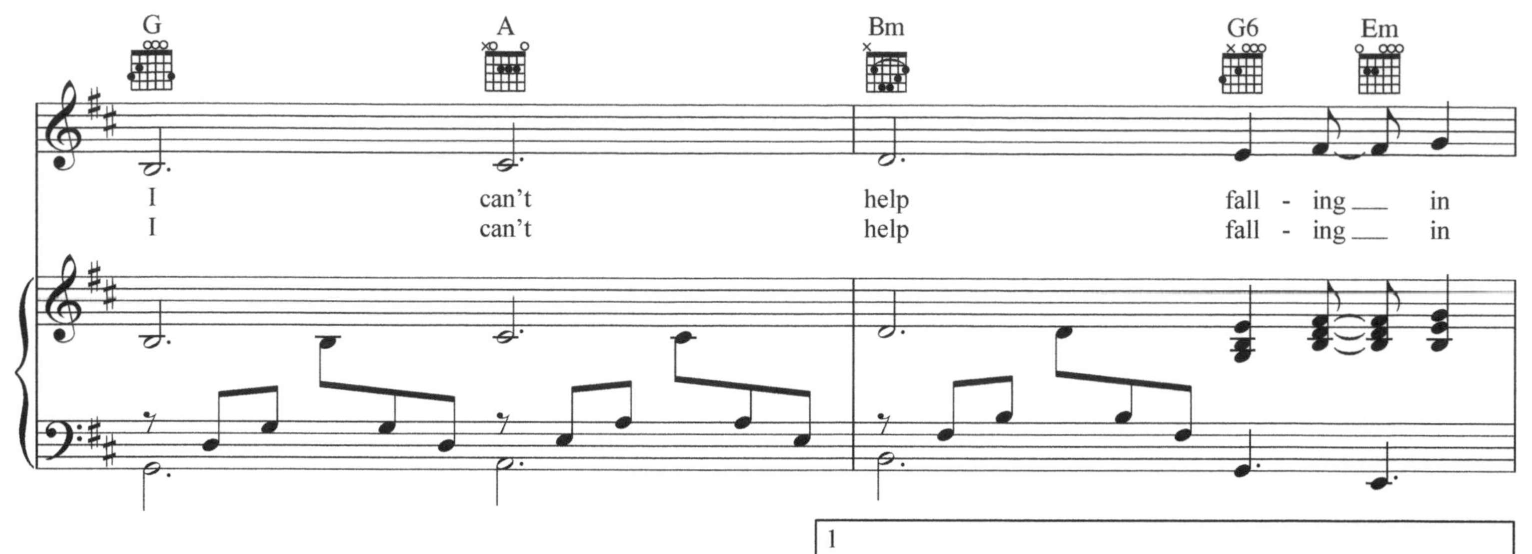
G
A
Bm
G6
Em
I can't help fall - ing in
I can't help fall - ing in

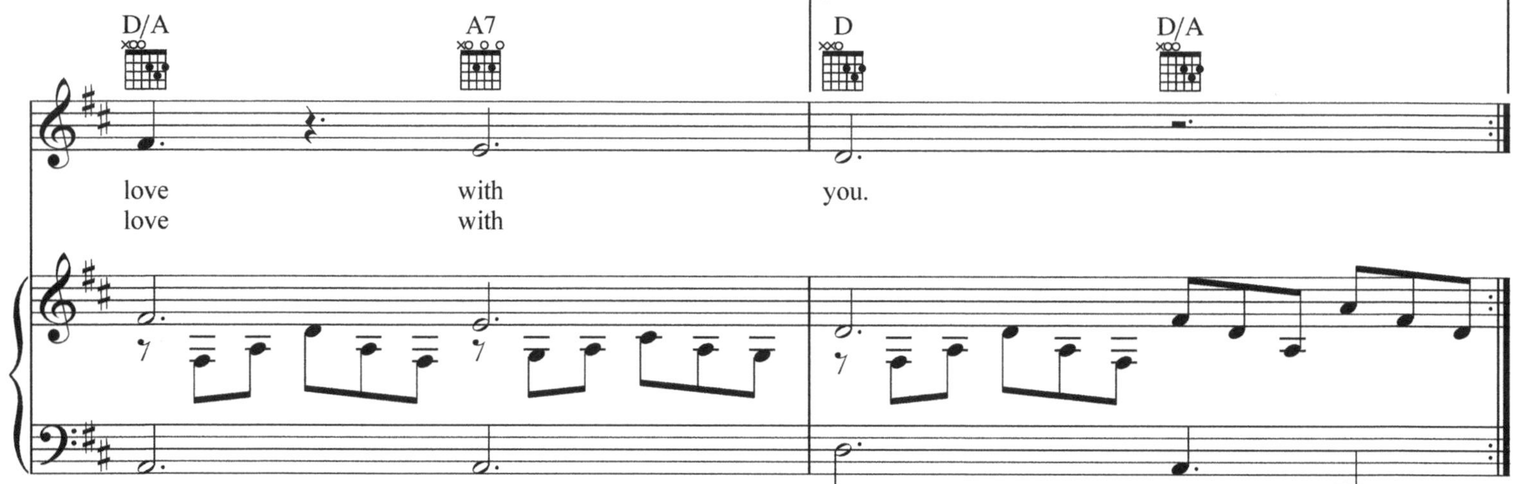
1
D/A
A7
D
D/A
love with you.
love with

2
D
F♯m
C♯
you?
Like a riv - er flows

F♯m
C♯
F♯m
C♯
sure - ly to the sea,
dar - ling, so it goes;

F♯m
B7
Em
A7
some things are meant to be.

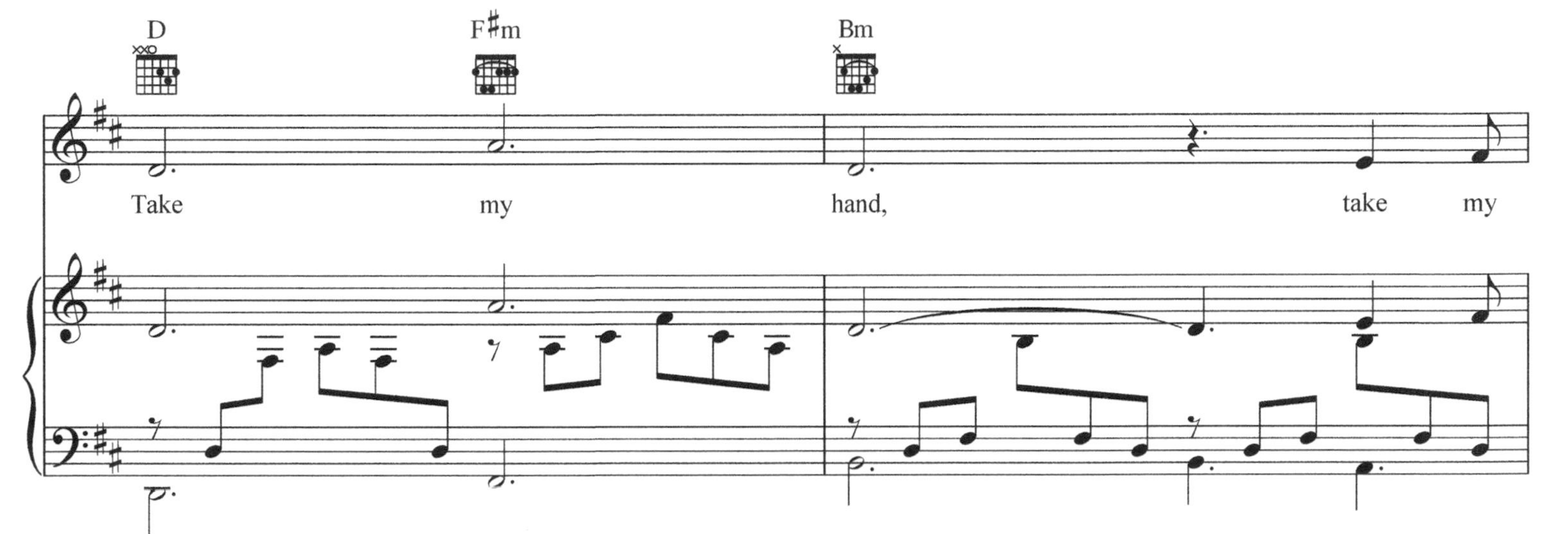
D
F♯m
Bm
Take my hand, take my

G
D/F♯
A7/E
A7
whole life, too, for

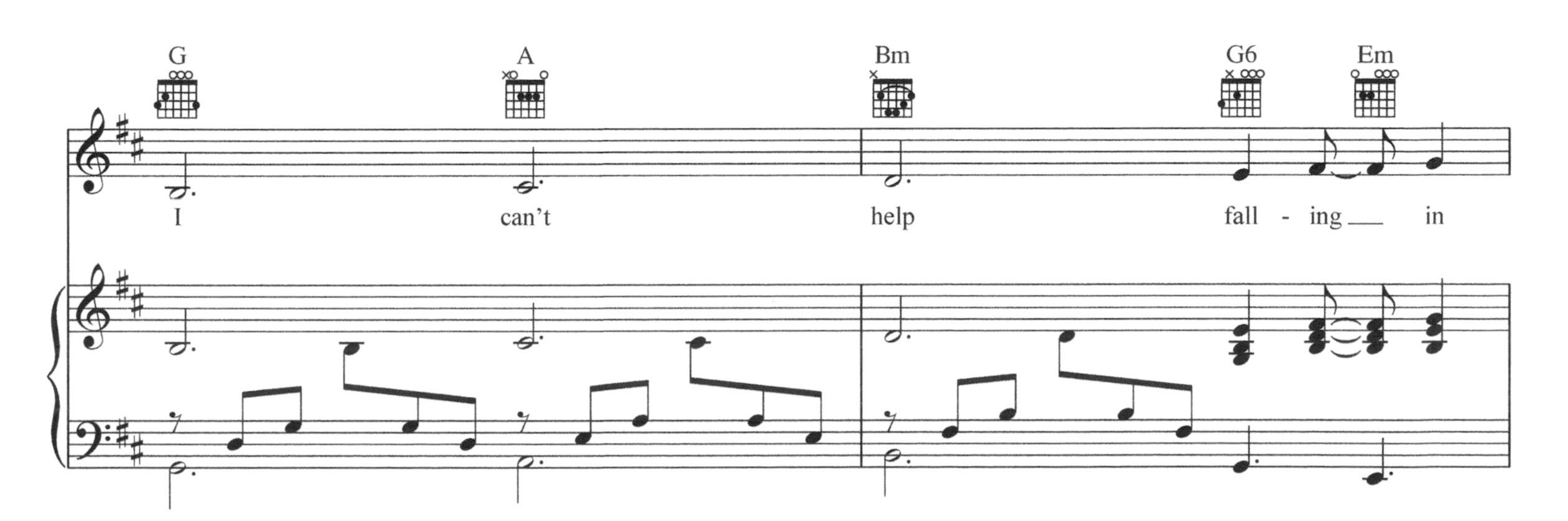
G
A
Bm
G6
Em
I can't help fall - ing in

1
2
D/A
A7
D
D/A
love
with
you.
D
G
A
you.
For
I
can't
Bm
G6
Em
D/A
A7
help
fall - ing in
love
with
rit.
D
you.

BLUE HAWAII

from the Paramount Picture WAIKIKI WEDDING

Words and Music by LEO ROBIN
and RALPH RAINGER

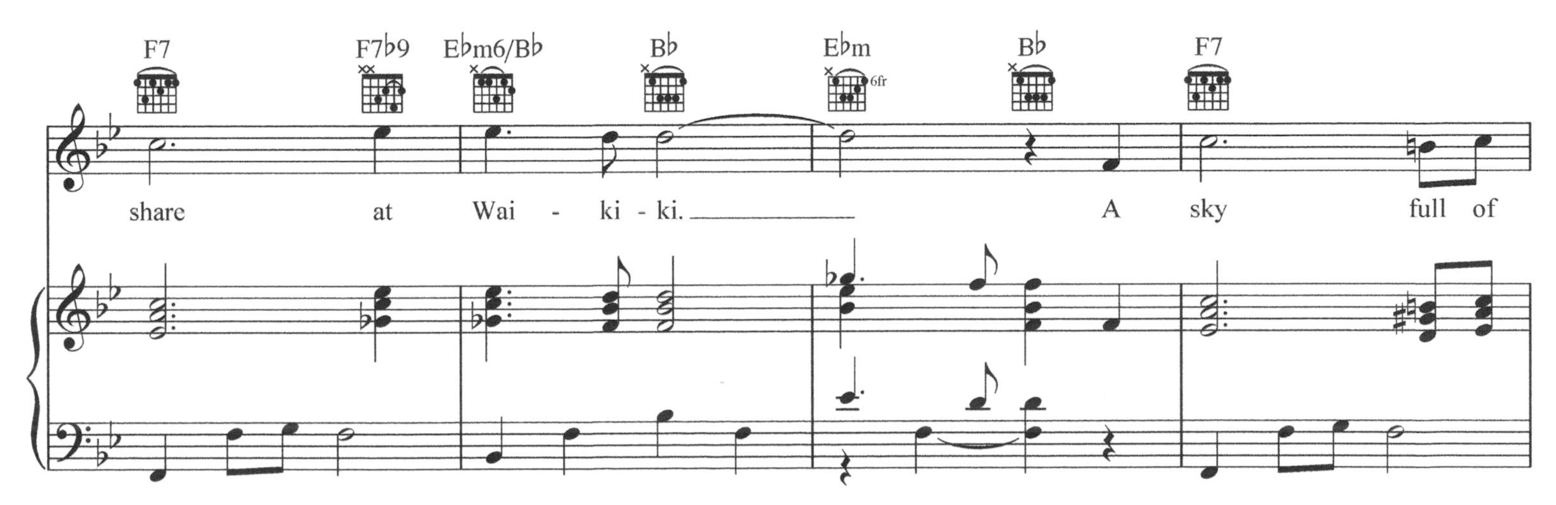

D7
Gm
3fr
Gm7
stars and soft far - a - way gui - tars, it

C9
F7
3
seems to be ___ on - ly a rev - er - ie. ___

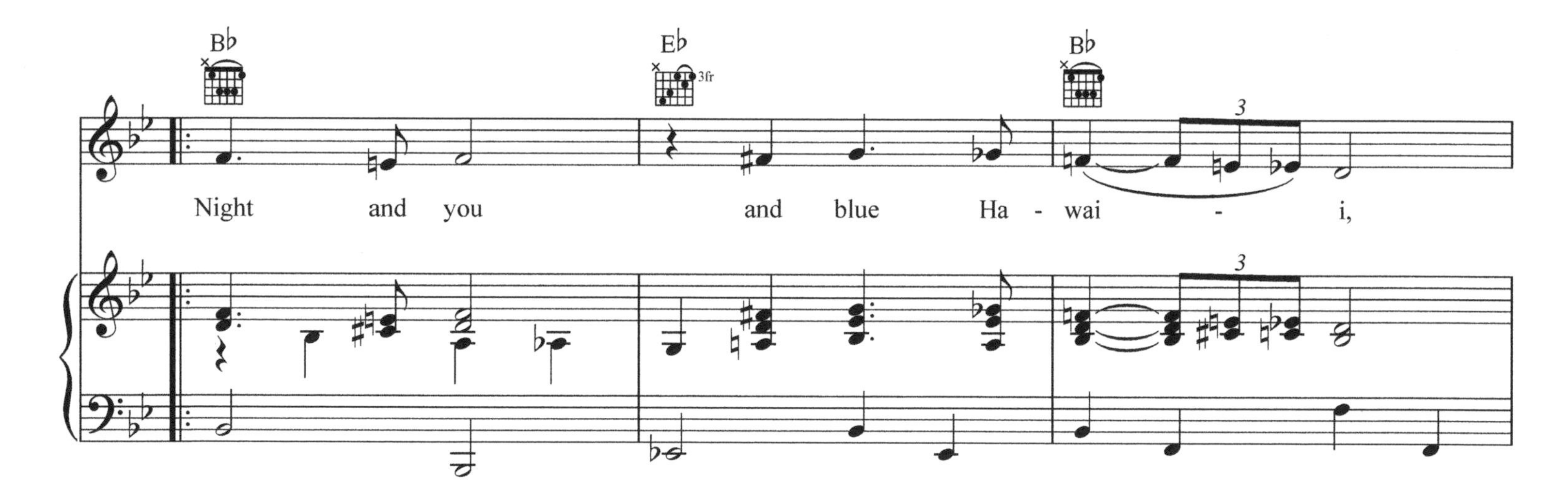
B♭
E♭
3fr
B♭
3
Night and you and blue Ha - wai - i,

G7♯5
C7
F7
B♭
3
the night is heav - en - ly and ___ you are heav - en to me. ___

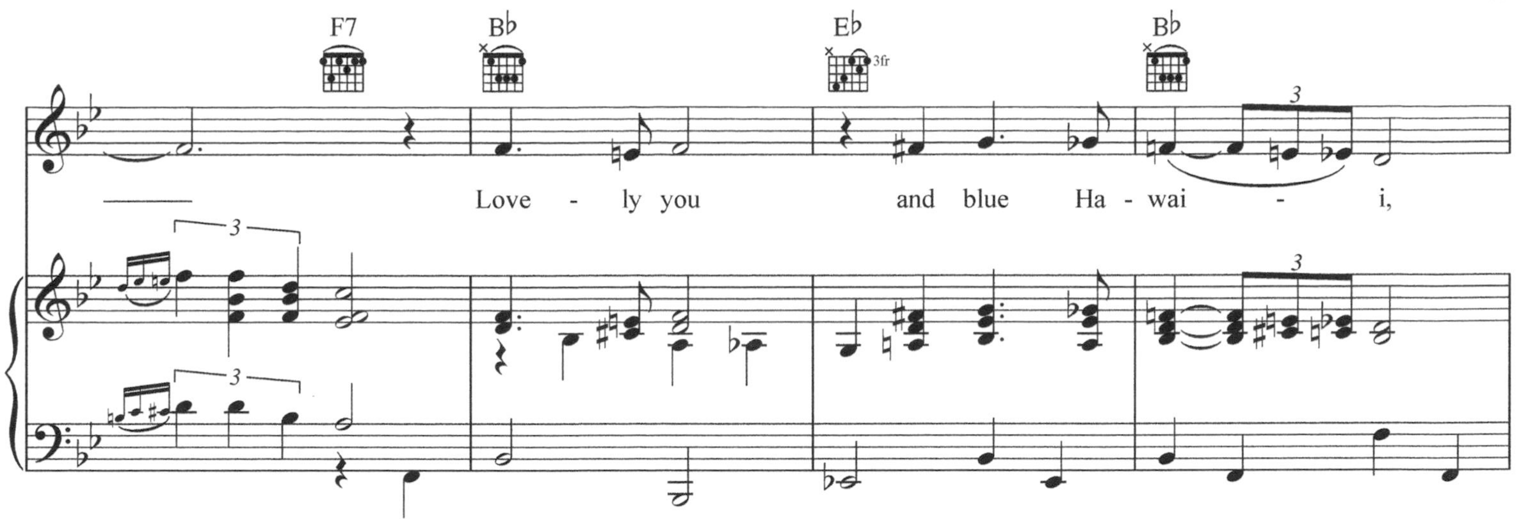
F7
B♭
E♭
3fr
B♭
3
Love - ly you and blue Ha - wai - i,
3
3
3

G7♯5
C7
F7
B♭
E♭6/B♭
with all this love - li - ness there should be love.

B♭
B♭7♯5
6fr
E♭
3fr
Come with me while the
3
3

B♭
C7
moon is on the sea. The night is young
3
3

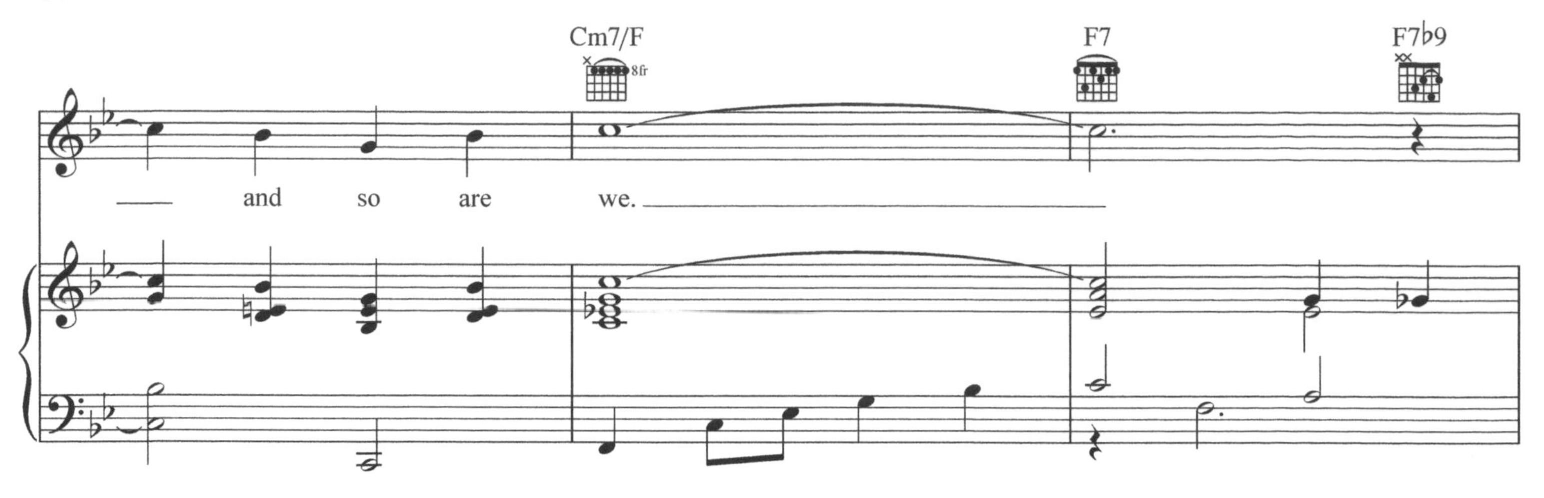
Cm7/F
8fr
F7
F7♭9
and so are we.

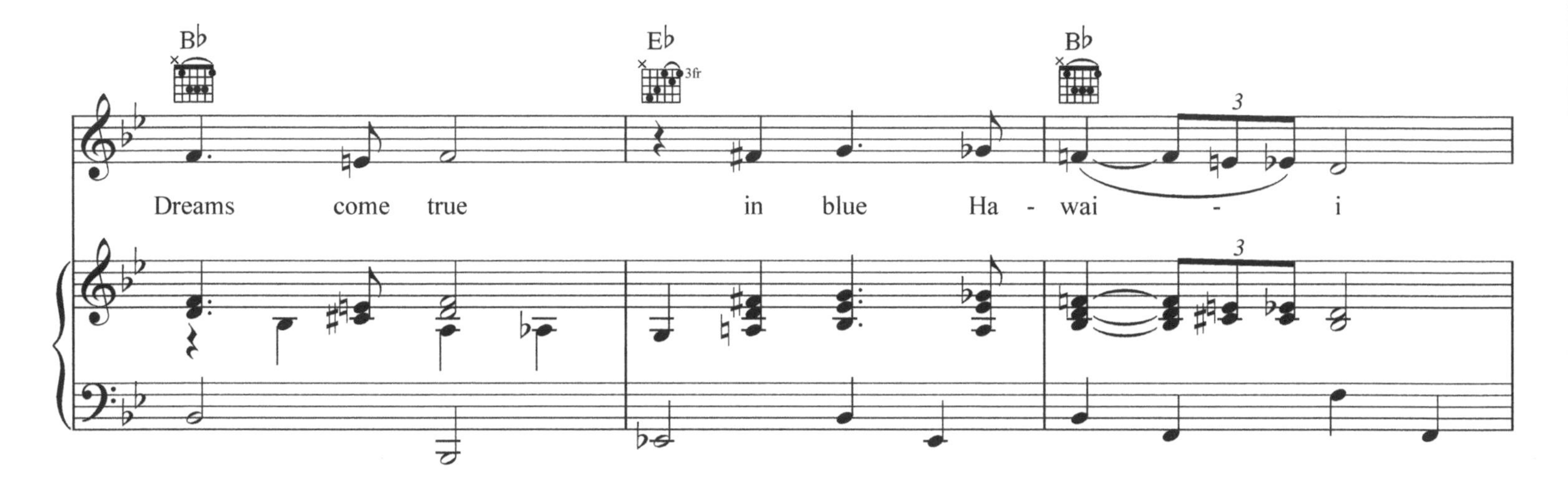
B♭
E♭
3fr
B♭
Dreams come true in blue Ha - wai - i

G7♯5
C7
F7
and mine could all come true this mag - ic

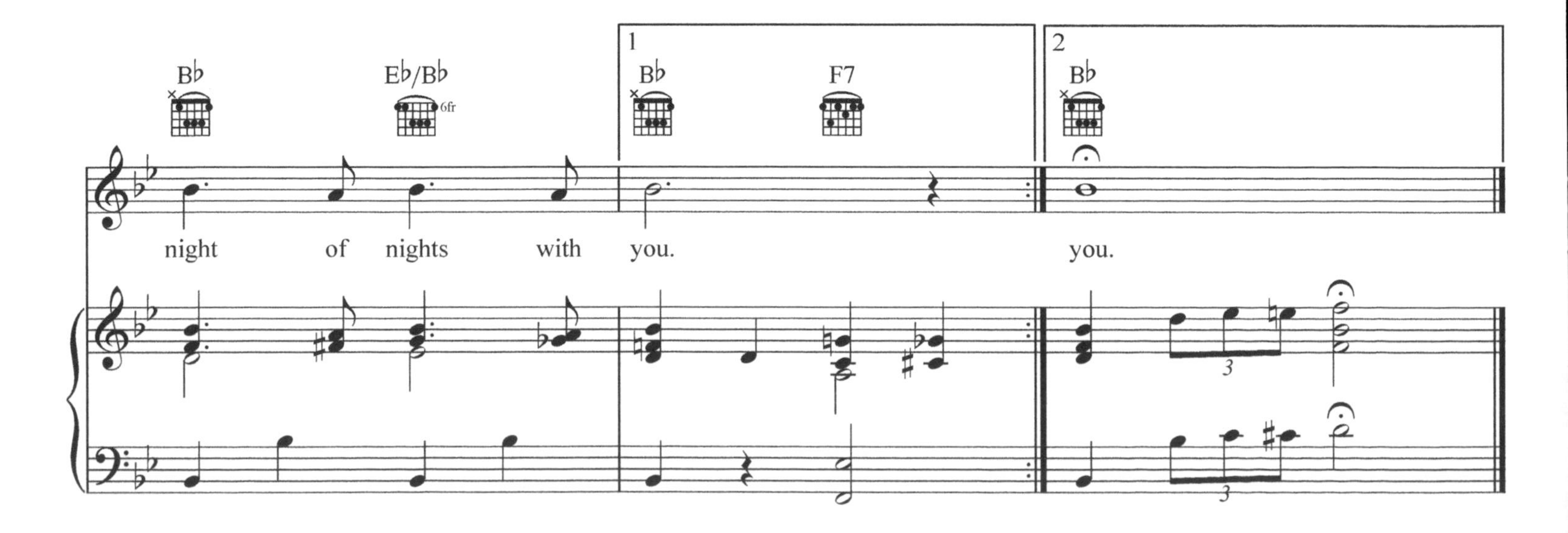
B♭
E♭/B♭
6fr
1
B♭
F7
2
B♭
night of nights with you. you.

NO MORE

Words and Music by DON ROBERSTON
and HAL BLAIR

B♭
C♯dim7
F7
I close my eyes and clear - ly my heart re - mem - bers.
Oh, how I wish I nev - er had caused you sor - row.

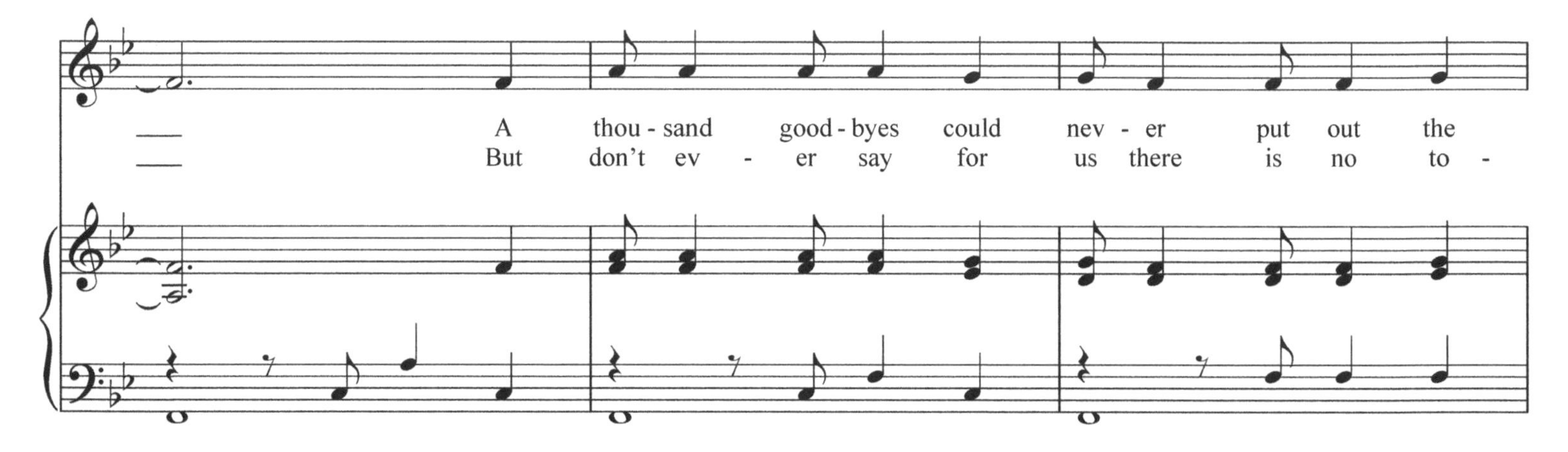
A thou - sand good - byes could nev - er put out the
But don't ev - er say for us there is no to -

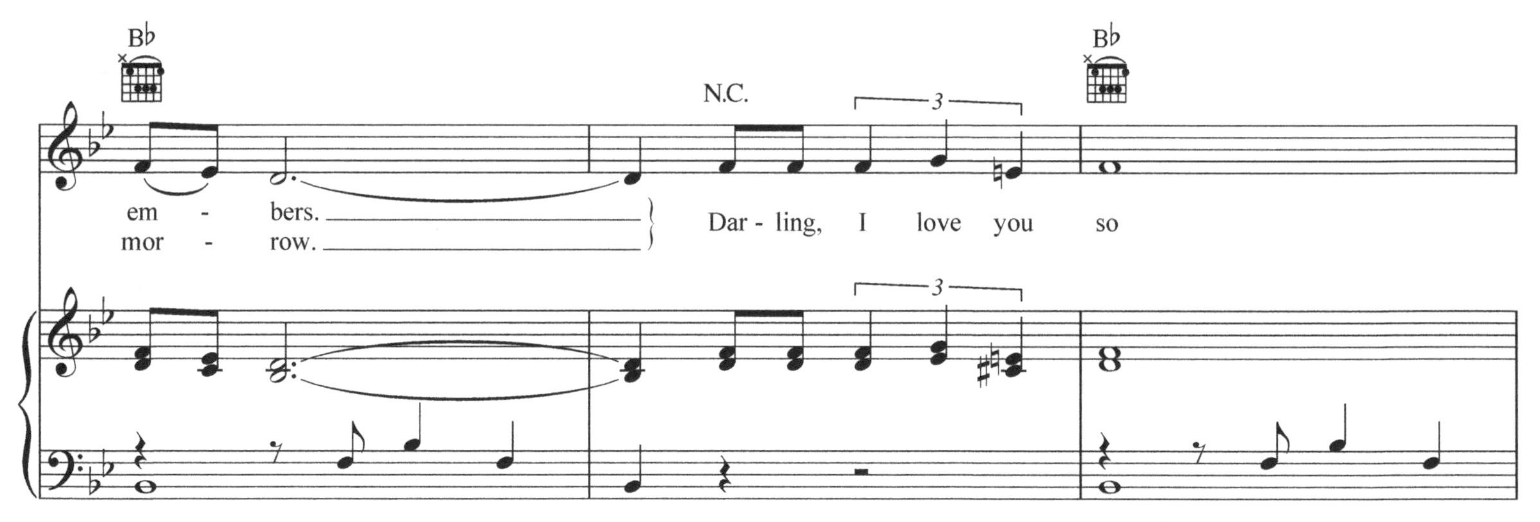
B♭
N.C.
3
B♭
em - bers.
mor - row.
Dar - ling, I love you so

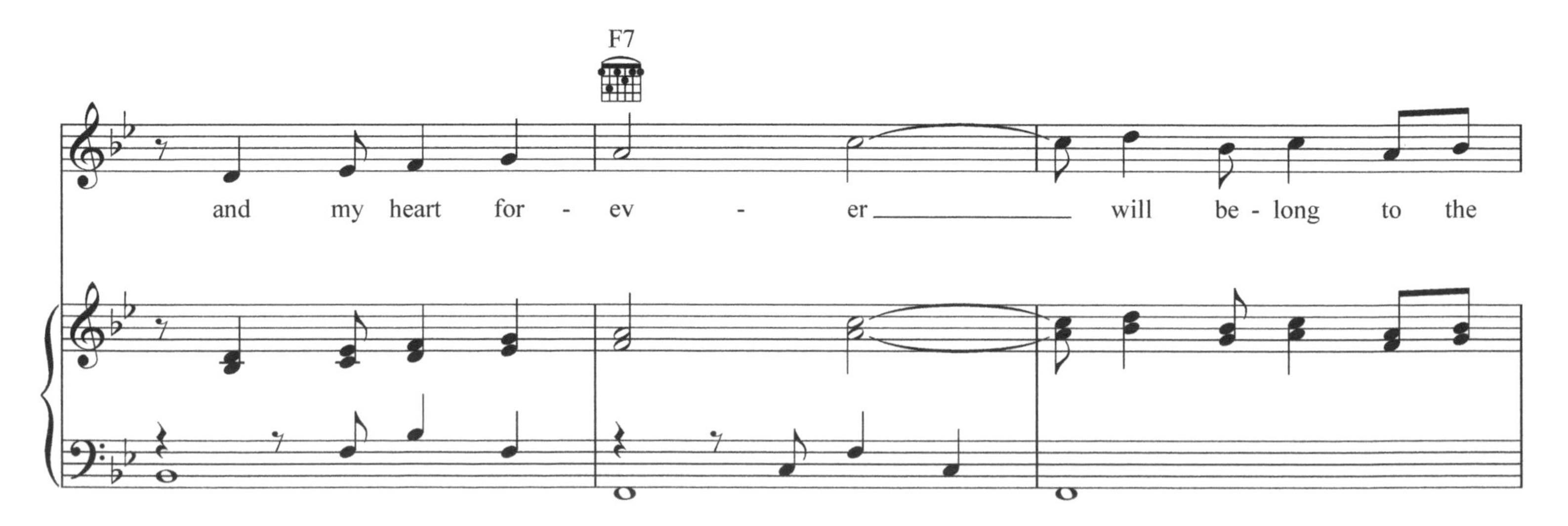
F7
and my heart for - ev - er will be - long to the

Cm7 F7 B♭ N.C.
mem - o - ry of the love that we knew be - fore. Please come back to my
B♭ F7
arms. We be - long to - geth - er. Come to me. Let's be
Cm7 F7 B♭
sweet - hearts a - gain and then let us part no more. No
F7sus F7 B♭ E♭m B♭
then let us part no more.
rall.

KU-U-I-PO
(Hawaiian Sweetheart)

Words and Music by LUIGI CREATORE,
GEORGE WEISS and HUGO PERETTI

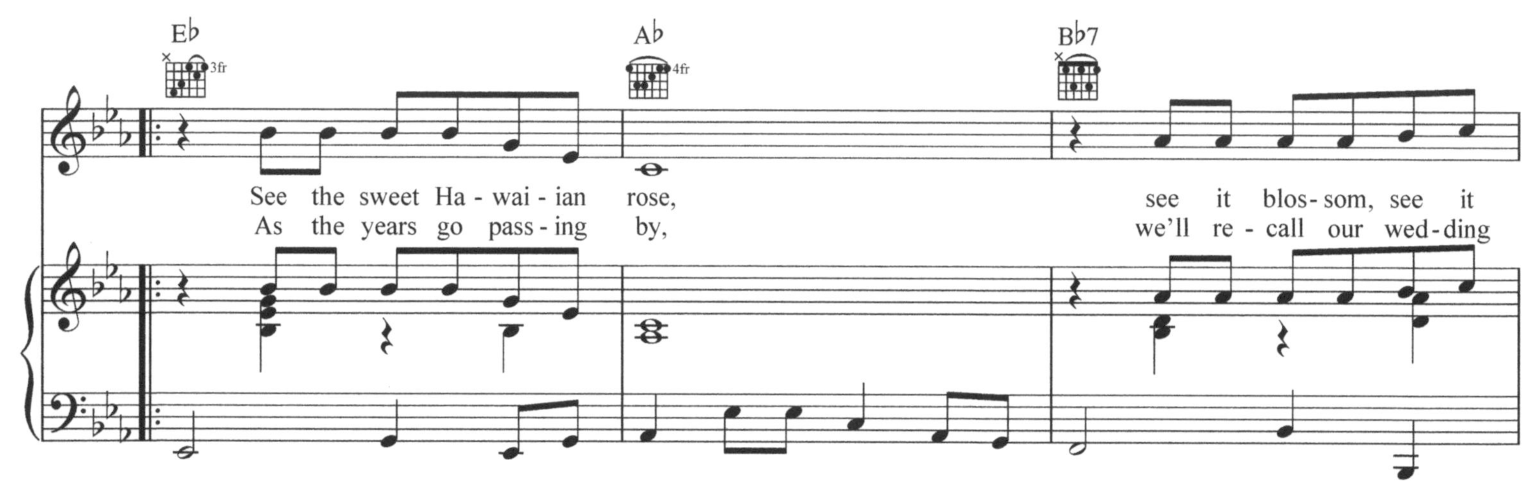

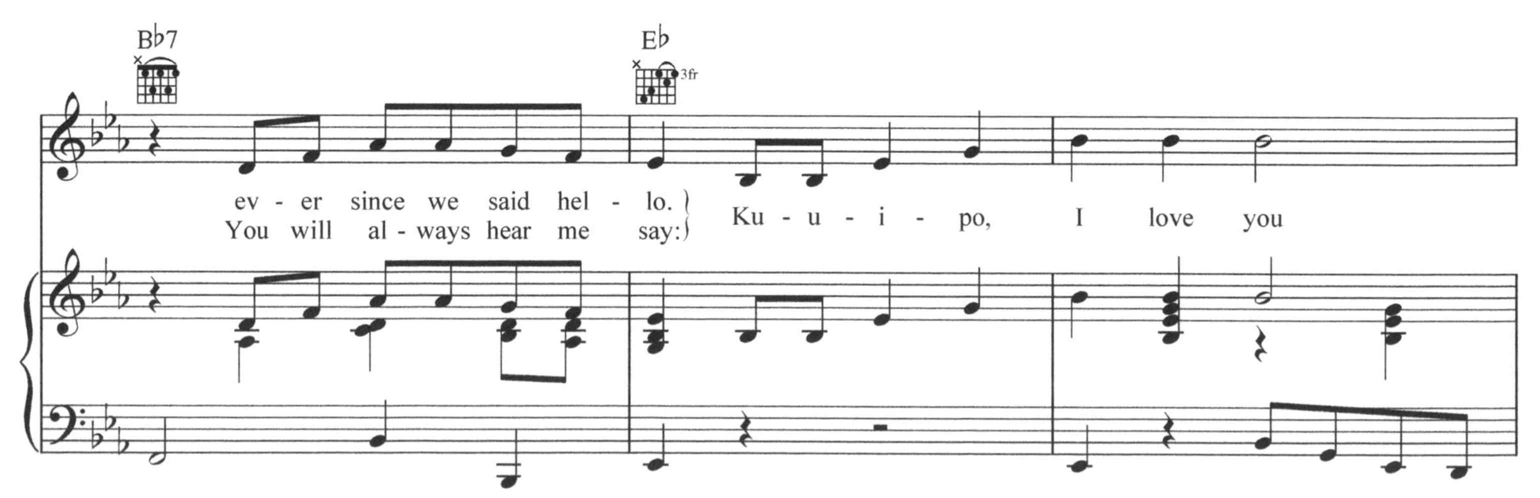

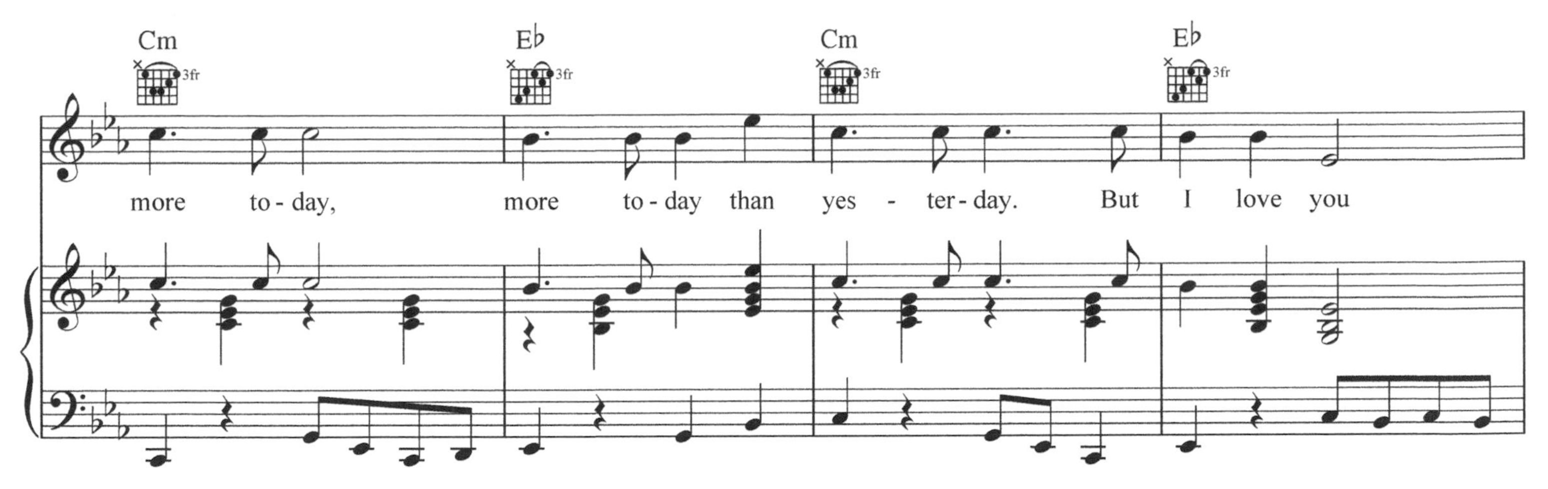
Cm
Eb
Cm
Eb
3fr
more to-day, more to-day than yes - ter-day. But I love you

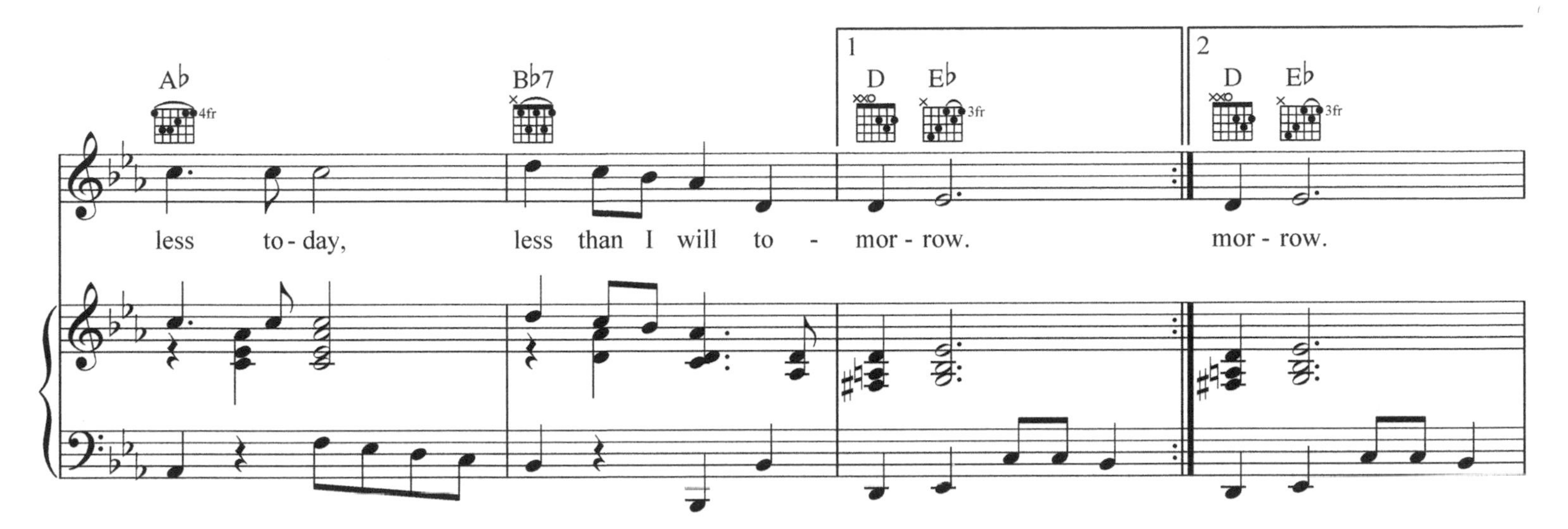
Ab
4fr
Bb7
1
2
D
Eb
less to-day, less than I will to - mor-row. mor-row.

Eb
Ab
Bb7
D
Eb
Ku-u-i - po, ku-u-i - po, you're my Ha-wai-ian sweet-heart.

Eb
Ab
Bb7
D
Eb
Ku-u-i - po, ku-u-i - po, you're my Ha-wai-ian sweet-heart.
rall.

THE HAWAIIAN WEDDING SONG
(Ke Kali Nei Au)

English Lyrics by AL HOFFMAN and DICK MANNING
Hawaiian Lyrics and Music by CHARLES E. KING

Slowly, with much warmth

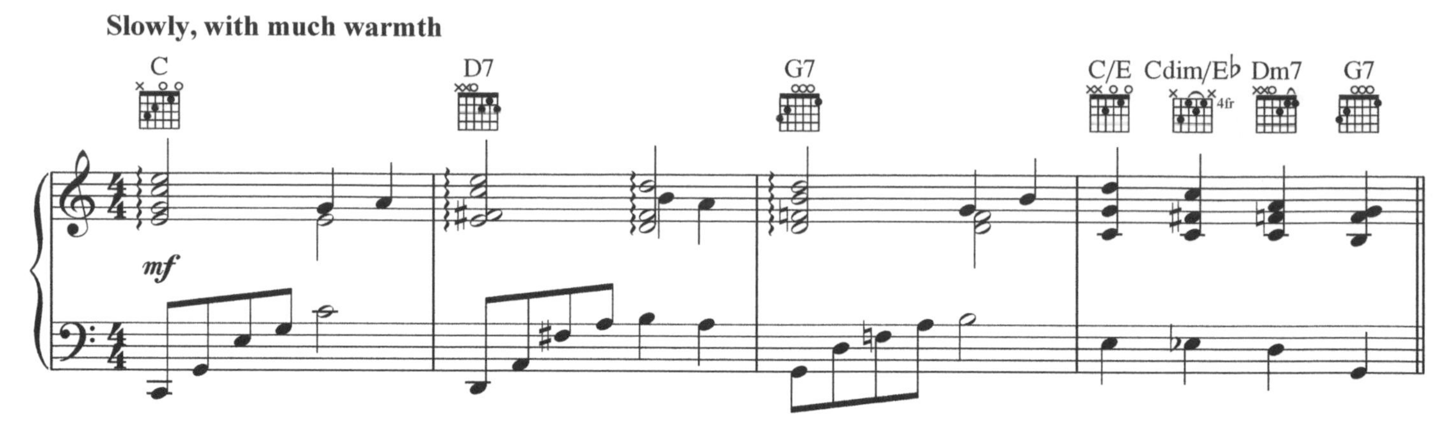

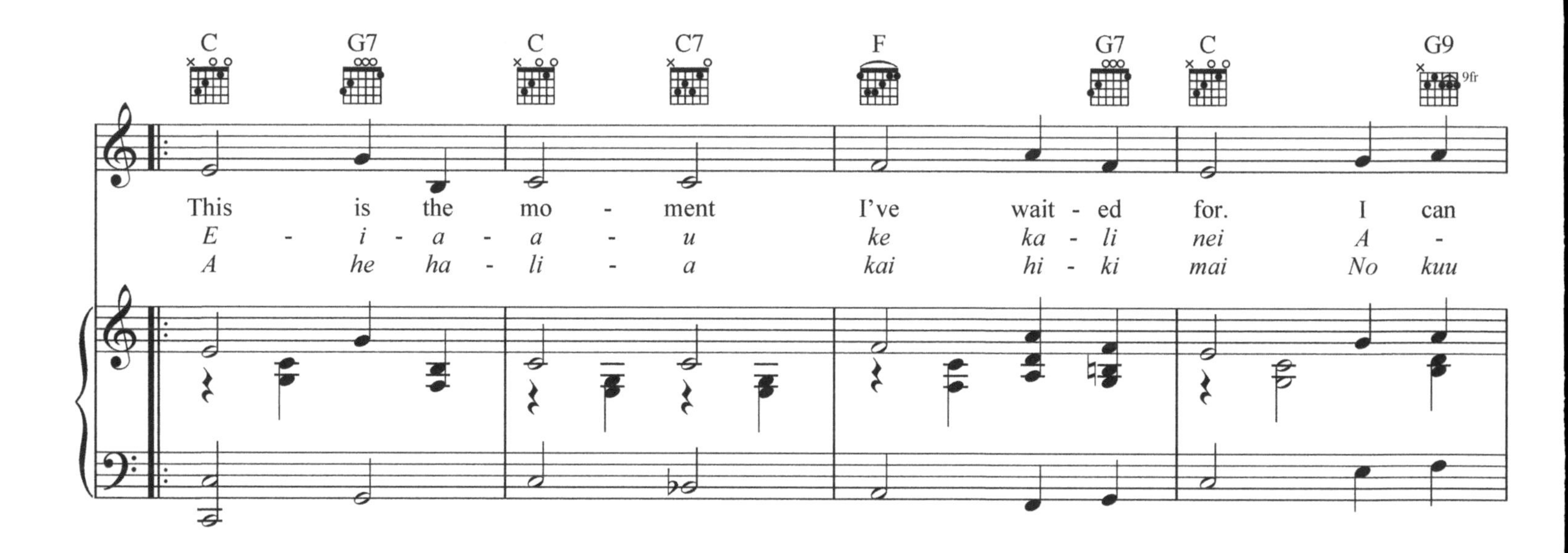

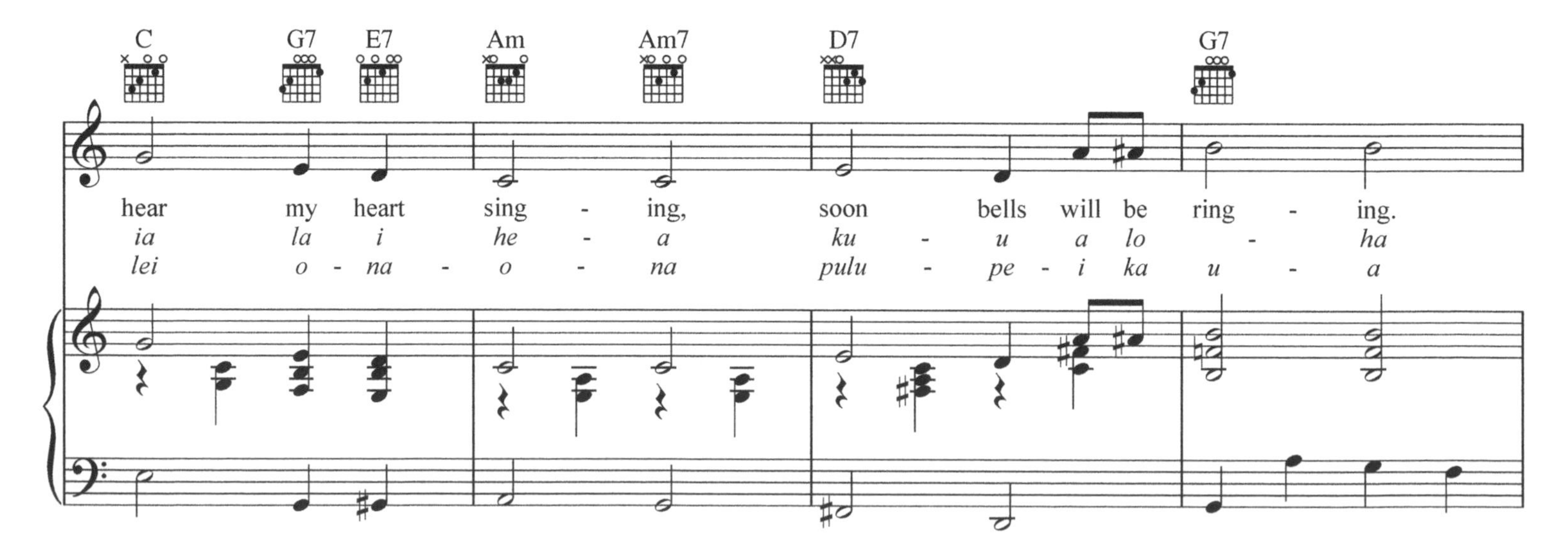

C Cdim D7 G7 C
3fr
This is the mo - ment of sweet "A lo - ha,"
E - i - a a - u ke hu - li ne - i
Au - he - a o - e kai - ini a lo - ko
G9 G7
9fr
I will love you long - er than for - ev - er, prom - ise me that you will leave me
A lo - a - a o - e e ka i - po Ma - ha ka i - i - ni a ka
Na lo - ko a - e ka ma - na o Hu - 'e la - ni a - na i kuu
C G+ C A7 D7 G7
3fr
nev - er. Here and now, dear, all my love I
pu - u - wai. U - a si - la pa - a ia me
ki - no. Ku - u pu - a ku - u lei on a
C Cdim G9
3fr 9fr
vow, dear, prom - ise me that you will leave me nev - er,
o - e Ko a - lo - ha ma - ka - mae e i - po
o - na A'u i kui a la - wa i - a - ne - i

G7
C
I will love you long - er than for - ev - er.
Now that we are
Ka - 'u ia e le - i a - e ne - i la
Nou no ka i -
Me ke a - la pu - a pi - ka - ke
A o oe kuu
F
D7
G7
C
A7
one, clouds won't hide the sun.
Blue skies of Ha -
ini A nou wa - le no
A o ko a -
pua kuu pua lei le - hua
A'u e li - 'a

D7
G7
C
wai - i smile on this, our wed - ding day.
I do love
lo - ha ka'u e hi - i - po - i mau
Na'u oe e
ma - u nei hoo - paa ia iho kea - loha.
He lei oe

A7
D7
G7
1
C
G7
2
C
you with all my heart.
heart.
lei na'u oe e lei.
lei.
na'u he lei oe na'u.
na'u.

EARLY MORNIN' RAIN

Words and Music by
GORDON LIGHTFOOT

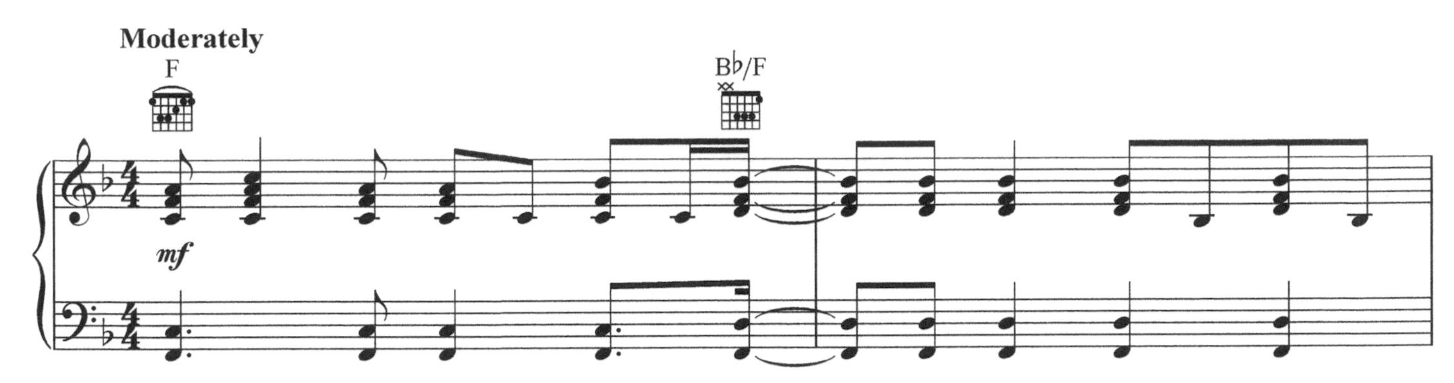

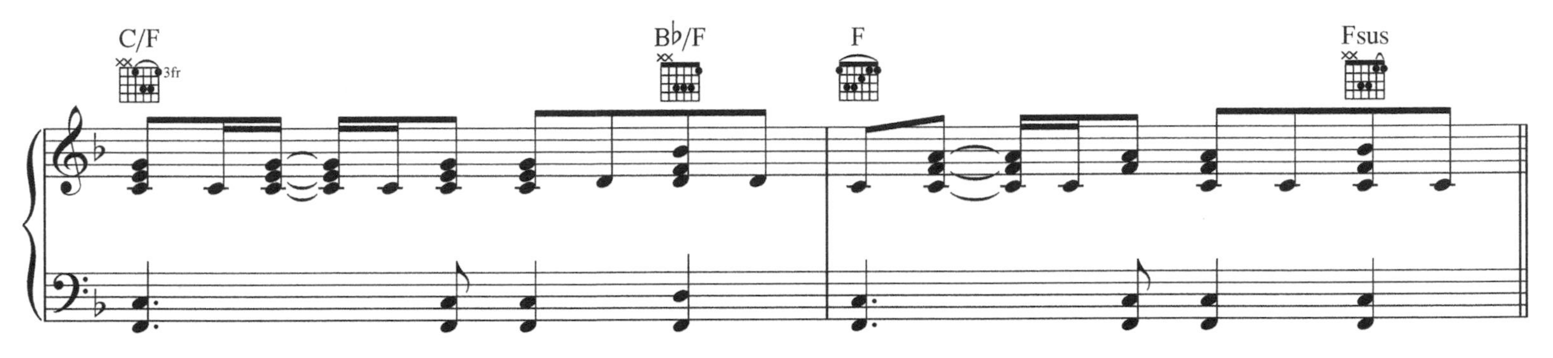

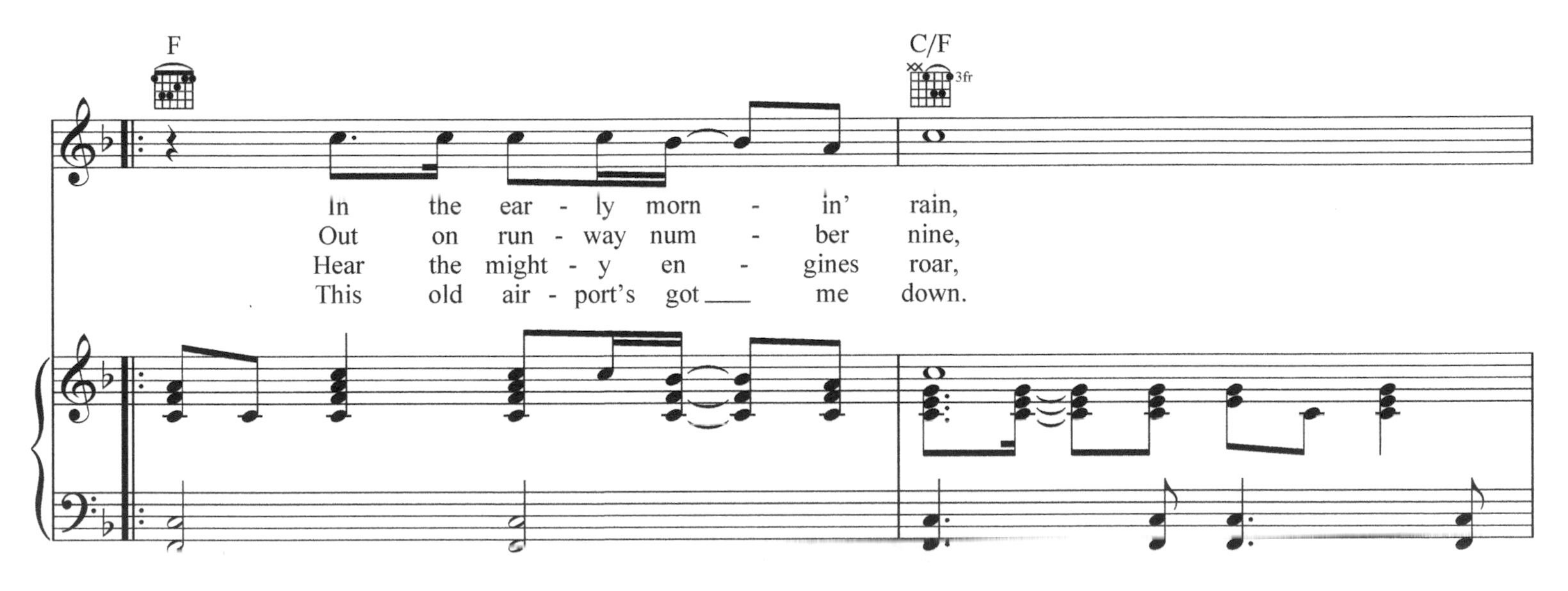

F
Bb/F
with an ach - in' in my heart,
And I'm stuck here in the grass,
She's a - way and west - ward bound.
'cause I'm stuck here on the ground,
F
Bb/F
and my pock - ets full of sand.
where the cold wind blows.
Far a - bove the clouds she'll fly,
as cold and drunk as I can be.
F
Bb/F
I'm a long way from home,
Now the liq - uor tast - ed good,
where the morn - in' rain don't fall,
You can't jump a jet plane
C/F
3fr
F
Bb/F
and I miss my loved ones so.
and the wom - en all were fast.
and the sun al - ways shines.
like you can a freight train,

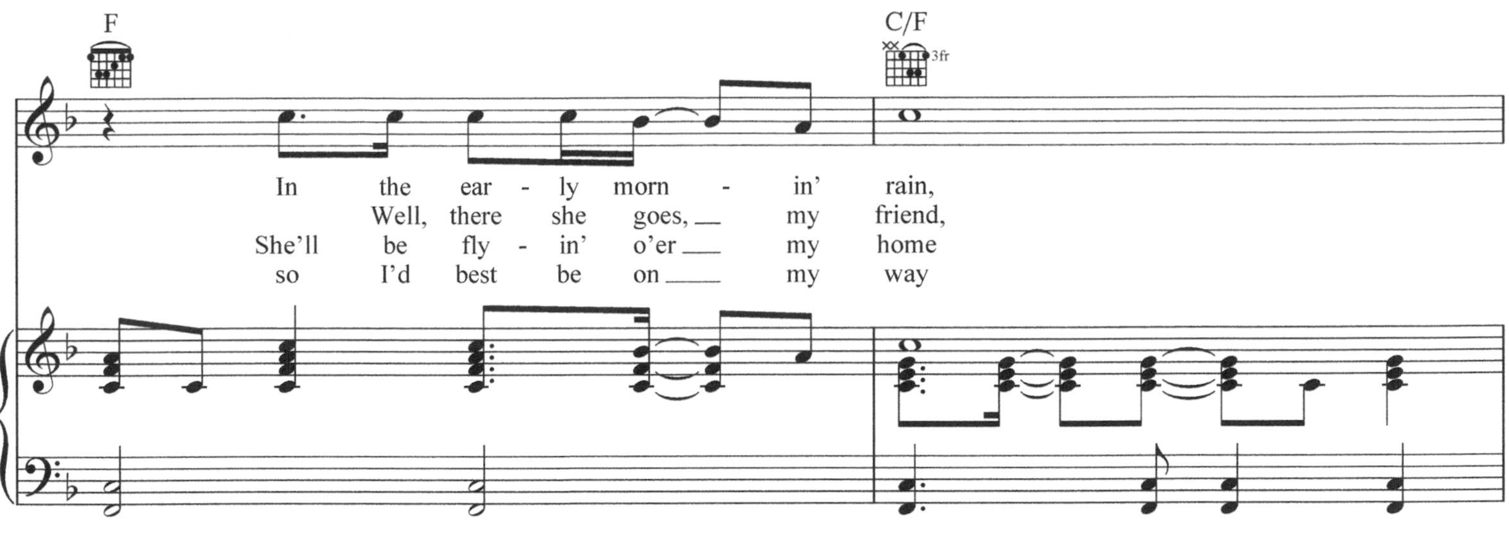
F
C/F
3fr
In the ear - ly morn - in' rain,
Well, there she goes, my friend,
She'll be fly - in' o'er my home
so I'd best be on my way

1
B♭/F
F
B♭/F
no place to go.

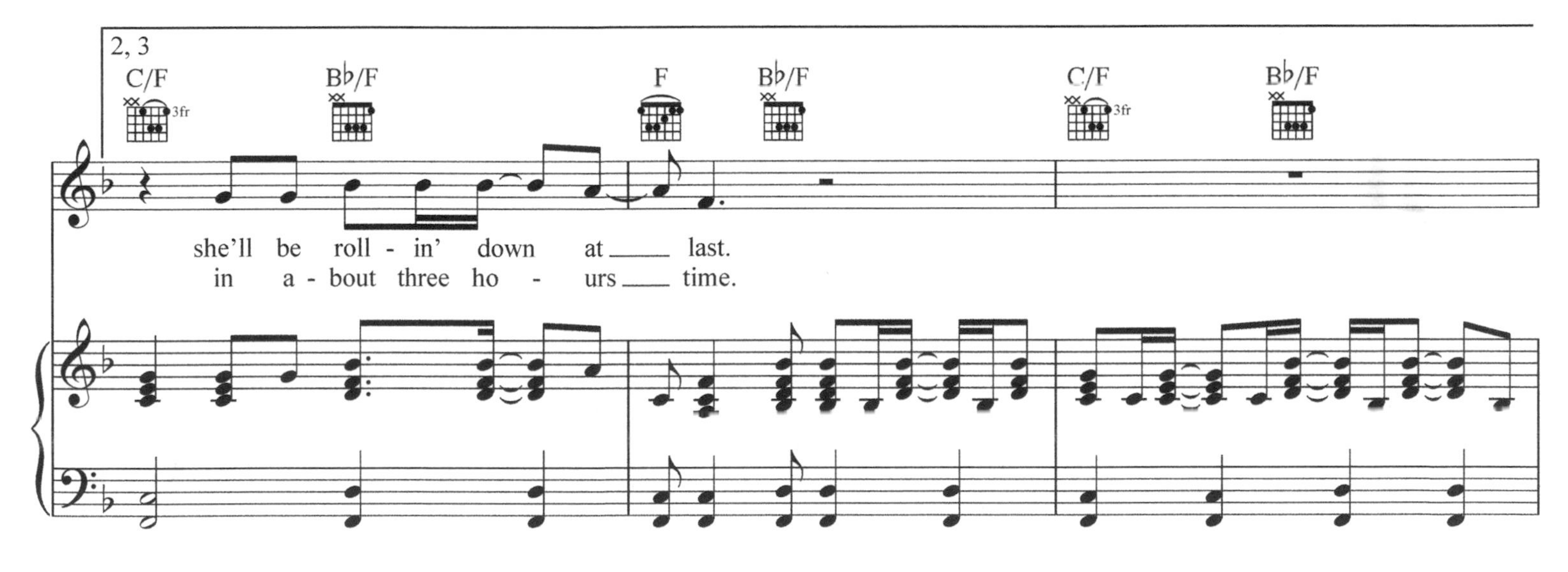
2, 3
C/F
3fr
B♭/F
F
B♭/F
C/F
3fr
B♭/F
she'll be roll - in' down at last.
in a - bout three ho - urs time.

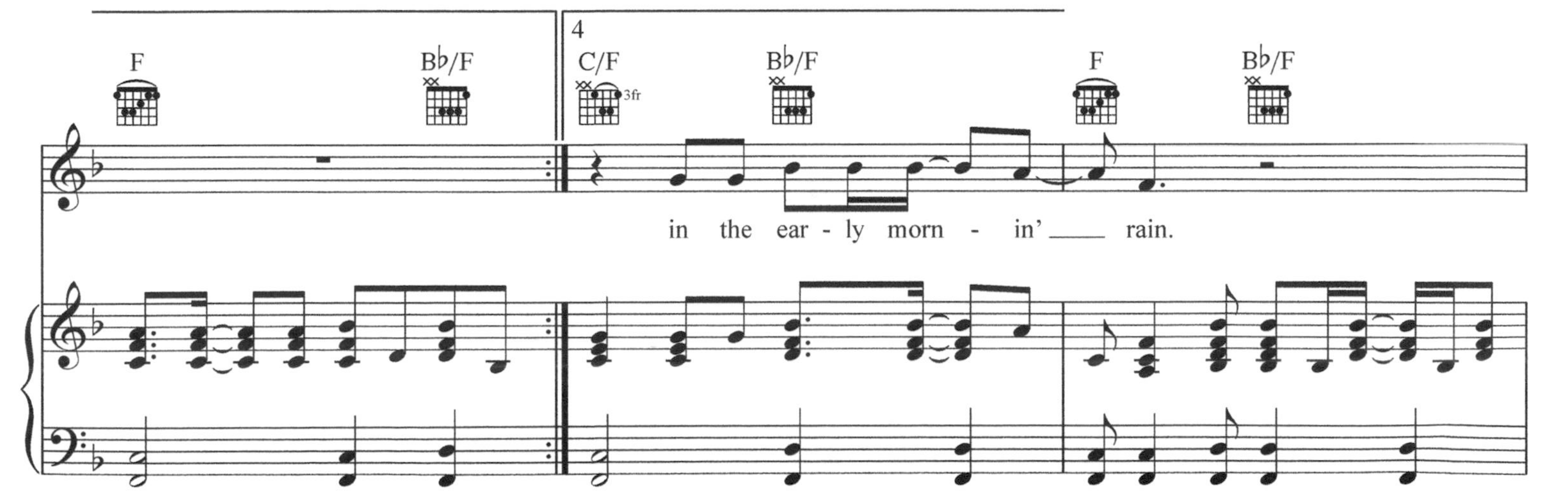
F
B♭/F
4
C/F
3fr
B♭/F
F
B♭/F
in the ear - ly morn - in' rain.

F
B♭/F
You can't jump a jet plane

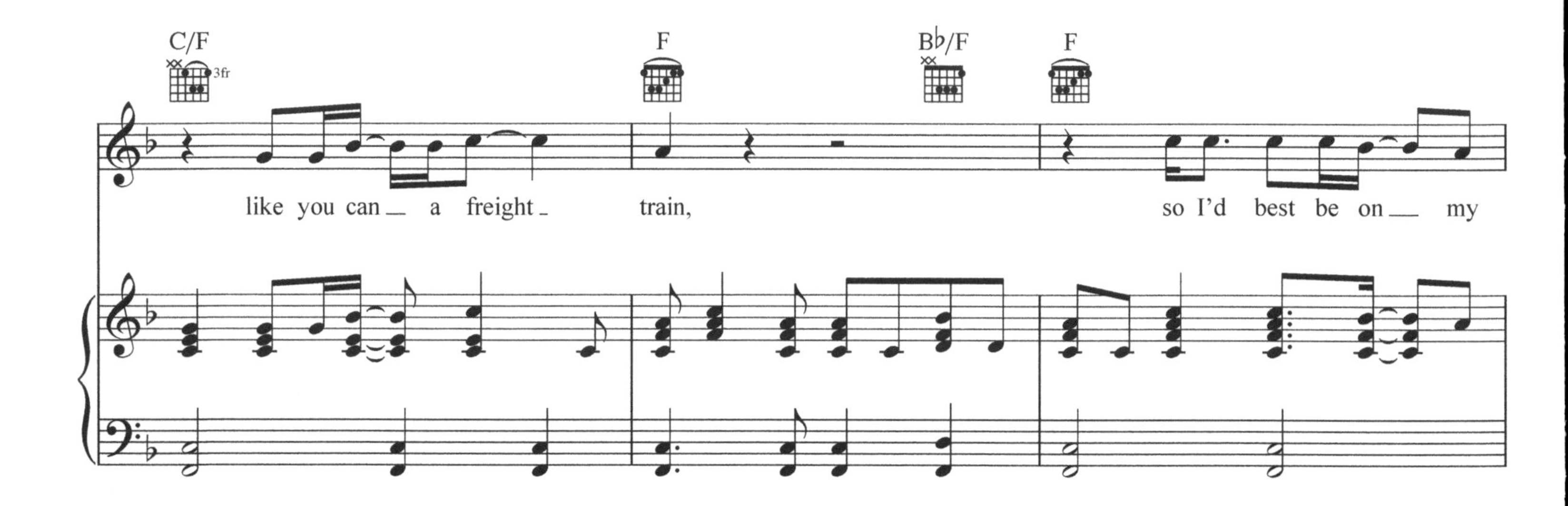
C/F
3fr
F
B♭/F
F
like you can a freight train,
so I'd best be on my

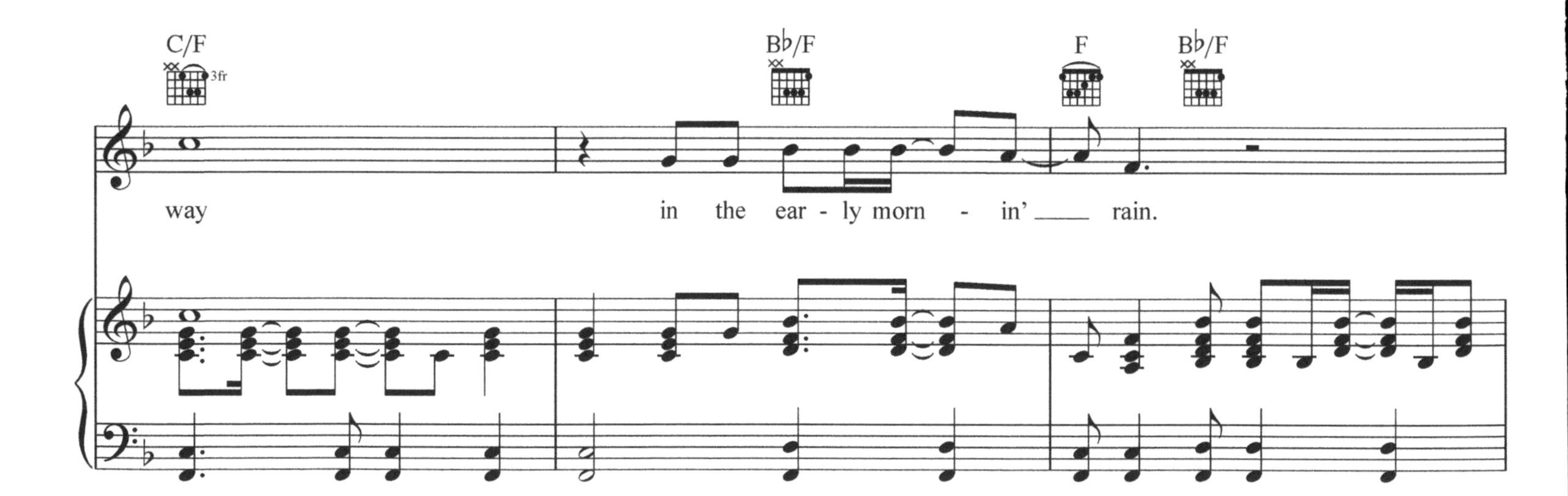
C/F
3fr
B♭/F
F
B♭/F
way
in the ear - ly morn - in' rain.

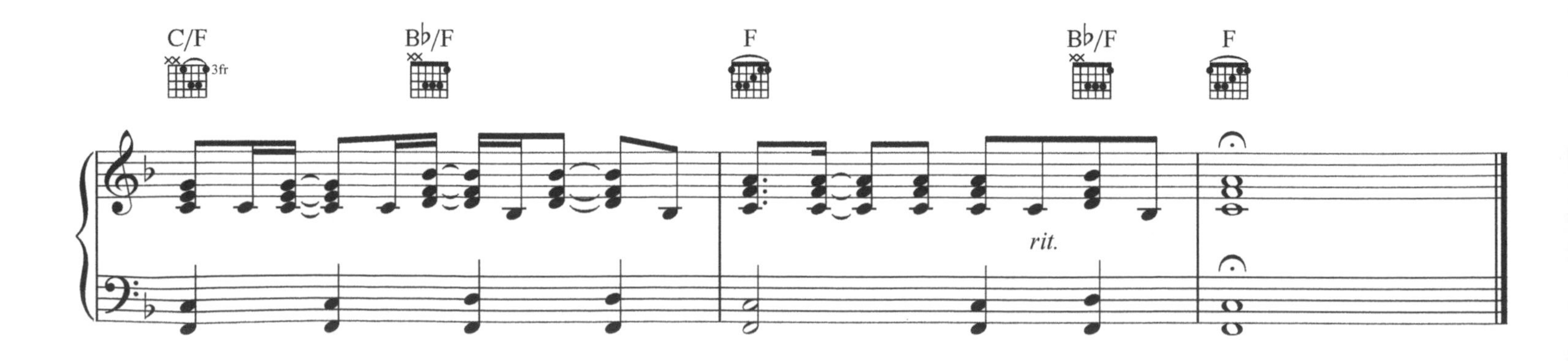
C/F
3fr
B♭/F
F
B♭/F
F
rit.